I0168658

Writers Block Publisher LLC

www.writersblockpublishlingllc.com

www.cdavisllc.com

PROLOGUE

The Date

RICHARD CHECKS HIS WATCH for the third time. Emerald is late. She said that she would be here at eight, and it is now 8:15. He is getting anxious. Where is she? He tries to relax. This is just Emerald; it's not a date; she is just a friend, no his associate, no an acquaintance, someone whom he knows from work. She is just a girl. Emerald is not new in town anymore. She has been in L.A. for over a year, and knowing her; she doesn't know anything about L.A. And tonight is the night that she needs to be out. So Richard thought it would be nice to escort her.

He is the star of the movie she wrote, called *The Topaz Chronicles*, and tonight is the premier party. This movie has already received good reviews. An action movie that has been predicted to be the blockbuster hit of the summer. Also, this is the movie that brought Richard out of his ten-year hiatus. At one time, he was a well-known celebrity, but soon after too many box office flops, Hollywood got weary of him, and he got weary of Hollywood, and so Richard thought it would be best if he disappeared for a while. He remembers the day last year when his agent called and told him about a lead role and how this girl Emerald Dixon, wrote a seven-book series also called *The Topaz Chronicles*. While writing the screen play she had Richard in mind for the lead role. Richard seemed uncertain; he never heard of the book. When he read the script, he knew that this was the role was for him. And now this girl is late!!!

One would think that on top of her wanting him for the part, she would at least have the courtesy of showing up on time. This is only the biggest night of his career! This is his comeback after ten years. Richard runs his fingers through his hair and tries to relax.

This is typical for Emerald Dixon, the shyest girl in the world. She is a twenty-six-year-old African-American woman from Pittsburgh, Pennsylvania, who is afraid of her own shadow. She hides behind her glasses and always has her hair in her eyes. To Richard, she reminds him of Adrian, from the movie *Rocky,* awkward and shy. So, of course, she would show up late; the less she is seen, the better. Emerald does not like large crowds of people. Besides, what does Richard need her to show up for? He is the star. Yeah, she may have written the screenplay, and yeah, she was the assistant director and producer. Yeah, technically, she is the backbone of this project, but her presence isn't really needed.

However, Emerald is a nice person. She is kind of cute, but she is defiantly not his type. What is Richard going to do with a backward black woman who is afraid of her own shadow? Why is this girl late? Despite her shortcomings, Emerald has a brain; she is an English teacher working on her doctorate. While working on the movie, Richard would find her studying, and a few times when her computer decided to have a mind of its own, Richard invited her to his place to let her type a few term papers and do research on the internet. So in the course of a year, he has gotten to know her. So this night is not a date, just two friends premiering their movie. This is more business than anything. It's like; if I see you, I see you.

Emerald didn't plan on coming at all. Richard couldn't understand why the creator would not show up. He saw her at one of the interviews that was promoting the movie. He had to talk her into coming.

"Just meet me at the premier party," He said to her, almost giving up on convincing her.

Reluctantly she gave in and said that she would come and that she would be there at eight, and now it is eight-thirty. Now, why is she late? It would be just like her to get scared and not show up.

Richard takes in a deep breath and decides to mingle and make small talk with the crowd, and if he sees her, he sees her.

As Richard turns around to greet fans and friends, he sees Emerald standing in the doorway surrounded by mobs of people, from famous celebrities to local fans trying to get a piece of Hollywood. Richard can tell by the way she is looking around that she is looking for him. Many people from the press and media are trying to take pictures of her. Richard can see that she is getting overwhelmed. Quickly, he approaches to help her get away from so many people. As he approaches, he is caught off guard; Emerald looks beautiful tonight. She is absolutely breathtaking. It is no wonder why the media is trying to take pictures of her. She is wearing a long flowing red silk dress with spaghetti straps. Emerald's hair is pulled from her eyes in a bun, and she has tiny gold studs in her ears, and a thin gold necklace is around her neck. On her feet, she wears gold four inches platform sandals; her cute toes are painted red. Emerald doesn't have her glasses on. Richard can see her dark brown eyes. She is beautiful. Who would have thought that she is this beautiful?

Suddenly he realizes that he is nervous.

Why am I nervous? He says to himself. *I am Richard DeMarco l can approach girls.*

"Hi," He says nervously.

"Hi, I'm sorry I'm late." She says.

"Did you get lost?"

"No, the cab came late."

"You took a cab, Em; I could have had the limo pick you up," He says.

Emerald shrugs her shoulders.

"Can I get you a drink?"

"Ginger ale," She says.

Richard remembers that Emerald only drinks ginger ale when she is nervous.

Richards leads her to a vacant table. As she sits down, Richard gets the ginger ale. He is still in shock at how lovely she looks.

Man, does she look good, Richard says to himself.

6

Emerald is a nervous wreck. Her stomach is doing cart wheels while her heart is pounding rapidly in her chest. She is out on the town premiering a movie with Richard DeMarco, the man she has been in love with since the tenth grade. While he was making movies, she was in Algebra class daydreaming about him. Now, she is out with him, she is not just hanging out, but the fact is she is hanging out with *Richard DeMarco*. Richard is so handsome; he looks so good. He is tall, standing at six feet, two inches. His dark brown hair is tussled. He is wearing all black, a black silk shirt with black slacks. In Emerald's eyes, it is a crime for a man to be that handsome.

This movie is supposed to be the kick-off for the summer movie season. The first action-packed adventure and she is behind it. What an honor! It is based on her seven-book series, which she had written when she was fifteen years old. And now, eleven years later, her story has come to life. Emerald is in another world right now. She is trying to keep everything in focus.

Come on, Emerald, relax, don't have a panic attack; she coaches herself.

The media and paparazzi are out taking pictures and talking with celebrities. Some celebrities are out showing support to their fellow colleagues in the movie. There are so many famous faces.

Richard returns back with the ginger ale. Emerald sips the drink, and quickly she drinks it.

"Are you okay?" Richard asks with a grin.

"I'm just nervous." She says, taking in a deep breath. "This is all so new,"

"Relax, this is your night." He tells her, smiling.

"Tonight is your night; you're the star of the movie." Her words are sweet. He smiles at her.

Music plays in the background.

"Want to dance?" Richard asked her.

Before Emerald can tell him no, Richard stands up and reaching for her hand. He leads her to an empty spot on the dance floor. To her surprise, a slow song come on.

Oh great, Emerald says to herself, *A slow song.*

She has only danced to a slow song a few times, and that is because she isn't much of a dancer, so now dancing with Richard DeMarco, not a good idea. However, as much as she does not want to dance with Richard DeMarco, she does want to dance with him. She put her arms on his shoulders, and he places his hands on her waist, and slowly but instinctively, they began to move and sway with the beat.

The song is Simply Red's version, *The Lady in Red.*

How ironic, Richard says to himself,

She is in red, and the lyrics are what he is feeling. He has never seen her look as lovely as she does tonight. He has never seen her shine so bright. He hardly knows this beauty by his side, and he will never forget the way she looks tonight. This is the lady in red, dancing with him, cheek to cheek. As they dance, Emerald looks around the room. There are so many people. Although she can see their mouths moving, she can't hear their voices, as if someone has pushed the mute button, and the only noise that she can hear is the music.

She is dancing with Richard DeMarco.

Man, do you smell good. Emerald says to herself.

She wants to lean closer and get intoxicated by his scene.

Emerald felt so good in Richard's arms. He wants to pull her in close, so he could feel her body next to his.

Slowly, very slowly, they make eye contact, and as their eyes meet, they lock. At this moment, they are able to read each other, like reading a book. What Richard is reading is that she really likes him, and it is the same for her. Emerald can see that he really likes her. This is funny, Richard would have never thought that she would catch his eyes, but she has. Emerald feels like she is going to faint. Quickly she looks away.

Don't look away, Richard said to himself.

It is dangerous looking into the eyes of Richard DeMarco's, but somehow Emerald is daring enough to look back into those eyes. He wants to kiss her. Her lips look so full, and her lip gloss is making them seem enticing. Her eyes say that it is okay to kiss her.

Should I kiss her here? Should I kiss her now? He wonders.

He looks around the crowded club, wondering who sees them. No one seems to notice them dancing. Richard looks back at her, and slowly, very slowly, he leans in, and their lips meet. It starts out as a small peck. He looks down at her, wondering if it is okay to do it again. Her eyes say yes. Richard leans in and kisses her softly and gently on the lips. He kisses her passionately, tasting the cherry-flavored lip gloss. She is a good kisser. Richard doesn't want to stop; he doesn't care who is watching. Eventually, he stops and looks down upon her. He smiles at her, and she smiles back and rests her head on his shoulders, and they continue their dance.

The song is over, yet they can still hear the music in their hearts. Richard and Emerald stop dancing. She is startled by the sudden noise; it is the people's voices as if someone had turned the mute button off.

"Would you like another ginger ale?" Richard offers.

"Yes."

Walking back to the table, Emerald begins to wonder what is going to happen next. She just kissed Richard DeMarco, and he just kissed her. Richard is wondering the same thing.

Is she okay? I just kissed the shiest girl in the world?

Disturbing their thoughts, a reporter from an entertainment television program abruptly approaches the two of them. A man has a camera in their faces, and the reporter is loud and overly friendly.

"Richard DeMarco and Emerald Dixon, how are the two of you tonight?"

"Good," Richard says, smiling.

"Let me ask the two of you few questions. Tonight is a big night! You're coming out of a ten-year hiatus and making such a big come back; what is going on in your mind?"

"A lot, this movie is a big deal," Richard answers. "I'm glad that it's taking off the way that it is. I am nervous and excited at the same time. This is a great film. I worked with a lot of great and talented people."

"Speaking of great talent, Emerald Dixon, the author of *The Topaz Chronicles*, you wrote the series when you were just fifteen years old. Did you ever think it would come to this?"

"No, this is very exciting," Emerald answers modestly.

"You wrote the screenplay, you were the assistant producer and director, and the rumor mill has it that there is a sequel in the making. Is there anything else for you?"

"Just working on my doctoral," Emerald answers.

"Well, congratulation to the both of you; thank you for talking with us."

The reporter shakes both of their hands and leaves as quickly as she came. Richard looks at Emerald and can tell that she is getting overwhelmed. Within' the past half hour, a lot has just happened, the crowd of people, the movie, the spontaneous reporter, and the kiss.

"Still want that ginger ale?" Richard asked.

"Oh yeah," Emerald says, inhaling a deep breath.

"Come on,"

They walk to their table, and Richard orders a ginger ale for Emerald. She begins to drink it and then looks around. Richard looks at her. Where did this girl come from? This is not the Emerald he met a year ago, or is it? He is taken by her. He is nervous; he doesn't know what to do or say. Emerald looks at him; she is also nervous. He is getting ready to say something in regards to the kiss, but knowing this, she interrupts him,

"Is Hollywood life always this fast-paced?"

"Yeah, something like that," He answers.

He can't keep his eyes off her. As nervous as she is, she is glowing. The red dress compliments her brown skin. As she smiles, his heart melts. She has a pretty smile. He wants to laugh and cry at the same time. Where is all this emotion coming from? She is so beautiful; he never thought she would be this beautiful. At thirty-seven Richard can't believe that he doesn't know how to respond. He feels like he is on a first date with the prettiest girl in school.

"How's that ginger ale?" he asks.

"Good, so tell me, is every movie premier like this?"

"Yep, the summer is the season for action-adventure movies, and the pressure is really on when the first one comes out because that gets the ball rolling,"

"And this movie is the first," Emerald asks.

"Yep,"

Emerald takes a deep breath. Richard can tell that she is getting nervous again.

"Want some more ginger ale?" He asks.

"No, I'm okay,"

"Are you sure?"

"Yeah,"

"We still got a few more interviews." He informs.

"What?"

"See all those people over there," Richard points to several individuals in the club.

Emerald turns her head and looks to where Richard points to. Her eyes grew to the size of quarters.

"Relax, Em, we'll go together,"

Together hand in hand, Richard and Emerald work through the crowd of people. As nervous as Emerald is, she talking with the reporters seems like second nature. She laughs and jokes with celebrities and everyone wishing each other luck for any upcoming projects.

THROUGHOUT THE NIGHT, RICHARD never leaves
Emerald side for two reasons. One, he knows that she is too
nervous to deal with so many people, and two, he can't bring
himself to leave her side. Besides, she is so grateful. The
night goes on for hours.

RICHARD NOTICES EMERALD YAWNING

"You want to go home?" Richard asks.

"What?"

"You want to go? I can take you home," Richard said.

Emerald looks at her watch; it reads two a.m.

"It's way past your bedtime, huh?" Richard jokes.

"Actually, yeah,"

Richard and Emerald laugh.

"Come on." Richard takes her hand and escorts
Emerald out of the club. "Are you hungry?"

Emerald thinks for a moment,

"Yeah, actually, I am."

"I have some Chinese food, want to come over."

After spending a whole year together filming the
movie, Emerald and Richard have become somewhat friends.
However, from that kiss earlier, Emerald is a bit nervous about
going over to Richard's house.

"Sure," she agreed hiding her hesitation.

He remembers that Emerald loves Chinese good.

Together they walk towards the limousine that brought
Richard to the premier party. The chauffer gets out of the limo
and opens the door for them. Once everyone is inside and
settled, they ride off.

"Where to, Mr. DeMarco?" the chauffer asks.

"Take us to my place," Richard tells him.

The chauffer nods his head and then drives. Richard
looks at Emerald, who is still looking as radiant as she did
when she first came out tonight. He presses the button for the
partition to separate them from the driver. Emerald shyly

glances up at Richard, and he smiles at her. Nervously she smiles back and then looks out of the window. Richard takes Emerald's hand. He is going to say something in regards to the kiss.

"Em, you know-,"

Again Emerald interrupts,

"So, this is just the first movie premier, are there more?"

"Yeah, there is one in New York, one in London; there will be a few."

"Will I have to go?"

"Not if you don't want to," Richard chuckles. "Why, you don't want to go? We can, you know, hang out,"

"I have classes lined up, and well-," Emerald stammers.

"It's okay." He says, smiling at her.

Emerald nods her head and then takes in a deep breath. One night of this is enough.

RICHARD OPENS THE FRONT door as Emerald watches the limousine drive off and the gates. Together, Richard and Emerald enter inside. Emerald had almost forgotten how beautiful Richard's home is. She has only seen the first floor where his office is.

"Do you mind if I take my shoes off?" Emerald asks. "My feet are killing me,"

"Sure," Richard said. He is already in the kitchen preparing the Chinese food.

He puts the food into the microwave.

"I had almost forgotten how beautiful your house is," Emerald says, walking into the kitchen.

"Next time, don't stay away so long." He says, smiling at her.

Again, Richard makes an attempt to say something about the kiss. He approaches her and tries to take her hands into his, but the timer on the microwave sounds off.

Saved by the bell. Emerald thinks.

Within' minutes, they dine on Chinese food and root beer.

"This really hit the spot, thank you," Emerald says, finishing her meal and patting her belly.

"Let me guess, this is the only thing you ate today," Richard asks with sarcasm.

Another thing that Richard remembers is that whenever Emerald got nervous or anxious, she wouldn't eat. He remembers how antsy she would get when she would be working on an assignment. Emerald would get so nervous that she wouldn't eat.

"No, Mr. Smarty Pants, I had a sandwich," Emerald says, smiling.

"A sandwich," He said, shaking his head, "That is not good, Emerald. Three-course meals a day."

"Yes, Dr. DeMarco,"

"Did you get enough to eat?" he asks. Emerald nods her head. "Are you sure?"

"Yes,"

"Would you like to see the rest of the house?" he asks her.

Without waiting for an answer, he takes her by the hand and leads her through his home. Richard has a fifteen-room house. There is a day room, a sun room, a personal gym, an office, a few living rooms, a few different style dining rooms, a couple of guess rooms, of course, the master bedroom. The most impressive room is Richard's personal room, which he calls his Sports Room.

Richard DeMarco is a huge sports fan. Emerald thinks to herself.

Inside this room are tons of sports memorabilia. On his walls are photos of famed athletes like boxers, baseball players, football players, and hockey players, baseball players. Some of the photos Richard had taken with the athlete. Also mounted on his walls are autographed jerseys from various sports teams, from basketball to football, hockey, and baseball. On the shelves are autographs of basketballs, footballs, and baseballs. Richard's favorite sport is football. There is a section in the room that has every helmet from the NFL teams mounted on a shelf. Also in the Sports Room is a pool table, a small mini bar, and a large plasma T.V.

"I can spend hours here," Richard says.

Emerald looks around the room as if she is studying.

"This room is amazing." She says. "I noticed you have a few Pittsburgh items here." Her eyes are dancing. "You like the Steelers?"

"Yeah, Pittsburgh is a good team,"

Richard smiles at her; she smiles back. Nervously, Emerald takes in a deep breath and then looks around the room trying to find something to say. Slowly, Richard attempts to walks towards Emerald, but slowly she begins to walk around the room, looking at everything as if she missed something. Richard can see that she is playing hard to get, and Richard was willing to play.

Play with me. He says to himself.

He can't understand how she has captured him, but that does not matter because he is not going to let go. Slowly Richard follows her like a hunter slowly following his prey. Like a prey, she backs herself into a corner. Richard stands before her, smiling. He can see that she is getting nervous again.

Remember, she is shy. He warns himself. *Don't freak her out.*

Nervously Emerald starts to look around for something to say.

"So, ah," she began nervously. "How long did it take for you to set this room up? I mean to get it like you want it."

"A few months, I guess. I shopped on-line or got things from auctions or just meeting the athlete themselves and got their autographs."

He smiles at her and tries to catch her with his eyes. If only their eyes can lock again. That felt good; it felt nice. Richard places his hand on her cheek,

Relax, he wants to say.

Slowly she looks into his eyes, and their eyes lock. His eyes are softly telling her that she doesn't have to be shy. She doesn't have to run; it is okay.

"Did I tell you how beautiful you looked tonight?"

Caught off guard for a moment, no one ever complimented her before,

"Um, no," she says.

"You look amazing,"

"Thanks." Emerald replies blushing.

She tries to look away, but Richard doesn't let her.

"Don't look away," He says softly. "I like looking into your eyes,"

Emerald grins but looks away. She takes in a deep breath. Richard notices something is wrong. He backs away.

I'm coming on too strong. He says to himself.

"I'm sorry," he says. "I don't mean to come on too strong."

"It's okay." She says softly.

Her voice is like music; Richard slowly moves in closer. He gently lifts her head so he could look at her.

"Em, I like you a lot." He said. "I ah, I can't explain it, but somehow you captured me. Tonight's kiss earlier was nice, really nice and what I'm trying to say is that I guess I've always like you. I just didn't realize it until tonight. When we kissed, I didn't want to stop."

Emerald grins.

"Maybe I can kiss you again." He says, smiling at her.

Richard leans forward and kisses her softly and full passionately. Emerald slightly is caught off guard. Kissing Richard is like being caught up in the midst of the ocean of waves. At first, it was startling, yet, she allowed herself to be caught up in the waves. Emerald realizes that if she relaxes and let go and submerge into the deep and let the waves carry her along, everything will be okay. Richard loves kissing her; tasting her lips is like tasting something sweet. As they continue to kiss together, they move in closer to each other. Richard wants to pull her in, yet he doesn't want to scare her. She doesn't want him to let go. Richard pulls back and looks at her.

"Wow." She said breathlessly.

"Exactly," Richard responded. "There is more where that comes from."

Emerald bashfully smiles and looks away. She looks at the clock; it said, forty-thirty AM., where did the time go?

"It's really late." She said in almost a whisper. "I have an eight o'clock class,"

"Okay," he said, leaning in to give her a small kiss on the cheek.

Together they walk downstairs. Emerald picks up her sandals, and she carries them out. The ride home seems too short. The half-hour ride seems ten minutes. Richard pulls into the driveway, and together they walk to Emerald's apartment. "I had a wonderful time," He said as he put his hands into his pockets.

"I did too," She said smiling, "Thank you for getting me through this night."

"Sure, um, maybe I can see you again,"

"I'd really like that." She said.

"Tomorrow, if you're not too busy, maybe we can have lunch or dinner," Richard suggests.

"My last class is over at eleven-thirty. We can do something then,"

"I can pick you up, maybe carry your books." Richard teases playfully.

"That would be nice," Emerald said, smiling.

"So it's a date." He said.

"A date,"

Richard leans forward and gave her another kiss for the night.

"Goodnight," he said as he began to walk away.

"Goodnight."

Spring

I Love You

AS EMERALD ENTERS INSIDE Richard's house, she is greeted by Richard's dog. An Akita named Bugsy. Bugsy runs to Emerald with excitement.

"Hey, Bugsy, girl," Emerald said, rubbing her behind her ears. "How is my baby, huh, how is my baby,"

Normally Bugsy would not allow anyone to come into her master's house without the proper growl and the showing off of the teeth. She guards Richard like the armed forces guard the President of the United States. However, with Emerald, she is different. Bugsy has a soft spot for her. She guards Emerald like she guards Richard. Emerald rubs Bugsy behind the ears and rubs her tummy just the right way, causing this dog to submit to Emerald's charm.

Within' moments of Emerald's arrival, Richard comes from the back room.

"Hey, baby," Richard said smiling.

"Hey you," She responds.

They both walk towards each other and give each other a kiss. Bugsy starts barking.

"What?" Richard asks, irritated with the dog.

"Leave her alone," Emerald says with a chuckle.

Richard wraps his arms around Emerald.

"So, how was that paper?"

"I think I did okay." She says to him.

"So like an 'A' minus," He teases.

"Yeah," She smiles.

Richard leans forward to kiss her again. He loves kissing her. Whenever he would kiss her, he didn't want to let her go. Her lips are full and enticing, and her cherry-flavored lip gloss makes them taste like candy. He is so happy to see her. Richard hasn't seen his "Emmy" in two weeks. With her school schedule, Emerald needed time to study and

Richard was finishing up a project for an independent film that he was doing. So the both of them were busy. Nevertheless, they managed to call each other each day just to say hello.

Now for the next three weeks, neither of them had plans. Richard doesn't start working on another project for at least another month, and Emerald did have some time before working on another thesis. Since they have been dating, their schedule seemed to increase, leaving very little time to be together, so to Richard, these next three weeks are important.

They have only been dating for six weeks since that night of the premier party. Richard cannot believe how fast he has fallen in love. He has loved many women, but with Emerald, this kind of love is different. Richard finds himself thinking about her when she is not around. He feels lonely when she's not there to smile at him or for him to stare into her brown eyes. Everything about her is amazing. To him, it is the simple things such as her favorite color is purple and her favorite types of movies are gangster movies. Emerald loves to watch the sunrise. Also, there are a few things that they have in common, like their birthday days are in the same month, just four days apart. It broke Richard's heart when he asked about her parents, and she told him that they died in a car accident a few years ago.

Richard has wondered why he is so smitten by her. Emerald is not the average girl that he would date. She is completely the opposite of his type. She is eleven years younger than him. He has never dated a woman that much younger than him, but Emerald is mature. She is of a different race. That issue is moot, but Richard usually preferred blonds. Emerald is painfully shy, reserved, and very conservative. Richard is outgoing and liberal. However, despite their differences, he cannot imagine his life without Emerald.

Richard wants to tell her that he loves her, but when he says it, he wants it to be perfect. He had planned on how and when he will say those words. They would be said over a candlelight dinner. He will take her by the hand and gaze into her eyes and say,

"Emmy, baby, I never met a woman like you. You're amazing, I find myself thinking about you from the moment I wake up, and I am dreaming about you at night. What I am trying to say is that I love you."

Emerald will smile that sweet, bashful smile that melts Richard's heart every time and say:

"Oh Richard, I love you too."

But is it too soon to love someone? He barely knows her, but all that he does know about Emerald, he loves. Or is he in love with the possibility of being in love? Whatever the feeling it is, he loves it.

Richard can see that Emerald loves him. He can see it in her eyes. She hasn't said anything yet. Richard secretly hopes that in the midst of a passionate kiss that she would say it, and he will smile at her and says,

"I love you too, baby."

Richard knows better. His shy, innocent girlfriend, is not going to make the first move.

At the same time, Emerald is taken by Richard. It doesn't seem likely that Richard DeMarco, the handsome movie star, would like her. She doesn't consider herself beautiful, not like the girls she has seen him date. Emerald considers herself average-looking, definitely not beautiful. In her eyes, she is too skinny; she wears a size three in clothes. Emerald would do anything to have some type of form or definition to her body, like curves and hips.

Plus, Emerald is afraid of the world, the concept of life. To Emerald, she thinks it would be safer if she is hidden and not seen. In her eyes, she is a typical nerd, and she would rather be at home reading a good book or perhaps writing one. So the question in her mind is: Why would Richard DeMarco, aka Mr. Hollywood, want someone like me? He is a ladies' man; women love him; men want to be him. He has the body of a Greek god, well-formed and structured from spending two hours a day in the gym working out. He stands tall at six foot two inches. Richard has those dangerous dark eyes that she loves to get lost in. As of now, Richard has a goat-tee, but he is only wearing that for his upcoming movie. However, Emerald likes it.

Every time Richard looks at Emerald, it is like she is the only one in the world. She wants to tell him that she loves him, that she has loved him for eleven years since she was fifteen years old. However, this relationship may not last, and if she let her guard down and he breaks her heart, she will look like a failure. She is dating Richard DeMarco and living in a pleasant fairy tale. He is the handsome prince, and she is the fare maiden. Life to Emerald right now is a pleasant dream, and she doesn't want to wake up to have Richard truly see her for the person she is, a nobody.

If Emerald only sees what Richard sees? Yes, she is naïve, but that is what Richard loves, her innocence. He wants everything from her. He loves to hear her laugh. It is contagious, almost refreshing. Richard can tell that Emerald a bit intimidating by the Hollywood lifestyle, but he enjoys watching her eyes light up like a child on Christmas Day. He loves to watch her eyes light up as she experiences the Hollywood life, the fancy cars, and the first-class treatment at classy four-star restaurants. Watching her smile is like observing a sunrise.

Now with both schedules, free Richard has planned every single day, hour, and minute with his Emmy. He wants to establish a deeper foundation with her, because now after six weeks together, he wants to make sure they are exactly where they want to be with each other. This is a new kind of relationship for Richard, a relationship that he has never experienced before. He is looking forward to spending quiet nights together, making love until the sunrises only to set again.

Making love that hasn't happened yet, nothing more than passionate kissing, and when the passion becomes too overwhelming and the temptation is only an arm reach away; Emerald would put the walls of defense up and push him away. However, Emerald's defenses are intriguing to Richard. She is a mystery that he must solve. This woman has magically taken control of his heart, and the irony is she doesn't know the impact of the spell she has cast upon him; that is the innocence.

"I missed you," He said.

"I missed you too," She says back.

"Are you hungry?" He asks.

"Hmm, yeah," She answered.

"Want to go out to eat? Or do you want to stay here?"

"I want to stay here." She says, "I want a pizza with everything." Emerald's eyes lit up with excitement.

"Everything," Richard asked in a teasing way.

"Yes, mushrooms, sausage, pepperoni, and onions,"

"No, onion," he said smiling, "I might want to kiss you later."

Emerald grins,

"Okay, no onions."

While Richard orders the pizza, Emerald and Bugsy go outside in the backyard.

RICHARD FINDS EMERALD PLAYING with Bugsy. Richard grabs her hand.

"Come, take a walk with me,"

Leaving Bugsy behind to chase her tail, Richard leads Emerald into his rose garden. In Emerald's eyes, Richard's rose garden is like an enchanted forest. It is a large field decorated with a long and tall Victorian-style white gates that stretches for miles and filled with roses of many colors. The pathway is formed out of marble stone. Richard's roses are the traditional red, yellow, white, pink, and lavender. At the cool of the day, a soft, enticing breeze would slide through the garden and allow each rose to give off their scents, filling the air with an intoxicating perfume. To Emerald, it seems like there is music in the midst of the garden, that the roses and the wind hum a sweet melody. It is in the garden that Emerald can forget about the cares of the world and just be free. The times when she would hear the music, she would hum along softly, trying not to disturb the harmony. She can never disturb the melody because she has a beautiful voice. At night when the sun has set for the evening, and the moon is properly in the center of the sky, Richard would turn on the garden lights, causing the color of the roses to blend together like a rainbow.

"So tell me," Richard beings. "What do you want to do for the next few weeks?"

"What do you mean?"

"We have three weeks to ourselves, no prior agenda, no movies to promote, no classes to attend. I thought it be nice if we just spend these next couple of weeks together before our schedules get crazy again,"

"That would be nice," Emerald said.

"Would you like to take a trip?" Richard asked.

"Like, go to the beach or a picnic?"

"Um, a little more than that," Richard said with a chuckle, "Like a vacation, you said you always wanted to see Hawaii, would you like to go,"

"To Hawaii," Emerald asks.

"Yeah,"

"The state?" she asks again.

"Yeah," Richard says with a chuckle.

It is amusing seeing Emerald grasp the concept of just taking off and leaving for a few weeks without having someone to answer to. Other than living in California now, she has never been outside of Pittsburgh. To Emerald, going to Hawaii is not just a pick-up-and-go trip. This is a trip where she would have to plan, pack a suitcase full of clothes, and ask her neighbor to water her plants and check her mail. This meant planning ahead, weeks ahead.

"When would we go?" she asks.

"Tonight, tomorrow, whenever I have a beach house there."

"How long will we stay?"

"As long as we want," Richard smiled at her,

If Emerald said yes, they would go to Hawaii, Richard will wine and dine her, and she will have a wonderful time. However, the events that might take place in Hawaii, she was not ready for, such as sex. Emerald is still a virgin. Emerald never really had a relationship. She spent her life focusing on school, reading, and writing, alone in her own little world. As much as she enjoyed spending with Richard, she is not sure if she is ready for that step. She needs to figure out a way not to get talked into this trip.

"I just can't pick up and leave," Emerald said, making excuses.

"Emmy," Richard began. "You have plans?"

"Not, not really, but, it's kind of spontaneous, I have to pack and-,"

"We don't need clothes." Richard jokes.

Emerald laughs,

"What am I going to do with you?"

"Anything you want," He said with an impish grin.

Emerald sees and reads that look, and quickly she looks away.

"We don't have to go away." She says. "I just want to be here with you,"

"Baby, you just had a rough school schedule, and we just finished promoting a movie, plus we had a hectic few months. Don't you want to get away, a change of scenery?"

"In a strange sense, I am away, in this garden; it's so peaceful here. Sound silly, but in this place, 1 feel safe."

"Safe, you don't feel safe?" Richard asks.

"It's not that I don't feel safe, it's-" she said bashfully, "It's just I feel safe from the world."

Richard places his hands on her cheek, trying to make eye contact, "Why are you afraid of the world?"

"I'm not afraid of the world, it just that-well, you know; l-," Emerald stammers, then shrugs her shoulders.

"So shy," He says, smiling at her.

"I suppose," She says bashfully, looking away.

"It's okay to be shy," Richard told her. "It's good to have a place to run to when the world gets too crazy. That's why I made this garden. Sometimes after a long day, I come out here, and soon my mind is clear."

"Yeah," she said, smiling. "You understand,"

"Yeah, I understand," Richard says, smiling at her.

He decides to tell her that he loves her.

"You know Em, these few weeks together have been nice."

"Really,"

"Yeah," he says with confirming eyes. "I can talk to you about anything. You feel the same?"

"Yes."

"Really," Richard asks.

"Hmm, I've enjoyed spending time with you," Emerald assures him.

Richard smiles and wraps his arms around her, and leans forward to kiss her.

"I really missed you the past two weeks," Richard admits. "I miss seeing your face, kissing your lips, holding you."

Richard leans forward to kiss her again, and their eyes lock. He is about to tell her that he loves her,

Just say it, he encourages himself.

"Em, you are so special to me," Richard begins.

He is getting nervous; butterflies start to swarm around in his stomach.

Just say it, He tells himself again.

"Emmy baby, when I'm with you, I feel like I'm floating. Every time I look into those eyes, l just-," Richard takes in a deep breath. "Baby, what I am trying to say is I really like you."

He can't believe himself.

Why didn't you say it? He asks himself.

Looking into her eyes, Richard can tell that Emerald knows what he wants to say about to say. So he hopes that maybe she'll tell him.

Tell me, tell me. He said to himself. *Baby, just tell me.*

Then again, looking into those same eyes, he could see that she is not going to tell him. Emerald is relieved that he didn't say those words. She doesn't know how to respond. She is too afraid of the intimacy because he was too good to be true.

"I like you too," She says.

Richard grins and kisses her again.

OVER MOVIES AND PIZZA Richard watch Emerald watch the clock, and when it seemed late, she tells him:

"It's late; I have an early class in the morning,"

Any other night it may have been a justifiable excuse, but tonight, this night is just beginning. Richard stops the DVD in the middle of a good action scene; Emerald jumps.

"What are you doing?" she asks, "Turn that back on!"

"No," he said, standing up. "Besides, it docsn't turn out like you think. The hero doesn't get the girl, and he dies in the end, real ugly. Come on."

"What," Emerald asks as Richard grabs her hands.

"Just come on," He said, smiling.

Richard leads her into the middle of the living room. He turns the stereo on, and Luther Vandross's song, *Here and Now,* began playing.

"This is my favorite song. Dance with me," He says, taking her into his arms.

Together they begin to dance. It is sweet. It is like when they had first dance at the premier party. Like she did before, Emerald avoids eye contact. She takes a deep breath and leans in closer towards him.

"You smell good." She said, "What is that?"

"I don't know. Something from Ralph Lauren," Richard says her. "You're a good dancer."

"Really," Emerald asks doubtfully, looking up at him with her big doe eyes. "You really think so?"

Richard nods his head. Emerald's eyes look around the room. Richard can tell that she is getting nervous.

"Em," he said softly.

"Hmm," She responds, looking at him.

"What's the matter?"

"Nothing," she answers softly.

"Are you sure?" he asks.

Emerald nods her head.

"You are so pretty," Richard says, smiling.

Emerald bashfully looks away.

"Can I ask you a question?" Richard asks.

"Yeah,"

"What are you so shy?" he asks with a friendly smile.

"l don't know," Emerald answers taking in a deep breath, "l just, ah,"

Richard smiles and leans down, and kisses her on the cheek.

"You don't have to be shy when you're with me." Richard says, "Just be yourself."

Richard grins, pulling her closer towards him. He lets out a content sigh.

"You feel so good in my arms." He tells her. "I *love* holding you," He stresses the word love hoping that she gets the hint. Emerald starts to look around the room again. Richard grins as they danced in silence. This is nice. Richard loves this part of the relationship, being able to just be together. Richard wants to tell her that he loves her. As Emerald glances at the clock, she accidentally looks into his eyes; and they lock.

Now, Richard said to himself. *Tell her now.*

"Em,"

"Rich-,"

They both want to say something. Richard knows if he doesn't say the words now, he is not going to say it tonight, and tonight he has to tell her. Emerald sees that look again. She quickly tries to think of something to say, an excuse to leave, but she can't think of anything off the top of her head. Richard leans down to kiss her as Richard leans forward to kiss her, tasting her lips. As they kiss, Emerald begins to relax. She loves kissing Richard. Every time he kisses her, she wants to melt. Emerald finds herself in that ocean again, the same ocean she was in when she first kissed Richard, The Ocean of Desire, where she allows herself to submerge into the depth of the ocean and let the waves carry her along. Suddenly, it seems like out of nowhere, the waves are getting too rapid, and this kiss is simply too much. The waves are too strong; she can't relax anymore. Their kissing is becoming too intense. Richard cups his hands around her head, hoping that she will not break free, but she does. Richard stops kissing her and looks deep into her eyes.

"Rich-,"

"What, baby," He says as he kisses her again.

"It's late; I should go," Emerald said, pulling away.

"No," Richard said. "Don't, please-,"

Richard's body is shaking; where did all this tension come from? Does he need her that bad? He kisses her again. Again, Emerald submerges and again allows the waves to carry her. She let out a sigh of pleasure.

"This is nice, isn't it?" Richard asks whispering. "I can make you feel real good,"

Emerald takes her hands and places them on Richard's hands, then managed to remove them from her. She pulls away. She catches her breath—Emerald's body trembles with fear and delight.

"Em," Richard said reaching for her.

He places his hands on her waist to try to pull her to him, but she backs away.

"I have to go." She says, walking backward.

"Emerald, please, don't go."

"I have to; it's late. Rich, I'll call you in the morning," She tells him.

"It's not late. Time can stand still if you let it." Richard tells her with a smile. "Em, stay the night,"

Richard slowly walks towards her. He caresses her face slowly with his right hand, and with his left hand, he glides it up and down her arm.

"Let me hold you in my arms." He tells her, "Caress you and kiss you all over your body."

"l - I can't," she stammers softly.

"Why?" Richard said, kissing softly on her cheek.

She is so shy; he practically felt sorry for her. She is so fragile? Was she hurt in the past? The walls of defense stand tall, guarding her heart. If only she will let Richard in, he can begin to break the walls down. He wants to look her deep into her eyes and say, *Don't be afraid,*

"I just can't," she says.

Richard looks into her eyes.

"There is something you're not telling me."

"No, I'm just really tired."

"So, sleep here,"

"l-l don't think that's a good idea," She says, looking away.

"Why?"

"Because," she said, "things could happen." Richard grins.

"Would that be so bad?"

Emerald doesn't say anything,

"Em, I want to be with you," Richard says.

Emerald takes in a deep breath and then looks away.

"Em, what is it?"

"Nothing," Emerald answers, "This is, well-ah, difficult,"

"Difficult," Richard asks,

"Yeah," Emerald says proudly of the world that she used.

"What is difficult about spending the night with me?"

"It's not difficult," Emerald said. "It's just complicated."

"Is there someone else?"

"No," Emerald said in defense.

Richard can't believe what he just asked. He knows that there is no one else.

"Well, see," her stomach begins to tie into knots. "See, Richard, I really care about you, a lot, and well, um-,"

Emerald tries to collect her thoughts. She is going to tell him that she is still a virgin and soon he will break up with her. Richard is a man with needs, and right now, Emerald is not ready to give in to his needs. So tonight, the fairy tale will end. Emerald takes in a deep breath, ready to accept the end, this end. However, the thought of Richard no longer wanting her starts to upset her. All of a sudden, she is feeling warm, and it is hard to breathe. Emerald starts to have a panic attack.

Oh no, Emerald says to herself. *Don't have a panic attack. Be cool.*

Richard can see that this situation is stressing her out. Maybe he is putting too much pressure on her. Quickly he runs to her and grabs her in his arms. He can feel her heart racing. He begins to rub her back.

"Okay, okay, breath," Richard says softly.

He doesn't mean to cause her stress. He just wants her to open up to him.

"Breath,"

Emerald starts to take deep breaths trying to calm down. Just having Richard hold her is soothing. She is going to miss this when he leaves her. After five minutes, Emerald finally feels calm enough to tell Richard.

"I'm sorry," she says softly, "1 get these panic attacks every now and then."

"It's okay, baby." He says as he softly rubs her back. "Come, sit down,"

Richard leads her towards the couch. Together they sit down; Emerald takes in a deep breath and then looks him in the eyes.

"I have something to tell you," Emerald says. Richard nods his head, encouraging her to proceed. "I, ah, well," she stammers, "When it comes to sex, I'm not that experienced."

"Not that experienced? What do you mean?" Richard asks.

"I, well, I never-," she stammered, "you know,"

Richard thinks for a minute. Then he realizes what she is trying to say. She is a virgin, untouched. It explains why she is so reserved. This also explains the depth of her innocence. Richard doesn't know how to react. This information caught him off guard. He does not want to offend Emerald. He takes a deep breath and runs his fingers through his hair. It's quiet for a long time, neither of them doesn't know what to say. What does one say to something like this? If he was in high school, it's:

"Okay, my girlfriend is a virgin. We don't go all the way,"

But Richard is not in high school. He is a thirty-seven-year-old man who is sexually active. And his girlfriend just told him that she is a virgin. They don't have to go all the way tonight, but eventually, soon, he will want to.

The silence is uncomfortable to Emerald.

"You're a virgin," Richard asked, hoping that maybe she wasn't and this is a misunderstanding.

"Yes,"

"You never-,"

"No,"

Again, Richard takes in a deep breath, and again it is silent.

"I'm going to leave," Emerald says, standing up.

"What?" Richard said, now reacting in shock. "No, don't leave. We need to talk."

"What is there to talk about?"

"A lot, you just told me that you are a virgin. You just don't walk away!" Richard reaches for her, "Sit down, Emerald, please."

Emerald sits down next to Richard.

"I like you," Richard begins. "I care about you, so this, it's okay."

Richard waits for Emerald to respond. He sees that she doesn't. Richard prompts her.

"Is there a reason why?"

"No,"

"No," Richard said, waiting for her to continue; she doesn't.

Emerald is giving him one-line answers. He needs a conversation.

"Emerald, I need you to talk to me."

"What do you want me to say?" Emerald asked, growing antsy.

"Tell me why you're a virgin," Richard says, almost demanding.

"I never really had a boyfriend." Emerald replies, "I went to school and came home. Besides, why does this all matter?"

"It matters because I'm trying to have a relationship with you. I have a right to know if my lady is a virgin!"

"But you're going to leave soon, so what difference does it make what you know!"

"What?" Richard asks.

She looks away, feeling ashamed.

"It's only a matter of time when you say goodbye?"

"Goodbye; where am I going?" Richard asks.

He is confused.

"I don't know, to someone better," Emerald said, getting emotional.

"What are you talking about?"

Emerald hesitates. Richard takes his thumb and index finger and places them on her chin, and gently moves her face to look at him. She doesn't look at him.

"Look at me," he says softly.

A minute passes, and then Emerald speaks.

"Right now, I am living a fairy tale, a pleasant dream that eventually I am going to have to wake up from. I am dating Richard DeMarco, I am living every girl's fantasy, and two, me actually dating someone and that someone thinks highly of me, well it's a bit much to take in. So I figure, why tell him that I'm a virgin? He's not going to be around for long anyway."

Again, he doesn't know what to say or how to respond. She is more than shy and naïve; Emerald is insecure. Richard feels as insecure as she feels. Why would a person like Emerald, who is quiet, reserved, and conservative, want to date a movie star? To live that wild, fast-paced life is not the kind of life Emerald has known. Maybe in a matter of time, Emerald will leave Richard for someone more simple and quiet. Richard takes her in his arms and holds her. Gently he rocks her back and forth, gently rubbing her back. He's in love. He is so in love that he doesn't know what to do. Richard pulls away from her. He gently lifts her head and cups her face into his palms.

"Emerald, don't movie star me." He said coolly, looking deep into her eyes; they lock.

"I'm sorry,"

"I'm not going anywhere." He said. "Not unless you want me to."

"No," Emerald said, "But wouldn't you want someone, you know, experienced or interesting."

"Em, I'm thirty-seven years old; I experience all that I need to experience. Plus, Emmy, you are an amazing person." Emerald grins and then bashfully looks away.

"Are you waiting until you're married?"

"It would be nice, being with just one man, my husband, on our wedding night. French vanilla scented candles filling the room. Roberta Flack playing in the background, but I don't know. I'm too much of a hopeless romantic. I still believe in fairy tales, wishing that one day, this charming stranger would come and sweep me off my feet and take me off to this faraway place. Sounds dumb, huh?"

"No," Richard tells her. He grins, "Roberta Flack, huh?" Emerald grins.

"Which song,"

"*The First Time I Ever Saw Your Face*,"

Richard leans in and kisses her softly on the lips.

"Emmy, you deserve that fairy tale. I hope one day I can make that fairy tale happened for you because I want to make love to you."

"I want to Rich; it's just-,"

"Shh-," Richard said, placing his fingers on her lips." There is no rush whenever you're ready. All I want for you is to talk to me. Whatever it is you need to tell me, tell me. No matter how silly you may think it is. We're in a relationship now, I mean, if you want to be."

Emerald smiles,

"Are you sure you want a relationship with me, having panic attacks? I can get pretty high strung,"

"We all have panic attacks," Richard says, pushing her bangs out of her eyes. "And as long as you want me, I'll be here to see you through them."

Emerald looks into Richard's eyes and realizes that it is okay to let down those defense walls. Emerald smiles. Richard leans forward to kiss Emerald.

"Em baby, stay with me tonight. We don't have to do anything; I just need to have you next to me,"

Emerald nods her head. Together they lay back on the couch. Emerald rests her head on his chest and falls asleep to the sound of his heartbeat.

<u>To Family</u>

Richard drives into the driveway. He looks over at Emerald. She stares out of the window and holds an empty bottle of ginger ale in her hands. Emerald has been quiet the whole trip. Her stomach is in knots, and her throat feels like there is something stuck inside. Emerald can't believe the size of the house. It is a large estate that Richard had brought for his parents a few years back, a Victorian-style home with a well-furnished lawn and flower boxes along the windows. There is a swing and a small table on the front porch. Emerald wonders how many rooms are in this house. Yesterday Richard had talked her into this meeting.

◆

He was at her apartment for a quiet dinner. Emerald loves to cook, especially for Richard, because he is easy to please. She had prepared a steak, sautéed with onions also she prepared carrots and a baked potato. Richard waited until after dinner before he brought up the subject of meeting his parents. So after a few glasses of wine and a full belly, maybe Emerald would be too full to not say no to this potential meeting. So they sat on the couch, and Richard is massaging Emerald's shoulders.

"Dinner was good, babe." He said.

"Hmm," Emerald said, enjoying her massage, "thanks."

"Um, you got plans this weekend?"

"No, nothing that I can think of," She answered, tilting her neck towards the left.

"I have to go out of town to New York; want to come?"

"What's in New York?"

Richard is from New York. He was born and raised in Manhattan. It never dawned on Emerald that he was trying to get her to meet his family.

"A meeting," he answered.

"So then why should I go?" Emerald asked. "I'd just be in the way,"

"Um, this meeting involves you,"

"Me? I'm not trying to meet anyone,"

Richard stopped massaging Emerald and waited for Emerald to catch on to his plan.

"Who are you trying to get me to meet?" she asked, then thought for a moment, and then it registered; his family. *Why else would this meeting involve her in his hometown?*

"No!" she said, then quickly got up and went into the dining table to begin to clear the dishes.

Richard followed her.

"Emmy, you don't know what you're saying no to,"

"Yes, I do! You want me to meet your family."

"Okay, so you do know what you're saying no to, but, baby, come on. It's time, don't you think?"

"No, do you see me introducing you to my family?"

"Emerald, your family members, are dead," Richard commented.

"Not everyone; I have some cousins," Emerald said.

Richard gave Emerald this look saying, *No one cares about your cousins.*

"Listen to me," He began.

Richard followed Emerald into the kitchen and began to put the dishes into the dishwasher.

"We've been together for a few months, and my parents really want to meet you. They want to meet this girl who has my head spinning. There is no need to be shy. Besides, there is someone very special I want you to meet?"

"Who,"

"My Nonna," Richard said. "My gram,"

"You're grandmother?"

"Yeah," Richard said. "My grandma Maria, she's my dad's mom. She is very old fashion and traditional, and I want her to meet you; I want her blessing."

"You're old-fashion Italian grandmother. Yeah, you'll get her blessing all right," Emerald commented sardonically.

"What?" Richard asked, confused.

"Richard, you and I have a lot of difference," Emerald said. I'm twenty-six, you're thirty-seven, and what if they're not okay with-," she hesitated, "the interracial thing."

Richard was quiet for a moment. He did not care what people thought of his relationship. He dated many women of all races, shapes, and sizes. His motto is; Who cares? As long as you're happy. To him, Emerald was his girlfriend, who happens to be black, not his black girlfriend. Also, Richard dated younger women before but not as young as Emerald, yet she acted more mature than some of the older women that he had dated.

"I don't see an interracial thing," He told her, taking her hands, "l didn't think you saw one either."

"I don't, but there are some people who still think it's wrong."

"Then let them be them and let us be," Richard told her. "I don't care what people think. My folks don't care if you're plaid and you're from Mars."

"I know that they know that I am black, but are they cool with it?" Emerald asked, walking back toward the dining table to collect more dishes.

"Yeah, they're cool," Richard said, also collecting dishes.

"And the age difference, I'm a lot younger than you."

"As long as you're legal, my parents don't care."

"So I can be an eighty-five-year-old Martian," Emerald asked with a grin.

"Well, I don't know about all that," Richard answered, laughing.

He put his arms around Emerald and hugged her. "Everything will be okay. I promise, baby. So come, okay?"

"No," Emerald walked back into the kitchen.

"No, Emerald, come on," Richard followed her.

"No, I don't know these people. I am going to be in a town I don't know,"

"I'm not sending you there by yourself; just say something to them?"

"I don't need to go across the country to say something. Call them up on the phone, and I can say hi."

"It's more than that." Richard said, putting the dishes into the dishwasher, "They want to get to know you," Emerald looked at Richard.

"You already planned this, didn't you?" Emerald asked.

Richard doesn't answer. As he placed the last dish down, he slowly looked up at her.

"They are up there waiting for me, aren't they? Richard, why did you plan something like this without checking with me first?"

"Because I knew you would say no."

"And you still planned this?"

"Emerald, you need to go. They want to get to know you,"

"Why can't you tell them about me?"

"What good is it me telling them about you?"

"Say, 'Mom, Dad, this is my girlfriend Emerald Dixon, she is a writer working on her doctoral.' See, that was easy."

Emerald poured the soap into the dishwasher, closed it shut, and turned it on.

"I can't do it, Richard; it's too much. Plus, what am I supposed to do when I get there. What am I supposed to say to them? I don't know anything about them, what they like, what they dislike, what they do, what they don't do. What if one of them says something that offends me, and what if I say something that offends them. There is no place for me to hide when I need to get away because if I want to be alone, they won't understand that it's just me, they'll think I'm being rude, and I don't want them to think that I'm being rude, because I am not rude, I am a nice person. What if they ask me a bunch of fifty million questions? What do I do? I don't do anything, what if they ask me about the book, ah- that stupid book-,"

Richard quickly wrapped his arms around Emerald. She was having a panic attack. Her heart was racing; she was breathing hard.

"Okay, okay," Richard said, rocking her in his arms. "Breath,"

Slowly Emerald began to calm down. It was quiet for a long time. Richard rubbed the small of her back. The last thing he wanted was for Emerald to get stressed out, especially like this. He wanted her to meet his family because she needed to meet his family.

"I have to go, don't I?" she asked quietly.

Richard didn't respond. His silence meant that she needed to go. Emerald took in a deep breath.

"When do you we leave?" she asked.

"Tomorrow at noon,"

Richard looked down at her. Her eyes were wet from tears.

"Everything will be okay," Richard said to her. "Pack for three days; we're staying all weekend."

Emerald nodded her head. Richard leaned down to kiss her on top of the head.

"I'll pick you up tomorrow, okay,"

Richard walked out of Emerald's apartment. Emerald sighed. How hard could this be? She would go, smile pretty, meet and greet the family and then leave. Say the pleasant, "How do you dos, it is very nice to meet you," and then she can come home, sound's easy.

◆

Richard takes his hand and gently guides Emerald's face towards his. They make eye contact, and their eyes lock. Richard sees the nervousness in her brown eyes. Although looking into his eyes, she sees peace; she needs to feel his peace in her heart. Richard leans forward to kiss her. There is something magic about Richard's kisses. They would ease the tension she would be feeling. Emerald takes a deep breath.

"Come on," Richard instructs.

Together they open the car door and step out. They walk hand and hand to the front porch. Before Richard can open the door, the door swings open from the inside. An older woman around sixty stood smiling in the doorway.

"They're here!!!" she calls out towards the back. "Richey!"

"Hi, Ma," Richard said as he and Emerald walking in.

He gives his mother a big hug. Soon several people came forward. "Ma, Dad, I want you to meet-,"

Richard reaches for Emerald, who is hiding behind his back. Slowly she emerges like a deer peeking from behind a tree. She gives a sweet and innocent smile.

"Emerald," Richard's mother says smiling, "You're right Richard, she is beautiful."

"Nice to meet you, Mr. and Mrs. DeMarco," Emerald says sweetly, extending her hand.

"Call me Carolyn, and I'll take a hug if it's all right."

Emerald hugs Carolyn.

"I'm Jacob, honey; I'm Richard's father. This is David, Richard's brother, Laura and Elizabeth, Richard's sisters, and their husband, Brian, and Michael,"

"Nice to meet all of you," Emerald says, smiling. She takes in a deep breath.

"Richard told us you were very shy," Jacob says, taking Emerald's hands, "But listen, don't be here because we're all family, okay,"

Emerald glances at Richard. He smiles and winks at her.

"Where's Nonna?" Richard asks.

"She's napping." Laura answers.

"Emerald, honey, come sit down and make yourself at home," Carolyn told her.

Richard takes Emerald's coat. Then Carolyn escorts Emerald into the living room.

"Where are your bags?" Jacob asks.

"They're still in the car." Richard answers, "David, come on and help me get them."

As David and Richard go get the luggage out of the car, Carolyn, Jacob, and the rest of the family talk with Emerald.

"Richard told us about your book as soon as he got the part in the movie," Laura says. "I went and got it, and Emerald, it was good."

"We are avid readers, Emerald," Carolyn says. "I had the series long before it became a movie. It is an honor to have you in our home,"

"Thank you," Emerald says.

"When Mom called us and told us that Richard was coming home to visit, and he was bringing you, we had to meet you," Laura says, smiling.

"Yeah, we all try to get together for a weekend whenever Richard comes home," Jacob adds.

"Can I get you something to drink?" Elizabeth asks.

"Ginger ale, if you have it," Emerald says, taking in a deep breath.

Elizabeth nods and leaves to get Emerald a ginger ale,

"I need to use the restroom." Emerald says, standing up.

"First door on the left, dear," Carolyn says.

Emerald heads towards the back. Still nervous, she goes into the first door on the right.

When she opens the door, it is not a bathroom but a guest room. An elderly woman is sitting at the vanity dresser, brushing her hair. She has long flowing silver-gray hair that hung down to her back.

"Excuse me." Emerald says. "I am looking for the bathroom,"

"That's quite all right, dear." The woman says, "Can I trouble you for a moment? I just woke up from my nap, and I need a little help brushing my hair, can you?"

"Sure," Emerald says.

Emerald walks inside the room and closes the door behind her. Emerald notices the sounds of Ella in the room. "Forgive me, I am a big fan of Ella's," "Who isn't?" Emerald says with a grin.

Emerald takes the brush and begins to brush the woman's hair.

"Wow," Emerald says, smiling. "Your hair is so thick and soft."

"Thank you," The woman says, looking up at Emerald through the mirror. "I was told Richey's lady friend is colored, but I was not told that she is beautiful. I've should have known better; all the colored women that I have met were lovely women."

"Thank you," Emerald says bashfully.

"What is your name, dear?"

"My name is Emerald,"

"A beautiful name for a beautiful girl," the woman says. "I am Richey's grandmother Maria DeMarco; I'm Jacob's mother."

"Nice to meet you, Mrs. DeMarco,"

"Maria will be fine, dear," Maria told her. "For the first month of Richey's life, I cared for him. His mother got ill after his birth, so from the moment he was born, he and I had a special bond,"

"That's beautiful,"

"How old are you,"

"I'm twenty-six." Emerald answers.

"What is Richey doing dating a baby?" Maria states with a chuckle, "Can you braid my hair, then wrap it in a bun."

"Sure," Emerald says.

The song *Summer Time* came on,

"This song, this song is my favorite," Maria said, "I have heard a lot of remakes, but-,"

"Only Ella does it right," Emerald says with a chuckle.

Maria smiles at Emerald.

Meanwhile, outside at the car, David and Richard are getting the luggage. David is so happy to have his big brother home to visit. Richard is the oldest child, and David is the youngest. At thirty-one, David still looks up to his big brother, and now that Richard is home, David can't wait to hear the adventures in Hollywood.

"So, how long you staying?" David asks.

"Just until Sunday, Emerald has classes."

"Tell me about your girl."

"What do you want to know?"

"For one, does she have a sister?" David asks, smiling.

"No," Richard says and then playfully punches David on the arm. "She's an only child."

"She is really pretty."

"Yeah, she's a cutie," Richards says. "Hey, listen, let me tell you something. Emerald is very, very shy. I mean, like Adrian from *Rocky* shy. So do not ask her a bunch of questions."

"Yeah, okay," David says.

As Richard and David enter the house with the luggage, they see their grandmother and Emerald coming from the back room.

"Richey!" Maria says, smiling.

"Hi Nonna," Richard says, approaching his Maria.

He leaned forward to kiss her on the cheek.

"That's my boy." Maria says, smiling, "I was just talking with your lady friend. She likes Ella."

"Looks like you made the cut, kid," Jacob jokes.

Everyone laughs. Richard leans in to kiss Emerald on the cheek.

RICHARD AND HIS FATHER sit in the den talking. Richard and Jacob enjoy the time they have together. It is more than the typical father and son time; it is their bonding time. Jacob looks forward in spending time with his son, and Richard enjoys getting wisdom from his father. After a crazy, hectic, busy year of filming and flying around the world, there is nothing like coming home to Mom's cooking and that time with his father. They would watch any kind of sports game on television, talk about current events in the world, or about life as a man. This meeting is especially important because of Emerald. Jacob is able to see how fond his son is of the young lady. He is able to see something different in Richard's eyes, not the normal look Richard would give to a woman he had feelings for, but this look said that Richard has finally found that one that will hold onto his soul, and every time he looks at her, his eyes would dance.

"What do you think?" Richard asks.

"I think she is a very lovely girl," Jacob says, smiling. "She is sweet, charming, and I think your grandmother's in love with her."

Richard laughs, "I had to talk her into coming. I told her that this was a meeting."

"Why?"

"You have to understand, she is very shy," Richard explains.

Jacob nods his head.

"Why is she so shy?"

"I don't know. She just is,"

Jacob nods his head.

"What is it about her?" Jacob asks.

Richard takes in a deep breath and sighs.

"I can't explain it," Richard says with a smile as bright as a kid in a candy store. Jacob smiles, "I have finally found someone who is everything."

"Everything?" Jacob asks.

"She is everything I want in a woman. Emerald is smart. She is working on her doctrine. She likes to laugh. She is so innocent and pure,"

"Pure?" Jacob asks with a chuckle

"Yeah," Richard says. "Emerald is different. And, the strange thing is, she is so innocent and pure that I don't know what to do with her."

Jacob gives Richard a perplexed look.

Richard takes a deep breath. He wants advice on how to love Emerald and how to be a positive and good man in her life. Jacob always gives his sons wise instruction. He encourages both his sons to think with their heads and their hearts so they can be a better friends and now, in Richard's case a better boyfriend.

"Emerald is still a virgin," Richard says. "And I want to be with her, but yet I don't."

"How does she feel about it?"

"I told her that we can wait until she is ready." Richard answers.

"So, what are you confused about?"

"Just say we do have sex, and later on down the line, we break up; she won't be pure for anyone else. I can't bear to know that I took the one thing that only she would give to a husband. Emerald is a gem, a rare gem that fell right into my lap, I almost missed it. I almost let her get pass me. With this gem in my life I have to care for it, but if I have to give it away I want to give it the same way I receive it; blemish free and unstained. But if and when we do make love, I want to make sure that it's really okay."

"Do you love her?" Jacob asks.

"Yes," Richard says.

"I mean love, her. Not just love her, but-,"

"Dad, I love her. I do. We haven't said it to each other yet."

"You just don't want to be having sex with her, but you want to be making love to her." "Yeah," Richard says.

"Rich, I can tell that you care a great deal about her. And considering the circumstances, you don't want to ruin something or someone special. I shouldn't have to tell you what to do. Whatever happens, remember she is a lady. Treat her with respect,"

Richard nods. Jacob continues.

"You know me. I am an old fashion kind of guy. Considering the topic of sex, a woman's first time is her only time. Yeah, you have the born-again virgins, and that is okay, but the first time should be done with honor, love, and respect. This gem should not be handled with the basic gentleness but with the kind that only you can give. No one can value your gem the way you value it, even if you have to give it away. With a gem that rare, you shouldn't want to give it away."

Richard ponders on his father's words.

Emerald enters the den. Jacob watches Richard's face light up. Jacob also sees the way Emerald looks at his son as if he is the only one in the room. There is the evidence that Jacob needs to see to know that they are truly in love.

"Dinner is ready." She informs.

Both men stand up. Richard takes Emerald by the hand, and together they enter the dining room. Carolyn approaches Jacob.

"What do you see?" she whispered to her husband.

"A daughter-in-law," Jacob whispers.

As Carolyn smiles, they enter the dining room.

The table set for eight is covered with a wine-colored table cloth. Carolyn decides to use her good china for this occasion. There is a bouquet of roses for the centerpiece, a large pan of lasagna and various pasta dishes like penne with vodka sauce, chicken cacciatore, and fettuccine alfredo. Also, there is placed on the table with a plate full of garlic bread, and the red wine is in the wine bucket next to the table. Everyone takes their places at the table, with Jacob sitting at the head of the table and Carolyn sitting on the opposite end. Once everyone is sitting down, Jacob stands and raises his glass for a toast.

"I like to make a toast," Jacob says. "I am so happy for this gathering. We like to get together as much as possible, but with a movie star for a son, it is hard,"

Everyone laughs. Jacob continues.

"However, we do try the best that we could to come together in love. I like to toast to family. To my lovely wife for forty years, she is still by my side. I am happy that my mother is here. Last but not least to our special guest, Emerald. We are honored to have you in our home. Please do not feel like a stranger because you're not; I speak for everyone here when I say welcome to the family. So I toast; to family." Emerald looks at Richard and grins.

"To Family," Everyone said.

Summer

The Perfect Night

EMERALD DABS JUST A touch of perfume behind her ears and then gently teases the curls in her hair. She is so excited because tonight is a special night for both Richard and her. Tonight is their six-month anniversary, and for Emerald, this night is special. This is the first serious relationship that she has had, and Richard is the man of her dreams.

Two weeks ago, Richard was at Emerald's apartment eating dinner.

◆

Emerald had barbecued chicken breast, made-a salad, and had chicken flavored rice. Emerald loves cooking for Richard. He noticed that she was acting a bit unusual, more than her normal shy and awkward self.

"How is the chicken?" she asked. "Would you like more ice tea?"

Emerald was fidgety and antsy. This was typical Emerald, but tonight she was making too much of a fuss over him.

"Are you eating?" Richard asked.

"Yeah, in a minute," She said.

Emerald was tense. How does one bring up a subject that may seem silly to some, but to her, it is important? And how would she imply how important without seeming childish? Emerald wanted to celebrate their anniversary. Richard is a thirty-seven-year-old man who had plenty of relationships in the past and did not think much of those silly monthly anniversaries. Plus, Richard has a packed schedule, he is working on a new movie, and Emerald is lucky to see him at least twice a week, so maybe he just doesn't have time to have an anniversary celebration.

"Em," Richard said. "sit down,"

Emerald put another piece of chicken on his plate.

"Okay, in a minute." She told him, "Um, do you know what your schedule will be like next Thursday?" she asked him as she walked back into the kitchen.

"My schedule," Richard asked, thinking. "I think I'm off that day."

"Really?" she asked with excitement as she poked her head out from the kitchen. "As in no plans?" "None that I can think of," Emerald walked slowly to him.

"Well, I was wondering- hoping, that maybe we can do something,"

"Something, what's something?"

"Um, dinner; whatever," She told him as she poured more ice tea into his glass, then quickly walked back into the kitchen to put the ice tea back into the refrigerator. Slowly Emerald came back from the kitchen. Richard was eating,

"Is everything okay? Can I get you anything else?"

"Everything is fine; come sit down." He told her.

She grinned then walked to the table, but she didn't sit. Emerald began to straighten things out on the table, like aligning the centerpiece. Richard definitely knew that something was bothering her. He pushed his chair back from the table. He grabbed her hands and pulled her to him.

"Come here," He said.

"What?" she said shyly.

"Come here," he said again.

Richard gently pulled her down on his lap,

"What is next Thursday? I mean, we can go out and eat any other night; we could have gone out to eat tonight." Emerald's heart broke.

He doesn't even know, she thought to herself.

"I just thought it would be nice to go out to eat. You're free; I'm free," she said, trying not to sound disappointed. "Sounds real nice, Emmy, but you're a homebody. You rather stay in than go out." He told her.

"Wow, you know me so well." She told him, embarrassed that Richard knew her so well.

"You're very antsy tonight," Richard said, tickling her at her sides, "You get really antsy when there is something on your mind. I know you; talk to me. What is next Thursday, our sixth-month anniversary maybe?" he said.

Emerald's face lit up with excitement. She leaned forward and kissed him.

"You remembered?" Emerald said.

"Yeah, baby, I remembered," Richard said to her, smiling.

◆

Emerald steps back to examine herself in the minor. She wants to make sure that she looks perfect for tonight. She wears a backless black dress. Normally Emerald wears her hair down, her bangs covering her eyes, but for tonight she curled her hair, and her bangs pushed back from her face. She wears a small pearl necklace and matching pearl earrings. This night has to be perfect. For the past month, Richard has been really busy with a new movie. He is starring opposite Nessa LaMonte, a beautiful actress with a body full of curves that can cause road damage if not taken seriously. She has long dark brown hair and big ocean blue eyes, and she is Richard's ex-girlfriend. They dated for four years and broke up three years ago.

Emerald has never had a problem with Richard working alongside beautiful women. She knows that he is just acting, but with Nessa, this is something different. Nessa, at one time, held a special place in Richard's heart, the same place that Emerald now holds. Emerald does not want to lose that place. Emerald's biggest fear is that old feelings between Nessa and Richard would rise, and they would miss what they once had and think that getting back together is a good idea. Richard will break Emerald's heart into tiny little pieces.

THE DOORBELL RINGS, STARTLING Emerald, breaking

her from her thoughts. It is Richard, right on time. He smiles at her as he steps into her apartment. Richard hands her a rose then leans forward to kiss her.

"Thank you," she says, smelling the flower.

"Emmy, you look lovely tonight." He says, smiling at her.

He takes her by the hand and gently spins her around, getting a full view of her dress. He smiles approvingly. Emerald looks at him then sees something in his eyes that seems alarming.

"Emmy, don't kill me," Richard said apologetically.

"What?" she asks nervously.

"Um, I completely forgot that the cast has this party to go to, it's nothing major, but I need to make an appearance. So we'll go for an hour, then leave, okay,"

She nods smiling.

"No more than an hour, okay?" Richard promises.

Emerald nods again.

"That's my girl," Richard says.

He kisses her on the top of the forehead.

Emerald grabs her shawl and her clutch handbag, and together they leave out of the apartment. As they step outside, Emerald is surprised to see a limousine waiting for them.

"Richard, you rented a limo?" she asks.

Her eyes wide with excitement.

Richard smile and escorts her into the car. Again, she gets another surprise. The limousine is full of rose peddles. Emerald smiles at Richard.

"You did all this?" Emerald asked.

"Yep," Richard said. "There is champagne on ice; tonight is our night. After this little appearance I have to make, I thought we go to a nice quiet restaurant. It's a new restaurant called Maretti's, and then there is a little festival at this local park, there will be some music, we can dance under the stars, and whatever else you have in mind, it's up to you."

"Richard, this is all so wonderful," She said to him.

"You didn't have to do all this. Just a nice dinner would have been perfect."

Richard leans forward to kiss Emerald. Every time he kisses her, her body trembles. She is so happy that Richard had planned a perfect night. However, in her heart, she already had plans for the evening. Only Richard doesn't know about her plans. Tonight is going to be perfect.

RICHARD LEADS EMERALD IN to a nightclub that is full of people. Tonight is the meet and greet party casting for the movie that Richard is currently in. Going from party to party can be somewhat mundane to Richard, but since his comeback six months ago, he has to make his presence known to let directors and producers aware that he is back on the scene. With Emerald on his arm, Richard smiles and waves to fellow celebrities out for the evening. He shakes their hands and gives the usual pleasantries.

To Emerald, this is too overwhelming, just like six months ago when she was premiering *The Topaz Chronicle*. There are too many people. She doesn't want to be here. She can wait for Richard to make his appearance and meet him at a restaurant. However, for Richard, she walks through the crowd of people. Emerald holds onto his arm and stays directly behind him, hoping that no one sees her. Together they walk to the bar. Emerald takes a seat on the stool.

"You want a ginger ale?" he asks.

Emerald nods her head. Richard grins. Richard asks the bartender for a glass of ginger ale.

Richard hears his name being called. He looks around to see whom the voice belongs to.

"Hey Richey, ole boy, what is going on?" says the person.

Approaching Richard and Emerald is Tommy Clayton, the film's director, a fellow costar Craig Brown, and not far behind them, is Nessa LaMonte. She looks radiant in a strapless dark purple mini dress. Her long and wavy dark hair hangs down her back.

"Hey Tommy, what is going on?" Richard says, smiling.

"Craig, what's up? Nessa, hello,"

"Not much, just having a good time," Tommy says, holding up his drinks. Then he looks at Emerald.

"Hey, Rich, how's it going?" Craig says, shaking Richard's hand.

Nessa and Richard gave each other a friendly hug.

"Who's your lady friend?" Craig asks, smiling at Emerald.

"Craig, Tommy, Nessa, meet my girlfriend, Emerald Dixon."

"*The* Emerald Dixon?" Craig says, smiling. "I feel like I'm in the presents of royalty, I've read *The Topaz Chronicle* series, and it is such an awesome book,"

"Thank you," Emerald says shyly.

"Emerald, this is Tommy Clayton, Craig Brown and Nessa LaMonte." Richard introduces. "Tommy is the director, Craig and Nessa are my co-stars,"

"I play the bad guy," Craig says proudly.

Emerald chuckles at Craig.

"It is nice to meet you all," Emerald says, shaking their hands.

"Very nice, Richey," Tommy says, smiling at Emerald, "so tell me, Ms. Dixon-,"

"Please, Emerald," Emerald says.

"Emerald, do you have any other books out there to make into a blockbuster? Tommy asks.

"No just that one," Emerald says with a polite grin.

"You're from Pittsburgh, right?" Tommy asks.

"Yes," Emerald replies.

"*The Topaz Chronicle* is an amazing series. It's a pleasure meeting you," Tommy says.

"The pleasure is mine," Emerald says.

"Rich, let me have a moment," Tommy says to Richard.

"Sure, Em, I'll be back," Richard says to her.

Richard leans forward and kisses Emerald on her cheek. Richard and Tommy step away. Emerald, Craig, and Nessa are alone. She is face to face with Nessa LaMonte. She is just as beautiful in person as she is on the television.

"I read your book. I was curious as to what the fuss was about," Nessa said, smirking. "You were fifteen when you wrote it."

"That's right," Craig joins. "A prodigy!"

Emerald grins bashfully.

"For the movie, I heard that you assisted in practically everything. Who did you have to sleep with to have that much clout?"

Nessa chuckles at her sardonic remark.

"Excuse me?" Emerald asks, appalled.

Nessa realizes her comment was offensive.

"I'm sorry, it's just a figure of speech. It's not everyone who has an overnight success," Nessa replies. "I've been in the business since I was twenty years old, and I'm thirty-five. I've yet to bring in a box office smash."

Emerald sips her ginger ale.

"My book is eleven years old. Not exactly an overnight success." Emerald says.

Is Nessa LaMonte jealous? Emerald asks herself.

"So besides write compelling novels, what else do you do?" Nessa asks.

"I have my teaching degree in English, and I am currently working on my doctrine," Emerald says.

"Brains and beauty," Craig compliments.

Emerald grins at Craig. Nessa looks at Emerald, wondering where did this beautiful woman come from. In Nessa's eyes, Emerald is too pretty to just be an average girl. An English teacher from Pittsburgh comes to Hollywood and makes such an impact. She has to be doing something else in her spare time- like modeling. Who comes to Hollywood to work on an English degree? Pretty girls don't come to Hollywood to do school work; they come out here to be seen.

"You don't act or model?" Nessa interrogates.

"No," Emerald says.

Nessa looks Emerald over, trying to find some kind of flaw. Sitting in front of her is the most beautiful girl next door.

Sensing the tension between the two women, Craig quickly changes the subject.

"So, do you plan on writing another movie?" Craig asks.

"No," Emerald answered quickly.

"So you plan on going back to Pittsburgh?" asked Nessa.

"I haven't decided yet," Emerald replies. "I been enjoying the success from *The Topaz Chronicles* and working on my doctrine. However, I might stay out here if there is a teaching position available."

"Teachers are special," Craig says. "I always said that if this acting thing doesn't work, I may pursue education." Emerald grins as she continues to nurse her ginger ale. "What grades do you or did you teach?" Craig asks.

"Before I came here, I was teaching the eleventh grade English, but what I really want is to teach college English Literature,"

Richard and Tommy return back to the bar.

"Okay, ready to go, baby?" Richard says to Emerald.

"Yes," Emerald said. "It is nice meeting you both."

Together Richard and Emerald left the club. Inside Emerald is aching. She wants to scream. How could Richard ever love someone as petty and simple-minded as Nessa? Although Nessa has the nerve to speak what was on her mind, unlike Emerald.

Boy, Rich, you really know how to pick em', Emerald says to herself. *You go from dating someone petty and simple-minded to someone shy.*

However, this is still her night. Despite Nessa's attitude and despite Emerald's insecurities, this is going to be a perfect night.

RICHARD AND EMERALD ENTERS Maretti's, she notices a few famous couples. Emerald wonders if anyone is celebrating their anniversary. Then again, knowing Hollywood, they could be celebrating their divorces. While they wait for their food, Richard and Emerald talk.

"Working on a book, nothing major; just brainstorming," She says.

Richard smiles at her.

"What is it going to be about?" he asks.

"Suspense with police," She says. "I've been doing some research on some cases on the internet. Next week I am going to interview the police chief,"

"Another series?"

"Of course," Emerald said smiling, "You know me. I love a good series."

Both of them laugh.

"Maybe this book will become a movie too, and you'll bring a washed-up movie star out from his hiatus," Richard says, sipping his wine. "Then again, you might fall for them, and-,"

"You have nothing to worry about. I can never fall for another. You're everything to me," She tells him, smiling.

Together they lean in and gave each other a kiss.

"You're everything to me too," He said, taking her hands and kissing them. "I find myself getting butterflies in my stomach whenever I am getting ready to see you. I'm smiling when I'm thinking of you. Just think, Emmy, a year ago, I was just an average man."

A Period of Time

"You were more than average man," She tells him with a chuckle. Emerald looks away shyly. "You were a movie star,"

"A worn-out movie star,"

"I didn't see it that way." She says, shaking her head.

"Oh," Richard says with intrigue. He smiles. "Tell me, Ms. Dixon, what did you see?

"I saw an actor who was choosing the wrong scripts. When you first came on the scene, you were playing the rebel; the bad boy. Then those parts became a bit redundant, and it was time for a change. Then you did a little comedy, a little romance, and that is good, but whoever wrote that material was horrible,"

"I've heard the saying that there are no bad actors but bad writers." Richard says, "But your writing made me look good,"

"It wasn't my writing; it was your performance," Emerald says. "It was your work that boosted my book sales. Your performance put my book back on the best sellers' list. Now my phone is ringing off the hook. People want me for interviews. People want me to write and produce things. I just-,"

"So shy," Richard says, smiling.

Emerald takes a deep breath and then sits back in her chair.

"The handicap that holds me back," she sighs.

"It's okay," Richard says, taking her hand. "The world thinks you're this empire of creativity, and really you're just the girl next door."

"Empire of creativity," She says with a chuckle. "I like that,"

"Everyone does not have the gift of words like you, Ms. Dixon," Richard says, smiling. "You wrote this series when you were fifteen, a kid. That makes you a child prodigy. Then out of nowhere, you came in and wrote the screenplay and assist in directing and producing the film. That is talent, extremely talented. And the movie is a box office smash. Your touch makes gold, and the world sees that, and they want you to give them gold,"

Emerald smiles bashfully,

"All this attention is really nice, but it's too overwhelming. I had my fifteen minutes of fame; I'm done."

"No sequel?"

"What's to sequel?" Emerald asks with a chuckle.

"What's to sequel? Em, come on, that's a seven-book series. I'm sure you can pull a movie from those volumes." Richard says to her.

"It's not the material." Emerald said, "The question is; what's the point? Some things you leave alone. Like there is no sequel to *E.T.* or *Forrest Gump*, two really good movies, why sequel them; leave them alone. If you keep bringing them into the public's face, then the public will get tired of them. Then they will become commercial, trying to make that extra buck and the real quality of the film becomes a joke."

"Just think about it," Richard suggests to her with a grin.

"I'm almost done filming."

"Three months of shooting, that was fast, compared to the movie we did together," Emerald says.

"Independent films are not that demanding," Richard tells her. "I like independent films because they're more intimate. Not so commercial. Besides, when you work with a great cast, the scene speaks for itself,"

"So you had a great team, huh?"

"Oh yeah," Richard says. "Howard Smith, Craig Brown, and Nessa LeMonte, she really talented."

There goes that name again; Emerald thought to herself as their food arrives.

Emerald lost her appetite, but she eats anyway. She is not going to let Nessa LaMonte's talented performance ruin her perfect night.

A Period of Time

AFTER DINNER, RICHARD TAKES Emerald to a music festival at a park. There are several round tables covered with white table cloths with a small floral centerpiece. The lights in the trees look like diamonds that are hiding among the leaves. Although there is not a star in the sky and the air is humid, the silver round moon that sits in the middle of the heavens makes the scenery seem like it was a cool night. A live band plays music as people dance. The atmosphere is very relaxing. There are no famous people here to plug movies. Everything is simple yet tastefully done.

The woman in the band begins to sing Emerald's favorite song, *The First Time Ever I Saw Your Face*, by Roberta Flack. Richard leads Emerald to a vacant spot, and they begin to dance. Emerald rests her head on Richard's shoulder, and they sway slowly to the beat.

"There is just something about this song that makes me want to fly." She whispers.

She remembers how she felt when she first laid eyes on Richard. Last year at the movie set filming *The Topaz Chronicles*,

◆

Emerald was sitting next to the director Dave Stevens when Richard approaches.

"There he is," Dave said, smiling shaking Richard's hand. "Rich, my man, how is it going?"

"Can't complain," Richard said smiling,

"Listen, I want you to meet someone. Emerald Dixon, she is the creator of this whole empire. I smell gold; you understand. She wrote the book, wrote the script, so I only thought that it would be fitting if she assisted me and seeing her work come to life."

"A renaissance woman," Richard said smiling.

He shook Emerald's hand. She vowed to never wash it again.

"Nice to meet you; I'm Richard DeMarco."

"Oh, she knows who you are. She personally requested you for this part." Dave said.

"Thank you," Richard said to Emerald.

Emerald smiled bashfully and then looked away.

"Now, she may be just the assistant, but she is running things. This is her vision," Dave said.

Emerald could not keep her eyes off Richard. There were knots in her stomach. Her heart was pounding inside of her. Richard was so handsome; he wore a pair of faded blue jeans and a black t-shirt.

"You know, at first, I never heard of the book. When I heard about the part, I read it, and wow, it is really good. When did you say you wrote it?" Richard asked.

"About ten years ago," Emerald answered him.

"Ten years ago." Richard seemed surprised. "I can't help but to ask how old you are. You seem pretty young."

"I'm twenty-five."

"Twenty-five!" Richard exclaimed.

"That means you were fifteen when you wrote it."

"Yes, hope that's all right," Emerald asked nervously, looking at Dave.

"That's right, Richey," Dave said, smiling brightly, "we're working with a genius."

"We must be," Richard said, smiling at Emerald.

◆

With her head resting on his shoulders, Emerald listens to the singer sing her favorite song. Richard is her Robert Flack song. The sun rises in his eyes, and the moon and the stars are the gifts that he gives. When she first kissed him, the earth moved in her hands.

"Richard," Emerald whispers.

"Hmm,"

"What was going on through your mind when you first saw me?"

"What was going on through my mind," he says, looking at her. He grins. "Well, I saw this intelligent yet painfully shy young lady."

That is not the response that Emerald is looking for, but she doesn't ask again. The song is over, and the singer begins to sing another slow song, *How Could an Angel Break My Heart*, by Toni Braxton. Emerald backs away.

Richard pulls Emerald towards him, but she shakes her head.

"I thought you liked this song."

"I do, but I don't want to dance with you to a sad song."

"Why not," Richard asks, smiling.

She shrugs her shoulders and attempts to back away, but Richard tightens his grip.

"Come on, baby, don't be so emotional."

"I'm ready to go," Emerald said shyly.

Dancing to that song will make Emerald sad because this song is what she is feeling. How can an angel break her heart? Why doesn't he catch her falling star? She wishes that she didn't wish so hard because maybe she wishes their love apart. How can an angel, Richard, break her heart? Emerald loves Richard so much. However, they still haven't said, "I love you," and Richard seems devoted to her. But will he break her heart?

It's been six months. Richard seems happy. Does he love her? Emerald knows that she loves him. She will always love him. Emerald wants more. Something needs to develop; a sex life. Emerald had always wanted to wait for the right perfect moment at the right perfect time. What time is more perfect with her man on their six-month anniversary, with the tunes of Roberta Flack?

Emerald looks up at Richard, and together they make eye contact, and suddenly their eyes lock. Richard is reading something, but he is not sure what her eyes are telling. Richard leans forward to kiss her, and she melts in his arms.

AT RICHARD'S HOME, HE pours Emerald a glass of white zinfandel.

"Richard tonight was wonderful," Emerald says, smiling.

He softly caresses her face. Emerald sits her wine glass down, wraps her arms around Richard's shoulders, and leans in to kiss him. Richard leans forward to meet her kiss.

"I have a present for you." He says.

"For me,"

"Yeah, wait here,"

Richard goes to his office, and within moments he comes back with a small gift box in his hands.

"Rich, you shouldn't have," Emerald says, shaking her head.

"Open it," He smiles.

Emerald opens the box. It is a silver charm bracelet with three different charms. The first charm is a book that represented her writing; the second charm is her birthstone which is the aquamarine. The third charm is an emerald.

"What's the emerald for?" Emerald asks.

"Me," Richard says.

"You,"

"I have grown very particular to emeralds."

"Because of my name,"

"Emeralds are precious stones, a mineral of beauty. You are precious; my mineral beauty,"

Emerald grins and looks away bashfully. Richard takes his hand and lifts her chin to face him. His eyes question what is on her mind.

"Thank you," She says. "You made tonight wonderful, and you didn't have to."

"Of course I did; you're my lady. I'll do anything for you."

"And I'll do anything for you."

"Just seeing you smile is enough for me," Richard says her.

Richard wraps his arms around Emerald, and they begin to kiss each other sensually and passionately. As they indulged in the Sea of Passion, Richard finds himself slowly caressing Emerald's body, gently gliding his hands up and down her back. As Richard places his hands on her hips, Emerald moves closer towards him. Slowly begins to rise on her toes, and soon she gently glides her pelvis into him. Richard's blood begins to feel warm, too warm at this moment. He pulls back.

"We better stop." He says in almost a whisper.

"It's okay," She whispers back. "You don't have to."

"What?" Richard asks. He is caught off guard.

Emerald looks at Richard long and hard in the eyes. Her stomach is full of butterflies.

"Tonight, I want to be with you." She says nervously.

"Tonight," Richard asks. Emerald nods her head and gives him a shy grin. "Are you sure?"

Again, Emerald nods her head with a grin. Richard is surprised. He knows this day might come, but he didn't know when and he defiantly did not want to push her. Richard loves Emerald, and he wants her first time to be special.

Richard slowly kisses her on the neck. He picks her up in his arms and carries her towards his bedroom. Emerald can't believe that tonight is going to be the night. She is going to have sex with Richard DeMarco, *the Richard DeMarco*, a fantasy that every girl has dreamed of. This is not going to be some type of casual trill. This is going to be romantic in many ways.

Richard gently places her on his bed. Emerald sits up on her knees. As Richard kisses her, he could feel her body tremble. Is this the tremble of excitement or of first-time jitters? He wants to take her clothes off and eat her alive.

Emerald is innocent and pure. As much as he wants her at this moment, there is something is missing. Emerald begins to undo Richard's shirt; he stops her.

"Emmy, wait." He says.

"What?"

"This-," he stammers. "This isn't right."

"What's not right?" she asks nervously.

"Us like this. I can't do this,"

"Why?"

"Because Em, it's not right," Richard says, buttoning his shirt.

"What's not right?" Emerald asks, confused. "What did I do?"

Richard looks at her with soft eyes.

"You didn't do anything, baby,"

"Then why don't you want me?" She asks feeling rejected.

"I do want you." Richard says with a chuckle, "More than ever, but just not this way. Baby, this is your first time. Don't you want it more romantic?"

"It is romantic," Emerald says as tears form in her eyes.

"There was the limo, the restaurant with the Roberta Flack song-,"

"Em, you're a virgin; you just don't lose your virginity because of a nice date." Richard tried to explain.

"A nice date!" she exclaims, feeling rejected. "This is more than just a nice date. This is our anniversary. Don't you get it? This is a big deal for me. I had a boyfriend for six months." Emerald says as tears rolled down her face.

"Em, you act as if you never had a boyfriend." Richard comments.

"I haven't, Richard," Emerald snaps. "The first guy I kissed is this Asian kid in the ninth grade. What part of me don't you get? I am a twenty-six-year-old virgin because no one wanted me. You are this fantasy come true who thinks something of me and now suddenly doesn't want me."

"I didn't say that I didn't want you. Every time I see you, I want to take you up and make love to you, but don't you get how special you are. There is a reason you're still a virgin."

"I'm still a virgin because no one wanted me. Look at me; I'm a scrawny black girl, a real pick of the litter! Who would want that?"

"Stop saying that about yourself because whoever ignored you was dumb,"

"If they were so dumb, then why did it take you a year to see something in me? A new dress and a premier party, and the next thing you know, you have your tongue down my throat,"

"Emerald, don't be crass!" Richard says sternly.

Emerald sits on the bed and buries her face in her palms, and begins to cry. Richard feels bad. He kneels down before her.

"Emmy baby, please, don't cry." He whispers, "You know I can't stand seeing a woman cry."

Richard takes her hands and pulls them away from her face.

"I want to go home," she says as tears continue to fall from her eyes.

"We're celebrating our anniversary," he said with a grin. "Emmy, don't cry,"

Emerald looks away. Richard senses that there is a greater issue than tonight being their anniversary.

"Emerald," he says her name. She looks at him.

"Talk to me. What's bothering you?"

"It's nothing," She says, looking away.

"Look at me," he orders softly.

Emerald looks at him.

"Don't tell me nothing," Richard says. "From the moment you brought up this anniversary, you haven't been yourself."

"I just don't want to lose you."

"Lose me?" he asks, confused. "I'm not going anywhere. Why do you think you're going to lose me?" Emerald doesn't respond.

"Have I giving you a reason to think that?"

"I just don't want to take my chances,"

"What chances?"

"The chances of losing you," Emerald said.

"Okay, now we're going in circles," Richard says with a sigh. "What chances?"

"Of not supplying your needs and you wanting someone else," Emerald said.

"Not supplying my needs, Emerald. What are my needs?"

"Richard, come on, you're a man with desires and needs; I may be naive, but I'm not dumb. How long will we go on without you asking me for sex?"

Richard can't believe the question. Here is a virgin ready for a productive sex life.

"There is no way to answer that question," Richard says. "Because tomorrow I might ask or next week, but Em, sex doesn't have to be in the picture right now. We're still laying the foundation of what we have, and I don't want to damage that. What we got right now is fine. I look forward to seeing you, hearing your voice on the phone, and I know that this is real because sex isn't in the picture,"

"What a load of crap!" Emerald snaps. "What man in his right mind turns down sex, free sex on top of that! Here I am your girlfriend telling you I want to be with you, and you're giving me a sappy love song!"

"Emerald, I'm not just gonna have sex with you!"

"Why not,"

"Because I love you," Richard exclaimed. "I want to make love to you."

Finally, those three little words are said. But Emerald is so caught up in her emotions that she doesn't notice.

"You loved your other girlfriends; how long did you wait to have sex with them?"

"What?" Richard asked.

He is shocked that Emerald asks such a personal question.

Emerald realizes what she asks Richard.

"I'm sorry, it's none of my business, I know. I don't even know why I asked, but-,"

Emerald stops, and she takes in a deep breath.

He thinks about the questions again. What does tonight have to do with taking chances and girlfriends? Why would Emerald worry about another girlfriend? Richard then realizes the root of the situation. There is an ex-girlfriend in the picture. Emerald is not worried about losing him to just any woman, but to his ex-girlfriend and Emerald is willing to do anything that she needs to do to keep that from happening, and Richard would have no reason to leave.

"Nessa," Richard asks.

Emerald takes a deep breath. As she looks at him, tears fall from her eyes. Quickly she wipes the tears from her cheeks.

"I'm not insecure." She says. "I'm not. I know you care about me. I also know that you that you have needs. Things that experience women can do for you."

"My relationship with Nessa was a lifetime ago," Richard told Emerald.

"I know-,"

"We broke up because we just couldn't communicate anymore."

"I'm trying to communicate with you, but we're not-," Emerald hesitated. "I thought that you wanted to have sex with me, and you were waiting for me for me to be ready."

"I am waiting for you,"

"I'm ready," Emerald says.

Richard shakes his head.

"No, you're not. I can see it in your eyes. Emmy, the eyes don't lie. You're not ready to make love to me because you want me; you just want to keep me from going elsewhere."

"I had a lovely time tonight." Emerald said, "I just wanted to-," Emerald thinks for a moment. "You said 'I love you,' didn't you?"

Richard nods his head.

"I love you," Richard said. He leans in to kiss Emerald, "I love you, Emerald,"

"I love you too," She said to him.

Richard kisses her again.

"I promise you, our time will come. But in the meanwhile, as long as I see you smile, that is my only need." Emerald hugs Richard.

"I'm sorry." She says. "I'm sorry, I got weird."

"It's okay," He says, rubbing her back.

After a few moments of just holding each other, Richard says;

"Emmy,"

"Hmm,'" she responds.

"Tell me about this Asian kid."

Emerald giggles at Richard, pretending to sound jealous.

Indian Sumer

Summer Time

NO WORDS ARE SAID. The quiet is just what the doctor would have ordered. Richard sits on the plane, staring out of the window, looking at the clouds. His dark sunglasses cover his tear-stained eyes. Emerald sits beside him and holds his hand. She never thought that she would be flying back to New York this soon? It was not that long ago that they were in New York so that Emerald could meet his family. Now they are flying back so Richard can bury his grandmother. Maria has died. She died peacefully in her sleep yesterday morning. Richard didn't find out until yesterday night while spending a quiet evening with Emerald.

◆

Richard was going to propose to her. He took Emerald to a nice and fancy restaurant. Then afterward, he brought her back to his home, and they sat in the den on the floor by the fireplace. There were engaged in a deep and passionate kiss. Richard pulled back, looked at her, and smiled.

"What?" she asked, smiling.

"I can kiss you forever." He said to her.

Emerald smiled bashfully.

"So, Dr. Dixon, what plans do you have after school," he asks.

"I'm not a doctor yet," Emerald said, smiling.

"No, but you'll be graduating in a month," Richard said. "What are you going to do after you graduate?"

"I hope to find a job," Emerald said with a chuckle.

Richard nodded his head with a grin.

"You plan on going back home to Pittsburgh?"

"No, I have gotten spoiled to the California weather," She told him with a grin. "And the people," She smiled at Richard.

They leaned in and kiss.

"Maybe, later on, you can find a permanent place instead of your apartment," He told her.

"Maybe," Emerald said.

"I might be up for a new part. Something really different from the roles I've taken before."

"Really," Emerald said to him. "What kind of movie?"

"It's something interesting," Richard said, "Finding the right co-star is the challenge."

"Anyone in particular? What kind of role is it?" Emerald asked as Richard took her hands and kissed them. He was hoping that she would catch on what he was trying to tell her.

"Emerald, will you be my co-star?" Richard said, smiling.

Emerald chuckled.

"Me, on the big screen? I don't think so."

Richard then looked deep into Emerald's eyes. Richard was about to say something, but the telephone rang. Richard sighed.

"Answer it," Emerald said.

"The machine can get it," Richard said, then finished off his wine. "Emmy, I-,"

The sound of the telephone ringing distracted him.

"Richard, answer the phone." Emerald insisted.

Richard sighed. He went to answer the phone. It was his mother telling him about Maria. Emerald saw the sad look in Richard's eyes. Immediately she walked to him and waited for him to get off the phone. He takes in a deep breath and then looks at her and tells her that his Nonna had died. He fought back tears, Emerald cried for him.

"Richard, honey, I'm sorry," she said softly, wrapping her arms around him.

He allowed her to hug him. He hugged her back.

Richard closed his eyes and allowed the tears to fall. His grandmother, Richard, used to call her Mama before he could say, grandma. They had a special bond from the moment he was born. When he was a baby, Richard spent every weekend with her, and they would play, take walks, and have such a wonderful time. Maria was the first one he told when he decided to be an actor. She was so proud of her grandson. Emerald didn't think twice when Richard told her about Maria. She packed her bags and joined Richard at the airport.

◆

As they sit on the plane, he kisses her on the top of her head, thanking her for being here. Then, he looks outside at the clouds and wonders which one of the clouds is Maria's soul resting on.

THEY ARRIVE AT RICHARD'S parent's house. Carolyn is waiting by the door. Although she is surprised to see Emerald, she is touched just the same. Carolyn gives Richard a big hug.

"Are you okay?" she asks.

"Yeah," He says.

He walks to the back room where Maria had stayed.

"Emerald," Carolyn said, taking her hands. "Thank you so much for coming; this means so much to us,"

"Of course, is there anything I can do?"

Carolyn leads Emerald into the den. Both women sit down.

"You know, Maria thought a lot of you." Carolyn said, "She just couldn't stop talking about how beautiful and how special you are."

"Maria was one of a kind," Emerald says.

"Oh, she was," Carolyn says, smiling as tears form in her eyes. "I can honestly say that she was more than a mother-in-law to me; she was like a mother,"

Carolyn quickly dabs her eyes with a Kleenex.

"And you were her daughter," Emerald says.

"Can I ask a favor for me, for Maria?" Carolyn asks.

"Anything," Emerald volunteers.

"Well, when you were here last, you were in the back yard walking along with the garden, Maria and I heard you singing. Emerald, you have such a beautiful voice,"

"Um, thank you," Emerald says bashfully. "Can you sing a song at the funeral?" Emerald sits stun by the question.

Sing in front of people who I don't know. Get in front of people? Who knows how many people. No, no, no!

"Okay," Emerald says, taking in a deep breath.

"Oh, thank you, Maria will love it,"

The telephone rings. Carolyn excuses herself to answer the phone. Emerald takes in another deep breath.

What did I just do? She asks herself. *Sing? I don't sing; I hum. What am I going to do?*

"Emerald," someone says, her name startling from her thoughts

Emerald turns to face them. Standing before her are Richard's sisters Laura and Elizabeth.

"Hi," Emerald grins.

Both girls hug Emerald.

"It's good to see you," Elizabeth says, smiling.

"I'm sorry about Maria." Emerald replies.

"Oh Emerald, you're so sweet," Laura says. "Where is Richard?"

"He's in the back room where Maria stayed," Emerald answered.

"Poor Richard," Laura says with a sigh. "She loved her Richey,"

Emerald nods her head, accepting the information.

"Where is David?" Emerald asks.

"He, Daddy, and our uncle went to pick out caskets." "Em, how long are you staying," Laura asks.

"Until the funeral,"

"What about your classes?" Laura asks. "You're graduating this month, right?"

"I got them covered," Emerald answers.

Carolyn is now off the phone and returns to the den. She smiles at her daughters.

"Hello girls," Carolyn says as she hugs her girls.

"How are you girls holding up?" Carolyn asks.

"We're okay." They answer.

"I have to run to the market," Carolyn says.

"Ma let us do something, you rest." Elizabeth express. "Emerald, make Mom rest, please,"

"Carolyn," Emerald says suspiciously.

"Mom took care of Maria," Elizabeth explains.

"Well then, you need your rest, don't you, Carolyn," Emerald replies.

Emerald takes Carolyn by the hand and leads her to the den to sit. Emerald plans for Carolyn to not lift a finger. Elizabeth and Laura leaves for the market.

FOR THE NEXT FEW days, Emerald assists the family with funeral arrangements. She also assisted with making the menu for the repass. She assists with arranging the obituary. Emerald makes sure that Carolyn rests. She offers a shoulder to Elizabeth and Laura. Although Richard has been quiet and aloof, he is impressed with Emerald's strength. During this time, she is not shy or reserve. Emerald is the first one in the morning to get up, and she is the last one to go to bed at night. While in bed, she lies next to Richard wrapping her arms around him, and falls asleep.

IT'S THE NIGHT BEFORE the funeral. Emerald sits outside on the porch swing. There is a cool breeze in the air. David comes from inside the house. He is carrying a plate with a sandwich and a glass of juice. She smiles as he sits down besides her.

"This is for you," He says.

"Thank you." She says, taking the plate and glass.

"You have been so preoccupied taking care of everyone else,"

As Emerald eats the sandwich, she looks up at the blanket of stars. Then she notices David looking at Emerald.

"What?" she asks. "Something on my mouth," Emerald begins to wipe her mouth.

"No - um," David says, feeling bad that he was starting. "I don't mean to stare, but you-," he hesitates. "You're so pretty."

"No, I'm not," She says bashfully.

"Yes, you are." He says with a chuckle. "I know beauty when I see it,"

Emerald begins to grow nervous.

"I don't mean to make you nervous," David says apologetically. "Richard said that you were very shy. He said that you remind him of Adrian from *Rocky*."

"He said that? Remind me to punch him later," Emerald comments as she sips her juice. David chuckles.

"Don't be mad," David says. "You're Richey's girl. I wish I find a girl like you. You're amazing?"

"Why?" Emerald asks. "Because I'm helping your family,"

"Yes," David answers quickly. "You barely know us, and you are so cool to be here. Plus, you're classy. When you were first here, you held your own. You're beautiful, classy, and considering what you do, you're intelligent. My mom and Maria, those are the only women I knew that had all those perfect qualities."

"Thanks," Emerald says shyly.

"I see that I'm making you uncomfortable," David says.

"You're not making me uncomfortable. I lost my parents a few years ago. I didn't have friends to help me through that time. Being here and helping any way I can is the right thing to do."

David grins at Emerald.

"Well, enjoy your sandwich." He says.

"Thanks,"

David stands up and then walks back into the house.

THE CHURCH SEEMS MORE like a museum instead of a place of worship. Large bouquets of flowers are placed through the church. Eighty-three candles lit for Maria's eighty-three years of life. In the front of the church lays Maria's body lays in a peach and gold casket. Carolyn had Maria in her favorite cream-colored dress. Maria looks peaceful, as if she is sleeping.

Richard sits with his family. Emerald wonders what is going on through his mind. She doesn't sit next to him but behind him. She wonders if he knows where she is sitting; he does.

Many friends and family come out to pay their respect for their beloved friend. In addition, many take turns to comment on their friend.

"Maria was a beautiful woman, the prettiest gal on our block." A childhood friend of hers says.

"I've never known a friend as dear to me as Maria." An elderly woman replies.

Everyone finishes giving their remarks. Then, the Pastor of the church stands up and reads the program.

"We will now be graced with a song sung by Emerald Dixon."

Richard is surprised to hear that Emerald, his shy girlfriend, is going to sing in front of people she doesn't know.

Emerald is singing? He thinks.

Emerald takes a deep breath. She still doesn't know what she is going to sing. Only Carolyn knew that she is singing. Slowly Emerald stands up and walks to the front of the church. She doesn't look like the typical mourner who wears black to a funeral. Emerald wears an all-white dress suit with matching high heels. Her long hair is in a bun, and she has tiny gold earrings in her ears. She can feel everyone's eyes on her. Her stomach is in knots, and her throat is dry.

What am I going to sing?

Emerald stands in front of the church. She steps forward in front of the microphone stand. Everyone's eyes are fixed on her. Her palms are sweating; her heart is pounding and thumping hard inside her chest. She closes her eyes and begins to sing Ella Fitzgerald and Louie Armstrong's version of *Summer Time.*

Emerald remembers that Maria loves this song. She begins without music, but soon the pianist accompanies her, then the rhythm of the drums, and soon the music begins to sound like a well-orchestrated symphony.

Summertime and the living is easy, Fish
are jumping, and the cotton is high.

Maria was now living easy,

Your daddy's rich and your ma,
Is good looking,
So hush little baby, don't you cry
One of these days, you're gonna rise up
Singing,
Yes, you'll spread Your wings
And you'll take to the sky

Maria is now flying in the sky with not a care in the world. Emerald doesn't think about the eyes staring at her. Emerald places herself in Richard's rose garden. The Enchanting Forrest that Emerald loves to get lost in. She imagines the soft and subtle gentle breeze flowing through the garden, the music that she hears from the wind that she sings along to. She can see Maria sitting in Richard's rose garden. This time Maria is young and beautiful, with long jet black hair and her skin the color of olive oil. Her eyes are dark brown, and they dance every time she smiles. There are no more aches and pains, no more brittle bones. This song is for her.

Yes with daddy and mommy
Standing by…

Richard sits shocked at Emerald's performance. He cannot believe that his girlfriend, his painfully shy girlfriend, is standing before people that she does not know and is singing. He has heard her sing before. She would sing softly in the garden, but now this is different. She is singing loudly with so much emotion. The shiest girl in the world is standing all by herself.

When she finishes the song she opens her eyes. Emerald had almost forgotten where she was. The people's faces startle her. Everyone applauding as they stand on their feet as they; their eyes are moist from tears. Emerald smiles bashfully and quietly goes to her seat.

RICHARD FINDS EMERALD on the porch sitting on the swing. It is quiet and peaceful. He sits down besides her and hands her a glass of ginger-ale. Quickly she takes a sip and takes in a deep breath. Emerald rests her head on his arm. Richard takes his hand and places it under her chin and gentle lifts her face to face him. The look at each other for a moment and then he leans forward kiss her softly on her lips. No words are said.

Okay

EMERALD PARKS HER CAR in the parking lot behind her apartment building. As she climbs out of the car, all she can think about is relaxing. It is Friday, and the acronym TGIF is much appreciated. She has had such a busy week regarding her upcoming graduation because she took time away from her school to attend Richard's grandmother's funeral. Emerald is beyond tired, and now all she wants to do is climb into bed, eat left over Chinese food, watch a good crime drama, and go to sleep.

Maybe in between this lackadaisical adventure, she'll call Richard. She hasn't talked with him since they returned from the funeral. She wants to give him space. He may need time to alone. Maria was very special to him. Space is good. Emerald remembers when her parents died, the last thing she needed was someone in her face asking,

"Are you okay?"

Emerald walks around the corner of her apartment building. To her surprise, she sees Richard sitting on the front step. He has a white rose in his hands. Emerald smiles and quickly walks towards him.

"Hey you," She says.

Richard hands her the rose. Emerald smells the flower and immediately becomes intoxicated with the pleasant fragrance. Richard takes her by the hand and gently pulls her to him. Emerald leans in to give him a kiss.

"Where've you been?" he questions with intense eyes causing them to lock with Emerald's.

"School, I had a ton of work to make up."

"I haven't heard from you," He states coolly.

"I assumed you needed some time to be alone,"

"Why?" Richard asks.

"Maria just died. I thought having some time to yourself is what you needed." Emerald explains.

"What I need is you." Richard states.

"I'm here."

Together they enter Emerald's apartment and walk onto the balcony and sit down.

"So, how are you holding up?" Emerald asks.

"I'm okay; I guess," He answers. "Things seem weird right now. You know, not having her around. I almost called home to talk with her."

"Maria told me that she took care of you when you were born."

"Yeah, my mother wasn't supposed to have children. Something about her uterus was pushed too far back; I don't know, anyway, before she knew it, she was pregnant with me. At eight months into her pregnancy, she went into labor. She lost a lot of blood and went into a coma for a week. Afterward for about a month, Maria took care of me. Maria would put me around things with my mother's scent, like pillows, sweaters so when my mother able to hold me, it would be like she was holding me all along,"

"To think, she wasn't supposed to have kids, and she ended up having four," Emerald said, impressed. "And you were a preemie, and you're six foot two."

"Yep, image that," Richard replies.

"I was a week and a half early," Emerald informs.

"Yeah, but you're tiny, so your miracle doesn't count." Richard jokes.

"Shut up," Emerald said, laughing.

Richard laughs with her.

"You know Emmy; you surprised me at the funeral," Richard says.

"I surprised myself." She replied with a chuckle.

"What made you do it?"

"Your mom asked me to. She told me that it would mean a lot to Maria,"

"It did. It meant a lot to me too. How did you know what to sing?"

"Ella," Emerald answers.

Richard grins.

They sit quietly for a moment allowing the cool breeze to soothe them. Richard then looks over at Emerald.

"Does the pain ever stop?" he asks.

Emerald doesn't look at him. She looks across the balcony and focuses her attention on a tree. She thinks for a moment.

How do I answer that question? She says to herself.

Slowly Emerald shakes her head. Tears forms in her eyes. Her parents have been dead for five years now. There has never been a moment when she is not thinking about them. To think, at twenty-seven, she is an orphan, no family whatsoever. Emerald remembers the day that she found out that her parents had died.

◆

It was a rainy Saturday night well into the midnight hour. Emerald was awakened by a loud knocking on the front door of her apartment. When she answered the door, she was surprised to see two policemen standing in front of her.

"Are you Emerald Dixon?" they asked.

"Yes," she answered.

"I'm Officer Smith, and this is Office McGovern." They introduced themselves.

"Yes," she replied nervously.

"There was an accident on Route 48, involving a Toyota Camry and a Nissan Altima,"

Emerald's father drove a Nissan. The police standing outside her door after midnight only meant one thing.

"Are your parents Mark and Sharon Dixon?" they asked.

"Yes, what-,"

"Ms. Dixon, there were no survivors," They informed.

Emerald gasps covering her mouth.

"I'm sorry, Ms. Dixon, but we're going to need you to identify the bodies,"

Emerald started to cry. Within the hour, the policemen took her to the morgue, where she identified her mother and father, both dead. There was no one to hold her as she cried; no one to comfort her. There were a few family members that came to the funeral, offering their condolences and their deepest sympathy. And after everything was over, she was left alone, mourning her parents.

Although this was a few years ago, sometimes she still cry at night.

◆

"No, the pain doesn't go away," Emerald finally says. "But it does get easier to deal with. The sun does eventually shines, and in time you learn to really appreciate things. Little things that once seemed non-existent now seem to matter, like watching a flower stand alone in a field or observing a sunrise. Rich, there is just something about a sunrise that takes my breath away. How the colors blend just right to make such a beautiful mixture."

"When does it get easier?"

"As soon as you let it," Emerald says, looking at Richard. "I still miss my parents. At times I cry at night because they're not here to see me and see what I have accomplished. I can't say, 'Daddy look, I co-wrote a blockbuster movie. Mama, I met the most amazing man who thinks the world of me'."

"See, that is the thing," Richard says. "It bothers me that I can't call Maria and tell her about a new part in a movie."

"So you share it with someone else, someone you love, and someone who will appreciate just like she did. I can't talk about my schooling with my parents, but I can share it with you, and I know that you're just as proud of me." Richard nods his head.

"Yeah, I am proud of you. I know your parents would be proud of you too, especially how you've grown."

"Sometimes people are removed from our lives so that we can grow," Emerald said. "In a way, I look at my parents' death as a push for me to come out of my shell."

"But your parents died before you came out here."

"Yeah, but if they were still alive, I would have never come here. The movie would have been done on its own. Coming out here was a step that I made by myself."

"So why do you think Maria died?" Richard asked.

"Well, for one, she was eighty-three years old, but maybe she was here just long enough to see you happy and in love and that is all she needed."

"Yeah, she told me to keep you."

"Your dad said that I made the cut," Emerald said, smiling.

They both said with a chuckle and said:

"Ella,"

Richard gets up and approaches Emerald. He stands in front of Emerald. He takes her hands and gently pulls her up. She stands up, and he wraps his arms around her.

"I wish I could have met your parents," Richard says. "I wished I could have comforted you the way you are comforting me."

Emerald rests her head on his chest.

"In a sense, you are comforting me."

He gently lifts her head so he can look into her eyes.

"Who did you look like?"

"They say my mom,"

"You have pictures?" Richard asks.

"Yeah, come on."

Emerald leads Richard into the apartment and into her bedroom. As he sits on the bed, Emerald goes into her closet and pulls out a photo album. She sits next to Richard, and together they look over the photos. Richard chuckles at some of the pictures of Emerald when she was kid. Most of the photos of Emerald when she was a kid, she was hiding behind her mother or father."

"So shy," Richard comments, smiling.

"I hated photos," Emerald says, chuckling.

"Your mother was beautiful." He said. "It is as if you two were identical, the same heartwarming eyes, that sweet smile. Emmy, why don't you have these pictures up?"

"Because when I came out here, I didn't expect to stay. I just came out here to make a movie, and in the meanwhile, I transferred my credits here so I wouldn't get behind,"

"And you end up falling in love with me." She nods her head and smiles.

"Yep, I would have gotten my doctrine and went back to Pittsburgh."

"Just like that," Richard asks. "You would have gone back to Pittsburgh after all the success here in L.A.," Emerald nods.

"Yeah," she answers. "I made a successful movie with Richard DeMarco, I'm good."

"Richard DeMarco," Richard chuckles with a sigh.

"But now," Emerald begins. "I am enjoying this new life with my boyfriend, Richard. I'm in no hurry to go back to Pittsburgh,"

He looks over at Emerald. She smiles and shyly looks away.

"Emerald," Richard says her name softly yet sternly.

Emerald turns her head to face him.

"Em, you are so amazing," he says to her in a softly.

"I'm just Emerald." She says modestly.

"No, you're this gem, this rare individual that has this special value."

"Oh, yeah, then what is the value?"

"Your heart,"

Emerald attempts to look away, but Richard doesn't let her. He gently places his hand on her face and turns her towards him. Richard leans forward to kiss her. Richard hasn't kissed his Emmy in two weeks. The first week was when Maria died, and this past week when Emerald was making up her schoolwork. Now it is like he is kissing her for the first time. He has missed her soft lips and that cherry-flavored lip gloss. He has missed the sweet smell of her perfume. He has missed holding her in his arms.

As he kisses her, Richard can feel himself getting aroused. He wants her here, and he wants her now. Richard doesn't want to wait anymore. He begins to kiss her harder, letting her know that he is aroused. He stops and looks at her. By the look in his eyes, Emerald can tell what is on Richard's mind. He looks into her eyes, making sure that this is okay. Her eyes say yes.

"Do you want me to stop?" he asks softly. Slowly Emerald shakes her head.

"Are you sure?" he asks in a soft whisper.

Emerald leans in to kiss him, and within moments they are lying down on the bed. Richard climbs on top of her and gently pressing his pelvis into hers. Emerald moans softly as she runs her fingers through his hair and kisses him passionately. Richard's body aches for her. It only makes sense that he takes her. As he softly kisses her along the neck, he slowly unbuttons her shirt. Richard caresses her stomach. Her body feels soft like silk. Then he takes his hands and glides softly up and down her legs. Then he unbuttons her pants. Her body responds to his touch. Richard is ready. He sits up to attempt to pull her pants down, but then suddenly, he stops.

What am I doing? He asked himself.

This girl is too special to simply screw, and that is what he was going to do. This girl is too special to just take, have his way, and when it's over, promise to love her later. If he takes her, he can ruin everything he has established with her, the foundation of their love. This is real love because sex is not yet in the picture. Richard doesn't need a good roll in the hay to prove his love or for her to prove her love. All they need to do is look into each other's eyes. Plus, this would have been their first night, her first night. Richard doesn't want their night or any nights to be like this.

Emerald reaches for him, but he pulls away. She sits up and holds Richard's face in her palms and attempts to kiss him, but he pulls away. Richard has never resisted Emerald's touch. She tilts her head to the side, questioning with her eyes.

"Emmy, I'm sorry." He says, his eyes tense. "We can't so this."

"Rich, it's okay. I'm ready." She says.

He looks at her. Hope and trust are in her eyes. Richard wants to cry. What did he almost do?

"I know I won't be much of a thrill right now," she says, taking his hands. "But if you're patient, I can learn,"

"A thrill?" Richard asks, offended. He stands up. "Do you think that's what I want is some trill?" Richard stands up. "If I touch you, I'll destroy everything,"

"No, you won't; I want you to touch me!" Emerald exclaims.

He looks at Emerald. She doesn't understand what he is telling her. She is so innocent. How could he have almost taken that innocence from her? He has to have her. He is longing for her but can't just take her. Even though she is his woman, his lady, the love of his life, morally, she is not his.

"Marry me?" he said, almost demanding.

"What?" Emerald asks, shocked.

"You heard me," Richard said, almost snapping at her.

Emerald doesn't say anything. She buttons up her shirt and climbs to the front of the bed.

"Marriage," she says.

"Yeah," Richard replies.

"Why?"

"What do you mean why?" he asks with a chuckle,

"Because I love you,"

"We never talked about marriage?"

"Okay," Richard says, sitting down on the bed. "Let's talk,"

Emerald is shocked at this sudden proposal. She is surprised at how serious Richard is. She doesn't know what to say.

"Why all of a sudden you want to get married?" she asks.

"All of a sudden," Richard asks. "Emerald, I've wanted to marry you for the longest time. With your school schedule and my work schedule, planning seemed impossible. But that night, when we were in the den, and my mom called telling us about Maria, I was going to propose."

"You were going to propose?" Emerald asks doubtfully.

"Yes," Richard answers quickly.

Emerald looks away. She takes in a deep breath. Richard doesn't like the reaction he is getting.

"What's the matter?" He asks her as he moves closer to her.

"I just never expected you to want to get married."

"Why?"

"I don't know," Emerald said. "Richard DeMarco doesn't get married."

"Don't do that," Richard scolded in a cool tone. "Don't movie star me. I'm not your movie star; I'm your man."

"I'm sorry," she says softly.

A moment passes.

"So, what are we doing?" Richard asks. "We're just dating to be dating?"

"No, but we don't have to get married," Emerald says.

"Yes, we do," Richard says. "Because I want to make love to you,"

"We could be doing it now!" Emerald snaps. "You stopped. Before, I could understand with my insecurities, but now, Richard, I don't understand."

"I can't touch you unless you're my wife," Richard said.

"Richard, that is old fashion," Emerald says, frowning.

"I don't care how old fashion it is," Richard tells her. "I'll ruin everything. Don't you understand how special and rare you are?"

"I'm only rare because I haven't been laid yet!"

"Don't talk like that!" Richard snaps. "This is not about getting laid. It's about the sanctity of marriage and the bedroom. If we have sex tonight, then we're just another couple screwing, but if were married, then it's a husband and wife, a union making love."

Emerald doesn't say anything. She takes in a deep breath. Richard stands up, then walks to her and kneels down on his knees before her. He looks deep into her eyes until they lock.

"I never loved a woman like I love you. You are everything to me. I can't breathe without you. I can't function without you. I can't imagine a life without you."

Emerald looks away.

"Emmy, don't you want to marry me?" Richard asks feeling rejected.

"Of course I want to marry you, but I don't think you're thinking with a clear head,"

"What is not clear about my love for you?"

"Rich, your grandma just died,"

"And-,"

"You're emotional right now," Emerald says him.

"Emmy, I was going to ask you before she died. I am not that emotional. I know what I want."

"You can have me; I am right here. You can have me at anytime,"

"It's more than that, Emerald. I want to come home from work; you greet me with that smile. I want to wake up in the morning with my arms around you."

"Then we can just move in together," Emerald suggests.

"No, that's not enough," Richard tells her standing up. "I don't just want to go on as your man, but as your husband, you're lifetime partner. Emmy, baby, what are you afraid of?"

"Nothing,"

"Yes, I can see it in your eyes."

"What if we end up like the rest of the Hollywood marriages. Married today, divorced tomorrow,"

"You're not getting away from me that easy; you know that," Richard says to her, smiling.

Emerald smiles back.

"Em, remember when you told me you wanted your first time to be on your wedding night, with the scented candles, Roberta Flack," Richard asking in a coaxing manner. Emerald smiles. "Then let that be us. Let's live that fantasy."

"What if I make you unhappy?" Emerald asks softly.

"How can that be?" Richard asked. "From the moment when we been together, I have never so been happier. I promise baby to be good to you. I will shower you with love and maybe jewelry," He winks.

Emerald giggles.

"I'll be good to you. I'll never hurt you," Richard said.

"I know,"

"You know," Richard said.

"Yes, I know you'll be good to me. You're good to me now." Emerald said.

Richard caresses her face.

"Marrying you will be a dream come true," she says.

"So let's dream, be my wife and let's live the life that others dream about."

All her life, she wanted this, to marry Richard DeMarco. A dream that all the girls in high school had, and now Emerald is about to have this opportunity to live this dream. She knows that Richard would give her the world. So why not marry him? Their first time can be right, not just a cheap thrill. She knows that he'll be gentle with her. It can be what Emerald always wanted, that magical night, with candles everywhere, and Roberta Flack playing in the background and with the man of her dreams,

"Okay," She says softly.

"Okay?" he asks smiling.

"Yes, okay," Emerald says, taking in a deep breath.

Richard stands up and takes her hands, and then gently lifts her up. He looks into her eyes. She smiles; he smiled back. "You'll marry me?" Richard asks.

"Yes," Emerald says with a chuckle, and then tears form in her eyes. "I will marry you."

Emerald wraps her arms around him, and Richard spins her around then kisses her.

"Okay, come on," Richard says, taking her hands and leading her out of the room.

"Where are we going?"

"To get married,"

"What?"

"We can honeymoon at my beach house in Hawaii," Richard says, smiling.

"How long will we stay?"

"Doesn't matter, you're done with your school. You graduate in a month. We can stay until then."

"Tonight, as in we leave right now?" Emerald asks.

"Right now,"

"Don't you think we're rushing this?"

"No, this is the perfect time," Richard says.

"Well, why don't we wait until after my graduation?" Emerald suggests.

"Because I start a new movie, and I won't be able to see you."

Emerald takes in a deep breath,

"Richard, I don't know-," Emerald

lets go of Richard's hand.

"What's the matter?" he asks.

"This is too sudden," Emerald says, shaking her head. "I have a lot to do. I have to pack and then ask someone to watch the place, and then where will I go when we come back?"

"What do you mean where would you go? You'll be my wife; you come home with me."

"There is too much to do; I just can't run off and get married," Emerald said.

Richard can see that she is getting overwhelmed. Richard cups her face in his palms.

"Listen to me, baby, it's okay to run off and do something crazy. Everything doesn't have to be planned."

"I know but-,"

"But what Emmy, this is our life. We can get married, have a wonderful honeymoon. Roast a pig on the island, no one to answer to; just you, me alone, and away from the world."

Alone and away is how Emerald likes to live.

"What about a dress?" she asks.

"We can get you a dress," Richard assures her.

"A white one," Emerald demands sweetly.

"No other color will be just,"

"Okay,"

"Okay." Richard says, smiling, "I'll let you pack. I'll be waiting in the living room,"

Emerald nods. Richard kisses her and then walks out of the room. Emerald takes a deep breath and then begins to pack her bags.

SHE APPEARS BEFORE RICHARD with two suitcases.

He grabs the suitcases from her.

"Are you ready?"

"Yes," She answers.

"Okay, let's go," Richard says, smiling at her.

Together they leave the apartment.

Great Expectations

IF EMERALD CAN THINK of one thing that she would not be doing when she woke up this morning that would be eloping with her boyfriend. She sits on the plane, rewinding back in her mind what she did today that has led to this event.

She woke up at eight o'clock. Then she is at school working on her thesis. By four o'clock, she meets with her publisher about her new book that will be released three months from today, and five-thirty, she is meeting with Dave Stevens, the film director of *The Topaz Chronicles*. They talk about the possibility of a sequel. By seven o'clock, she goes home and finds Richard on her front step, and two hours later, he proposes to her, and she accepts. That has been today.

Emerald thinks about the past year. First is the coming to L.A. to make a movie. Then when she thinks that was over, she starts to date Richard DeMarco, the actor. Emerald meets his family, and just last week, she assists his family in burying their beloved matriarch. Now, she is on her way to Hawaii to marry the man of her dreams.

Emerald is excited and nervous at the same time. She is going to marry the man that she has been in love with since the tenth grade. Emerald remembers daydreaming about him in high school. This is the same man who loves her. No more daydreaming. Now she is living the dream, her dream. She pinches herself to make sure that this is not a dream that she won't wake up in Pittsburgh.

Richard looks over and sees Emerald pinching herself. He grabs her hands.

"Are you okay?" he asks with a chuckle.

"Yeah," she says, smiling, feeling silly. "I am just making sure that I am wake, that this isn't a dream,"

"Then if this is a dream. Then I hope that we never wake up," He says, kissing her hands.

"You know, you're not supposed to see the bride before the wedding,"

"Who needs tradition, huh?" he asks her with a grin.

RICHARD AND EMERALD STEPS off the plan. She smiles at Richard when she sees a chauffeur standing next to a Rolls Royce waiting for them. She looks at him smiling. He winks at her. The chauffeur holds the door open for Emerald. He nods his head and smiles at her.

"Good morning Mr. DeMarco,"

"Gregory," Richards says, smiling and pats his arm.

"THIS HOUSE IS AS big as your home in L.A.,"

"Almost," He says with a chuckle. "Come on, let me show you around,"

Richard takes Emerald's hand and shows her around the house. To Emerald, it is a mansion. There is a back porch that leads to the beach. There are five actual bedrooms, two offices. Richard uses one of the offices for his work. There is a small greenhouse filled with all kinds of flowers. There is spa with a Jacuzzi, a large kitchen, a breakfast nook, a dining room, and a living room. To Emerald, this house is better than the one Richard had in California.

"Mr. DeMarco," Someone says.

Richard and Emerald turns around and see an elderly woman standing before them. Richard smiles at her.

"Elaine, hi," Richard says.

"Hello, this must be Ms. Dixon?" Elaine replies.

"Yes, Emerald meet Elaine," Richard introduces. "Elaine keeps this place looking good."

"Very nice to meet you, Elaine," Emerald says.

"Is there anything you need?"

Richard looks at Emerald,

"I'm okay." Emerald says.

"We're good Elaine, thanks." Richard says.

Elaine smiles and then leaves.

Richard turns towards Emerald. He takes her hands and kisses them.

"Unpack, okay, and then we can go shopping for whatever you need. Then we can go to the church. I know a pastor that has agreed to marry us.

"Okay," Emerald says, taking in a deep breath.

Richard tilts his head, looking at her.

"You okay?" he asks.

Emerald nods her head as her eyes search around the room. She takes in deep breaths.

"Em,"

"I'm okay," she says, looking at him. "Just taking everything in."

Richard grins and takes her hands to kiss them again.

"I love you," he tells her.

"I love you too," she says.

After Emerald unpacks, Richard and she leave the beach house to go shopping for a few odds and ends for their wedding.

THE CHURCH IS SMALL, but lovely. The pastor and his wife wait for them to arrive.

"Here they come." the pastor says, smiling at them as Richard and Emerald enter the church.

"Rev. Joe," Richard greets, extending his hand. "Glad you were available,"

"Glad I can be of help." The pastor says, shaking Richard's hands.

"Come along with me, honey." Rev Joe's wife Vikki says to Emerald.

VIKKI SITS AT THE piano and plays, *Here Comes the Bride.* Holding a bouquet of red roses, Emerald slowly marches down the church in a white, strapless all lace gown that give her body mermaid silhouette shape. Richard cannot believe how beautiful she looks. Her hair is not in eyes. Her long hair is full of curls and waves, giving her that old Hollywood glamour look.

Richard stands waiting for her looking handsome. He wears a black suit, his hair he combed is back; he too looks like Hollywood royalty.

Finally, she stands before Richard. They smile at each other. Joe smiles at the two. They are so happy. Joe looks at Vicki, and he smiles at her. She smiles back.

"We have our own vows, Reverend," Richard informed. Joe nods his head.

"If someone told me two years ago that you and I would be here getting married, I would have laughed. I cannot believe that I had a life without you." Richard begins to say to her, "Emerald, you are everything to me. You are my best friend.
You are so special, so amazing, and so wonderful. I love you."

"Richard," Emerald begins. "Thank you so much for accepting me for who I am. Thank you for being my best friend. I am the luckiest woman in the world because you love me,"

"Richard, do you take Emerald to be your lawfully wedded wife to have and to hold from this day forward, for better or for worse, for richer and for poorer, in sickness and in health, to love and to cherish, from this day forward until death do you part?"

"I do,"

"Emerald, do you take Richard to be your lawfully wedded husband to have and to hold from this day forward, for better or for worse, for richer and for poorer, in sickness and in health, to love and to cherish, from this day forwards until death do you part?"

"I do," Emerald answers smiling.

"By the powers invested in me, I now pronounce you man and wife. You may kiss the bride."

Richard and Emerald kiss each other.

RICHARD CARRIES EMERALD OVER the threshold.

"You're glowing." He says to her

Richard set her down.

"I'm so happy." She says, wrapping her arms around his shoulders, "I am the happiest girl in the world."

Richard leans forward to kiss her. He can kiss her all he wants. He doesn't have to stop because now she is his wife; she is his. Soon their kissing becomes passionate, and he begins to caress her along her body. Emerald pulls back.

"I'm going to change into something more comfortable," She says, smiling.

"Wait," He says, "Let's have a drink."

Richard gets to a bottle of Champaign and pours her a glass, and together they toasted.

"Emerald, you're everything to me,"

"I love you," She says. "I cannot believe that I am married. I'm totally changing my name, Emerald DeMarco, none of that Dixon-DeMarco stuff." Richard chuckles. "And I can't wait until we are together." She says, smiling.

"Yeah, you're that hot and horny for me?" he jokes.

"Shut up." She says, laughing. "But seriously, this is what you wanted. You wanted me pure for my wedding night."

"Our wedding night," He corrects. "I knew that we would get married. It was just a matter of when. Besides, it's what right. As close as we have gotten before, I couldn't image myself thinking of doing this any other way,"

"What do you think everyone is going to say when they found out that we eloped?" Emerald asks.

"I know my sisters are going to flip out because they weren't bride's maids. David, he could care less; all he wants is free booze. My parents, my mother is going to flip because she would want to organize some spectacular event. Besides, who cares? This is our life not theirs,"

Emerald walks to the window of the living room.

"Who would have thought that I'd be here, married to a movie star," She comments. "I used to sit in class and daydream about what it would be like getting married to the man of my dreams, but all of that seemed like a fairy tale, but here I am living that fairy tale. I'm here with you, married. I am a married woman,"

"Yep, and pretty soon, I'm gonna fatten you up with a bunch of babies!" Richard says as he picks up Emerald in his arms and carries her into the bedroom.

Emerald shrills with excitement!

"A bunch," she laughs.

"Oh yeah, ten maybe twelve," Richard says as they lay on the bed.

Emerald laughs. She looks and sees that there are several white candles already lit in the room. Her eyes question Richard.

"I had Elaine place candles in the room," Richard informs.

She grins.

"You are so beautiful," he says to her.

Emerald smiled bashfully.

Richard leans down to kiss her.

"Will you promise me one thing?" Emerald asks.

"Anything,"

"Right now, we're happy, and we're in love. Richard promise me that when we're still married for like fifty years, we will still be happy and still be in love." "I promise, baby," Richard says softly.

Then he leans in and kissed her again.

"I brought this nice little lacy thing a few months back, you know, for us in case, we-,"

"Sex clothes, huh?" Richard asks in a joking away.

"Yeah," Emerald says, laughing. "I'm going to put it on, okay,"

"Okay," Richard says.

A Period of Time

Emerald walks into the bathroom and Richard around into the bedroom. He can't wait until Emerald comes out. He changes into pair of silk black pajama pants and then sits down on the bed. In the bathroom, Emerald sits on the edge of the tub. Her stomach begins to tie into knots. As she rubs her stomach, she wants a ginger ale.

Tonight is definitely the night, she says to herself.

She can no longer not be ready. She cannot –not want to. Emerald looks at the 15 karat emerald cut white gold engagement ring. Emerald gulps; she shakes her head at the ring.

Emerald cut. She says, looking at the ring.

Richard wanted the emerald cut for obvious reasons. She shakes her head and takes in a deep breath. She is nervous and excited at the same time. She stands up and looks herself over in the mirror. Again like she did on the airplane, she pinches herself. She is married. She is a married woman. She is a Mrs.; She is Mrs. Emerald DeMarco. She is Mrs. Richard DeMarco. She is married to *the Richard DeMarco.* Emerald begins to feel light-headed. Immediately she holds on to the sink and slowly inhales and exhale.

Don't have a panic attack, she warns herself.

She waits for a moment and then gathers herself together. She stands up and looks herself over in the full mirror. She wears a long, white lace, night gown with a lacy over coat. She is please with what she sees. She smiles because she knows that Richard will like it. Emerald turns towards to the door but hesitates to come out of the bathroom. She backs away.

Stop it! She scolds herself. *This is really it. I can do this.*

Still standing still, Emerald shakes her head.

I'm not ready. Emerald sits down on the side of the bath tub. *Wait, this is with Richard DeMarco, the man of my dreams. I am going to have sex; make love to Richard DeMarco. He is going to be my first. I can do this.* Emerald bolts towards the door but then quickly backs away; n*o, I can't do this. I'm not ready, not yet; I'll just tell him. Richard will understand. He always understands.* Emerald walks towards the door again. She waits a moment and then backs again. *No, I have to have sex. This is my wedding night. Besides, it's with Richard; this is okay. He'll be gentle with me. What if he doesn't like my body? What if I do something wrong?*

Emerald backs away from the door again and sits down on the side of the tub.

The French vanilla-scented candles filled the air. Richard sits on the edge of the bed, anxiously waiting for Emerald. He stands up and attempts to knock on the bathroom door to see if she is all right, but he doesn't. He runs his fingers through his hair and slowly paces the bedroom.

Finally, she appears in the doorway of the bedroom. The light from the moon shines through the window spotlighting on her. She looks like a goddess. He grins and holds his hands out to her. She walks to him and takes his hands.

"Wow." He says, smiling.

Emerald smiles bashfully.

Richard lets go of her hands. He walks to the stereo and turns it on. Roberta's Flack song, *First Time I Ever Saw Your Face*, comes on Emerald smiles.

"You remembered." She says.

Richard nods his head.

"Come here," he says in a soft tone.

She walks to him. Richard gently takes her in his arms, and they begin to dance.

"We were dancing when I first kissed you." He whispers in her ear.

"Hmm," Emerald says, taking in a deep breath.

Richard feels the tension in her body.

"Are you nervous?" he asks her.

"No," she answers quickly.

"Look at me, baby," he says.

She takes in a deep breath and looks up at Richard.

The room is too dark for him to see the intensity in her eyes. Richard leans forward and gently kisses her lips.

Richard wants tonight to be perfect for her. After tonight, everything is going to change. He takes in a deep breath. He feels the pressure that is on him. If Emerald isn't pleased, then he failed. Then again, if she is pleased, then he performed well.

He steps back to admire his wife. Richard almost doesn't want to have sex with her. She is so precious. He feels honored that her first time will be with him. It is like she has been saving herself just for him and only him. They don't have to do anything tonight. They have their whole lives to make love. Richard has his whole life to teach her the art of love making. She is his wife now; there is no rush. As he holds her, he wants her more than he has ever wanted her. It would be foolish to wait.

Richard leans forward and kissing her passionately. His hands gently glide up and down her body.

As much as she enjoys Richard's touch, Emerald is nervous. He can feel the tension in her body. He pulls away and caresses her face.

"Emerald, relax, baby," He encourages softly.

She takes in a deep breath and nods her head.

"If at any time that you're uncomfortable and you want me to stop, just say so, okay," Richard says.

Again she nods her head but then questions why he would say that.

Why would I be uncomfortable? She asks herself.

Gently, Richard takes off her nightgown, letting it side down her body. He is amazed at her tiny body. Her form is structured and enticing. It is taking all of Richard's control not to take her and ravish her. With his index finger, and gently outlines her flat stomach, then moves his finger up towards her breast. Richard looks her in her eyes to make sure she's okay. She grins, encouraging him to continue. Richard's hands move to her neck, and then he locks his fingers in her hair. He gently pulls her head back and kisses her neck softly. Emerald moans softly. Richard begins to kiss her passionately. He places his hands on her waist and pulls her into him.

As she runs her fingers through his hair, Richard's hands caress her body. He can't wait any longer. From the way she kisses him, Richard can tell she too cannot wait any longer. Richard steps back and sweeps her in his arms and carries her to his bed, and gently lies her down.

Emerald lies still looking like a Greek goddess. Softly he caresses her silky skin while anointing her with kisses. This body is now his, and he is going to take each moment to explore it. Slowly he climbs on top of her. He can feel her body tremble beneath him. Soon they become one. He slowly and carefully moves inside her as if his life depends on it.

Emerald cannot believe what is happening. Finally, she is with the man that she has loved since she was fifteen years old. However, something is missing. Is this lovemaking? She feels him physically, but she can't feel him emotionally? She knows that it would be a new experience, but not like this. Emerald doesn't like what she is feeling. Making love to him is supposed to be special; where is the special? The man she has wait for all her life is not the man she wants to be with at this moment. She wants him to stop.

Is this what he meant? She asks herself. *Stop, stop,* she cries, but her voice cannot utter the words.

Emerald prays that he will stop. That he will get off of her and vow to never touch her again.

As Richard caresses her, he wonders if she enjoying herself.

She's okay, he says to himself. *She's not telling me to stop. Everything is fine. Emerald will have said something if she is uncomfortable.*

He doesn't want to stop. She feels so good to him. Richard hasn't been with a woman in over a year, and although this is more than just physical, he misses being with a woman, inside a woman.

Finally, it's over.

Richard kisses her on the cheek and whispers in her ear;

"I love you,"

Emerald is disgusted. She wants to throw up. There isn't enough ginger-ale in the world to settle her stomach.

RICHARD WAKES UP; IT'S the middle of the night. He reaches for Emerald, but she is not in bed. He sits up and calls out for her.

"Em,"

There is no answer.

"Emmy," Richard calls out again.

He climbs out of bed, puts his pants on, and looks around the house.

"Emmy,"

He finds her sleeping on the couch. She is wearing a thick, heavy sweat pants and a shirt. Emerald looks so peaceful he doesn't want to wake her up, but he gets down on his knees and gently kisses her lips. She finally wakes up.

"Hey," He says, smiling at her.

"Hi," She says, sitting up.

"What are you doing out here?" he asks.

"I couldn't sleep," She answers.

"Why couldn't you sleep?" he asks.

Emerald shrugs her head.

"Are you okay?"

Emerald nods her head.

"Come back to bed." He gently coaxes.

Richard takes Emerald by the hand and leads her back to the bedroom. As they walk into the bedroom, Richard looks at Emerald.

"I have something for you," He informs with a flirtatious grin.

"For me,"

"Yeah," He says, nodding his head.

"What?"

"Come see?" he says.

Together they walk into the bedroom. As Emerald sits down on the bed, Richard opens a drawer at the dresser and pulls out three small gift boxes. He walks back to her then sits down beside her. Richard hands her the boxes.

"What is this?" Emerald asks.

"Just open them," Richard presses gently. "I was going to wait until the morning, but I think now is appropriate."

Emerald begins to open the boxes. The first box is a marquise diamond pendant that is set in 14k white gold. The second box is a matching bracelet, and the third box is matching earrings.

Emerald is shocked at the expensive presents.

"Richard." She says, "What is all this for?"

"They're what you call wedding presents." He says, smiling.

"Wedding presents are toasters, pots, and pans." She says.

"Pots and pans are from relatives you normally don't see but are obligated to invite to your wedding. Diamonds are from a man to his wife because I love you." Richard said.

He leans in to kiss her.

"We didn't have a wedding," Emerald says. "I mean we-,"

He notices that she seems solemn.

"What's the matter?" he asks softly.

"I didn't get you anything." She says quietly.

"Oh, but you did," He says to her.

"I did." She asks.

"Yeah," He says, smiling. "You gave me the best gift that a woman gave give to her husband, you're virginity. You can only give that gift once, and you chose me. I'm honored."

Emerald looks away. At this moment, she doesn't feel very honorable. Richard gently takes his hands and gently lifts her face to face him. Richard senses that something is bothering her.

"What's the matter? Did I say something wrong?"

"No," she answers quickly and then grins.

"Do you like the gifts?" he asks.

"Of course, I like them." She says with a grin, "They're beautiful."

"Then what's on your mind?" Richard asks.

"Nothing, I'm a bit tired." Emerald answers.

Richard leans in and kissed her on the cheek.

"Emmy tonight was real special. Being with you-,"

Emerald looks away. Richard senses her distance.

"Emmy baby, what's wrong?" Richard asks as a knot forms in his throat.

"Nothing," she replies.

A knot is also forming in her throat. Emerald feels tears welling up in her eyes. Richard's heart broke. He has failed.

"Okay," He says softly.

He nods his head, accepting his defeat.

Emerald turns her face away to wipe the tears that fell from her eyes. Richard lifted her chin to look into her eyes.

"It's okay," He says to her.

She nods her head. Richard wraps his arms around her.

"What can I do?"

Emerald sits up. Richard wipes the tears from her eyes.

Slowly she shakes her head and moves away from Richard's touch.

"I just-," she hesitates to speak.

Emerald tries to explain how she feels, but the tears begin to flow from her eyes. She puts her head down, feeling ashamed.

"Okay," Richard whispers as he leans forward and kisses her on top of her head.

He wraps his arms around her and they sit quietly.

The Wedding

ONCE THE DEMARCOS FOUND out that Richard and Emerald eloped they insisted on throwing them a wedding party which included a formal wedding with a church full of people, a church full of flowers, and a reception for the world. Carolyn DeMarco wants to see her eldest son get married, not hear about it. Although the idea is welcoming to Richard, he hesitating to give his mother an answer as they talk on the phone.

"What's the problem, Richey," Carolyn asks with a sigh."It can be a lovely wedding."

"Because Ma, Emerald is shy, very, very shy. She is not one for crowds,"

"What crowd?" Carolyn says, looking at the list of five hundred names of guests and relatives that she has already invited, "Just a few people here and there. What about her family? I'm sure they would want to know and come,"

"Emerald doesn't have any family," Richard says, rubbing his temples.

"She has no family?" Carolyn asked doubtfully.

"Her parents died in a car accident a few years back, and she's the only child. She's basically an orphan. Ma, please, Emerald is painfully shy-,"

"Shy," Carolyn mimics sardonically. "Richey, how shy can she be? She's a famous author? Is she too shy when she does book signings?"

"She doesn't do book signings," Richard says. "She's too shy."

Carolyn lets out a big sigh. She likes Emerald and thinks highly of her but does not quite comprehend Emerald's personality.

"She sang at the funeral?" Carolyn states in hopes of proving her point.

"Yep, and hid outside away from everyone at the house, remember?"

Carolyn reflects back on that day of the funeral. She does remember Emerald staying outside on the porch for the most part of the day after the funeral, but she didn't think it was because she was shy. Carolyn thought she just needed some fresh air, all things considered.

"Why is she so shy?" Carolyn asks, now frustrated at her daughter-in-law.

"I don't know, Ma," Richard answers, taking in a deep breath.

"Well, why didn't you guys just invite us?" Carolyn whined.

"Ma, we just took off in the spur of the moment." Richard explains. Carolyn just shakes her head. Richard can tell that his mother is shaking her head.

"Ma, don't shake your head at me."

"I'm not," Carolyn says, shaking her head. "I just don't understand you at times."

"Ma, what is not to understand?"

"You meet this girl and tell us how special she is, it takes months for us to meet her, and then you run off and get married,"

"Ma, I told you that she is shy. Emerald is painfully shy. Now that the word is out that we're married, the media and paparazzi have not left us alone. They hide across the street, follow us everywhere. It's very overwhelming for her."

"Okay," Carolyn says, putting her hands in the air. "Listen, just talk to her, please, Richey. I'm sure that you can hire security and all that stuff,"

Richard sighs. He is getting a headache. Richard massages his temples.

"Okay, I will talk to her, but I am not making any promises,"

"That's fine, dear; just call us as soon as possible," Carolyn says, smiling.

"Okay," Richard says, sighing running his fingers through his hair.

"Okay, talk to you soon," Carolyn says.

"Okay, Ma,"

"I love you,"

"Love you too, Ma,"

Richard hangs up the phone, runs his fingers through his hair, and lets out a long sigh. His mother knows how to lay on the guilt. From the moment she found out about Emerald, his mother nagged him to meet her. He thought that was enough, now that he is married, she is going to nag him about this wedding reception. Richard wouldn't mind another wedding. He would marry Emerald every day, but he knows his wife. This is the last thing she wants to do to be bothered by a ton of people she doesn't know. Emerald has a lot on her agenda. She has finished school. Her graduation is in a few weeks. She is getting her doctorate in English Literature. She is also was working on a new book. Emerald is trying to move everything from her apartment into Richard's home and trying to find her place as his wife in his home.

Emerald has never lived with anyone except her parents. Living with someone is going to be a challenge. And to top things off, she is married; the married life is a lifetime challenge in itself. So this wedding reception just might be the straw that breaks the camel's back. Planning a wedding that is not needed because she is already married, and this wedding reception is just for show, not Emerald's style.

Richard and Emerald have been married for two weeks, and these two weeks it have not been a blissful honeymoon. The two weeks where man and wife stay in bed hiding from the world and make sweet and passionate love all day and all night. These past two weeks, Emerald makes it her mission to avoid Richard. Ever since they had first made love, Emerald finds reasons not to be around. When he wakes up in the morning, she is not there. She is either at school or out somewhere where she can write.

When Richard attempts to spend time with her, she'll avoid him by saying she has to work on her thesis or meet with her editor. When it comes to intimacy, they only made love once, their wedding night. Richard knows that she doesn't want to, so he doesn't push her.

◆

The next day after their wedding night, Richard insisted that he shows Emerald around Hawaii. He takes her to boutiques, buys her new clothes. Emerald wanted to stay out all night, which is not like her. Richard wanted to get back to the beach house, to talk or try to make love, but by the end of the night after the shopping spree, she went to sleep.

After a few days of shopping in just about every store, Emerald was ready to get back to California. She had a lot of work waiting for her, and she doesn't want to get behind. Knowing how organized and meticulous, she is, he agreed to go back home.

The past two weeks have been stressful for Richard. He's been having headaches thinking of ways to make his wife happy. No matter what he does, nothing seems to work.

She may smile, laugh, and talk with him, but she's not the same. Richard knows that Emerald isn't feeling good about the situation either; his house is stocked with ginger ale. Everywhere he turns, he sees a ginger ale bottle. If only she would talk to him, tell him how she feels so they could deal with this and move on.

◆

Not too long after Richard hangs up the phone with his mother, Emerald comes home. Richard greets her at the door.

"Hi." He said, smiling.

"Hey," She responded in a dreary way,

"What's the matter?" he asked, taking her bag from her.

"A long morning," She says with a chuckle.

Together Richard and Emerald walk into the living room and sit down on the couch. Emerald leans her head on the back of the couch.

"Can I get you anything?" he asks, caressing her arm.

"No," Emerald says, lifting her head up.

Emerald grins as she pulls away from Richard.

"I talked to my mother, and she and everyone is really happy for us." He said.

"That's nice." She says.

"I mean really happy." He says, giving her this playful grin.

Emerald looks at him and wonders why Richard is smiling at her that way; that smile is familiar. It wasn't the same charming smile that he gives. This smile has a hidden meaning.

"Why are you smiling at me?" she asks nervously.

"What I can smile at my wife?" Richard asks, caressing her face.

"Not like that," She says and moving his hands from her face.

Richard tries not to feel rejected. He continues to smile.

"You want something," Emerald accuses.

Richard starts laughing. His Emmy knows him well. Emerald begins to grow nervous.

"What, Richard, what do you want?"

"Emmy, relax," Richard says, smiling.

Emerald slowly takes in a deep breath.

"My folks want to throw us a wedding."

"We're already married," she says.

"Well, more so reception."

"Why,"

"Because they want to see us get married," Richard says.

Emerald shows no response; this is the type of silence that disturbs Richard because he doesn't know where Emerald is going to come from. She may explode and have a panic attack or run and hide from the world. She looks at him.

"Emerald,"

"So get married again; for show?" she questions.

"Something like that." He says, hesitating to answer. "But think about it, we didn't have a reception, no wedding cake to feed each other."

"No." she snaps. "Tell your mom thank you, but no thank you. I don't need to show off,"

"It's not showing off Emmy; it's having a reception for those who didn't make it."

"They didn't make it because we didn't invite them." She snaps again.

"We got married the way we wanted to, just you and me,"

Emerald stands up and begins to pace the floor. Richard stands up. She is about to have a panic attack.

"So basically, we do everything again. I get all dressed up, march down the aisle, having everyone stare at me. Then the reception, what do you do at a reception? Is it like one of those premier parties, talk and mingle? Who am I going to talk and mingle with? I don't know anyone! Who is going to be my maid or matron of honor? I don't have any friends. Richard, I don't have any family. The bouquet, who do I throw it to? A bunch of women I don't know! Who speaks for me? Am I just going to sit there in my new dress feeling dumb? How many people are going to be there? I know your mother, Richard, she is going to invite the whole world, and she is going to put me front and center like she did when your grandma died, and then everyone is going to get in my face, 'What's your name? What do you do? Where are you from?' Why do I have to do this? Why can't your family just send us a gift and be done with the whole thing? Then afterwards, what do we do afterwards? Do we go on another honeymoon, I don't have time to go through that again, I can't -,"

Richard grabs Emerald in his arms.

"No, Richard, no!" she cries gasping for breath. "Don't make me do this,"

Her body is trembling from anxiety. This panic attack is more than the possibility of being in front of people. It is the whole course of events that have taken place within' the past two weeks.

"Breath," he encourages softly. Emerald tries to break away, but Richard tightens his grip.

"Baby, don't fight me." He pleads softly, "Let me hold you."

Richard feels the tension in her body. She tries to take in a deep breath.

"Emerald, relax." He softly coaxes.

AFTER FIFTEEN MINUTES, EMERALD begins to relax.

"I'm sorry." She says, her face wet from tears.

"It's okay," Richard says, slowly rocking her in his arms.

She is still trembling.

TEN MINUTES GOES BY; Emerald is finally relaxed in Richard's arms. Richard didn't want to let her go. He is fighting back tears. He hasn't held her in his arms in so long; she feels good.

"Is this something that you want?" Emerald asks.

"I think it would be nice," he says softly.

"Okay, I'll do it," Emerald says softly, backing away.

"Are you sure?" Richard says, caressing her face.

Emerald nods her head and dries her eyes.

Richard grins.

"It can be a small wedding," he promises.

Emerald nods her head. Richard leans down to kiss her. He tries to kiss her passionately, but Emerald pulls away.

"I'm going to lie down for a while." She says to him.

"Okay." He says.

Richard stands, watching Emerald quickly walk away from him. He runs his fingers through his hair and sigh. His headache begins to increase.

EMERALD WAKES UP FROM her nap. She finds Richard in the kitchen, preparing to fix dinner. He greets her with a smile.

"Hi," she says.

"I was just getting ready to fix dinner." He says to her.

"I'm not hungry." She tells him opening the refrigerator and grabbing a ginger ale.

Richard notices that ginger ale in her hands.

"What's the matter?" he asks. "Nothing,"

"Nothing, huh?" Richard questions suspiciously. "Ginger ale; you're not hungry,"

"I guess I'm just antsy, these last-minute procedures for graduation, and now all of a sudden this wedding."

"Too overwhelming," Richard asks.

"No, it's fine. A small wedding, right?" Emerald asks with a grin.

"Small," Richard says, promising.

He walks to her.

"I know that the past few weeks been overwhelming, but if my folks get out of hand, say something,"

"Okay,"

"But in the meantime, you got to eat something," Richard says, putting his arms around her and then leans down to kiss her on the forehead.

"You need your strength. Let me fix you a sandwich."

She moves away from Richard.

"A turkey breast sandwich with provolone cheese," he suggests.

She nods with a grin. Richard prepares to fix her a sandwich.

"Just think, in one week, I will be completely done with school." Emerald said, "And l can finally sleep in,"

"You sleep in?" Richard asks sarcastically. "I thought that you enjoyed waking up before the birds to see the sunrise,"

"I do, but still, every now and then, I like to sleep in, but I can't. I have to hit the books."

"If you sleep in, we can wake up together," Richard says.

He stops fixing her sandwich and walks to Emerald, and pulls her into his arms.

"Maybe start off the day making love."

Emerald grins slightly and then tries to pull away, but Richard tightened his grip.

"Where you going?"

"No, nowhere," Emerald said nervously.

Richard senses that Emerald is nervous. The last time Emerald was nervous around him was when they had started dating. Richard knows where all this tension is coming from, but still, he doesn't say anything.

"Are you all right?" Richard asks pulling back from Emerald and returns to fixing her sandwich.

"Yes," She answers, finally relaxing.

Richard grins at Emerald.

"If I didn't know better, it seems as if I make you nervous."

Shocked by Richard's statement, Emerald takes in a deep breath and shakes her head, indicating that Richard's accusations are false. He finishes making Emerald's sandwich. Before he hands it to her, he approaches her. Richard stands in front of her. Their eyes lock. His eyes are cool; yet they penetrate through her causing a wave of anxiety to rise up from the pit of Emerald's stomach. To keep from exploding, she inhales slowly and then smiles.

"W-why would you make me nervous?" she stammers.

"I don't know, you tell me. You seem fidgety," Richard says coolly. "Maybe later we can go for a walk and talk."

Still holding in that deep breath,

"I need to work on my thesis." She

replies.

"Right," Richard says.

He steps back walks to the counter to grab the plate with Emerald sandwich. He turns back to face her and then hands her the plate.

"Here you go, baby,"

"Thank you," she says.

"You're welcome."

Richard walks out of the kitchen.

Emerald finally exhales.

RICHARD OPENS THE DOOR and welcomes his parents, brother and sisters into his home.

"Mr. Married Man." They all say, hugging him. "Congratulations."

"Thank you," he says, laughing.

"So, where is the little woman?" Jacob asks.

"Oh, Jacob," Carolyn admonishes; she laughs at Jacob's comment.

"I don't know. She out running around somewhere," Richard says.

"Don't know?" Jacob asks.

"She is graduating soon, huh? Is she excited?" Elizabeth answers.

"More nervous than anything," Richard answers. "Want me to take your things upstairs?'

"No," David said, "We can do it; we've been here before."

Richard nods his head.

"Richard, you look tired," Carolyn says.

"I'm okay,"

"Too much honeymoon." David implies smiling.

Richard grins.

"Let's get everything unpacked," Carolyn suggests.

David, Elizabeth, Laura, and Carolyn all leave for their rooms. Richard's family visits him plenty of time. Each one had a room that they had selected to stay while they visited

Jacob can see that Richard is stress. He has bags under his eyes as if he hasn't been sleeping. Although Richard is smiling, there is no light in his eyes.

"Want something to drink?" Richard asks his father.

"No, I'm okay," Jacob says.

Richard nods his head.

"Elope, huh?" Jacob said.

"Yeah," Richard says with a sigh.

"Whose idea was it?"

"Mine," Richard says with a grin.

"Everything okay," Jacob asks.

"Yeah,"

"You sure," Jacob asks.

Richard nods.

A sweet voice interrupts them. Both turn around and see Emerald.

"Hi," she says.

Richard walks to greet her with a kiss.

"Hello, daughter-in-law," Jacob says, smiling as he approaches Emerald.

Jacob gives Emerald a big hug.

"Hi, Mr. DeMarco-,"

"No, no honey, call me Jacob, or even Dad," Jacob says.

"Dad," Emerald says smiling, "I thought I would never get to say those words again."

Jacob smiles and kisses Emerald on the cheek.

"Welcome to the family."

"Thank you. I'm sorry I wasn't here when you guys arrived."

"We just got here, honey," Jacob told her. "I'm going to check on Carolyn and the others."

Jacob dismisses himself, leaving Richard and Emerald alone.

Emerald stands before Richard. She shyly smiles up at him. Her smile is sweet and endearing. Richard caresses her face.

"How was your day?"

"Okay," She tells him.

"Can I have a, hello Richard, love of my life, kiss?" he asks.

Emerald grins. Richard leans down to kiss her. Richard tries to kiss her passionately, but Emerald pulls back.

"I ah, I went to the market to get some food. I thought it be nice if we barbeque." Emerald suggests.

"Okay." Richard agrees.

Together Richard and Emerald walk in to the kitchen and begin to prepare dinner for the barbeque.

"l didn't know what everyone likes, so I got a little bit of everything, chicken, ribs, hamburger, salad," Emerald says him.

Richard nods his head as he washes his hands. He started to dice the cucumbers. Emerald begins to sort out the different meats. She begins to season them with the different varieties of salts and peppers.

"Emmy, is there anywhere, in particular, you like to go for our honeymoon?"

"What honeymoon?"

"Our second honeymoon," Richard says with a chuckle.

"Do you really think that is necessary?" Emerald asks.

"Yeah," Richard said with a chuckle, "When you get married, you go on a honeymoon. We can go to Rome, Paris."
"We already had a honeymoon," Emerald says.
"Besides, I don't really have time."

"Don't have time?" Richard asks feeling rejected.

"No, I had the whole six months planned out, with my book, graduation, me moving in, I just don't have time. We can do the honeymoon thing later."

"Honeymoon thing?" Richard asks. He is insulted. "Emerald," Richard begins.

Richard grabs her arm so that she can face him. She looks at him alarm, almost frightened. He isn't going to hurt her, but the look in Richard's eyes shows his frustration. Richard steadies himself. He sees that Emerald is nervous. He takes in a deep breath.

"I don't want those kinds of marriages where we see each other on the weekends. I want a wife, someone who I can come home to. Grant it that you have a life of your own. I do admire your independence, but I'm willing to cut my workload in half, doing one movie a year just so that we can spend time with each other. We didn't let our schedules get in the way of us before, let's not start now."

"Okay," Emerald says softly.

The continue cooking in silence.

"EMERALD HONEY, YOU OUT did yourself," Jacob says, sitting back in his seat.

"Everything was delicious." Carolyn agrees.

"Yeah, Richey old boy, you got the woman well trained," David jokes.

"David!" Carolyn admonishes, laughing.

Everyone laughs at David's jokes.

"I'm glad that you enjoyed everything," Emerald says modestly.

"I am looking forward to organizing this wedding, Emerald. "Carolyn says.

"Me too," Elizabeth says.

"When Liz and I were getting married, and our husbands were asking for our hand, Daddy scared them to death," Laura says.

"What?" Emerald asks with a laugh.

"Oh yeah," Elizabeth says smiling,

"Daddy said, 'No man is good enough for the DeMarco Girls,'" Laura says, smiling.

"Awe," Emerald smiles.

"That's right," Jacob says, smiling proudly.

"Jacob was very over-protected over his girls," Carolyn replies.

"So, how did they win you over?" Emerald asks.

"They were good boys," Jacob replies. "They promised to treat my princess like queens and give Carolyn and me tons of grandkids!"

Emerald grins.

"You know Emerald, Richard, you two can get started on those kids whenever you're ready. No rush," Jacob jokes with a wink.

Everyone laugh.

"What about you, David," Emerald asks. "Thinking about marriage?"

"Dad said he's not good enough for any woman." Richard teased.

Everyone laughs.

"That's it, laugh at poor ole Dave," David says, smiling.

"But honestly," David begins. "I'm still looking for that magic. The kind of magic that you and Richard have,"

Touch by his words. Emerald shyly glances at Richard. He smiles back at her.

Immediately, Emerald stands up and begins to clear the table.

"Emerald, let us help you," Carolyn offers.

"Okay, thanks."

Together the men went into Richard's Sports Room to watch ESPN Classic, and the women did the dishes and began planning the wedding.

IT IS WELL PAST midnight. Richard hears noises coming from the kitchen. Hoping it is Emerald, Richard walks to the kitchen only to find his father in the kitchen.

"Dad, what are you still doing up?" Richard asks.

"Emerald's barbeque chicken was calling me," Jacob says as he places the piece of chicken breast on his plate, "I'm telling you, son, that little girl is dynamite in the kitchen."

Richard grins. He takes his father's plate and places it in the microwave, then turns it on.

"Why are you still up?" Jacob asks as he sits down, "I figured you and Dave would have falling asleep watching those classic Ali fights."

"No, they went off an hour ago," Richard answers. "They're just showing some hockey highlights,"

"Emerald is asleep?"

"Ah, I don't know," Richard replies.

He reaches into the refrigerator and pulled out two bottles of water. Richard hands Jacob a bottle. Jacob watches his son pour water in a glass and then adds some kind of antacid.

"Is she writing?" Jacob asks.

Richard drinks his water. He finishes the drink completely.

"Don't know," Richard answers breathlessly.

"Don't know?" Jacob interrogates. "Do you know where she is?"

"I know where she is but-," Richard answers but stops when he sees the look that Jacob has on his face.

Jacob's eyes are intense, wondering what is going on with Richard and Emerald. "It's after midnight," Jacob comments suspiciously.

"Emerald has been so busy. Lately, it's hard to keep up with her," Richard says with a slight chuckle.

"Is that right?" Jacob replies with doubt. "Everything all right,"

Richard nods and gets another bottle of water from the refrigerator. He opens it up and takes a long drink.

"Yeah," he says, grinning. "Just a little-anyway, I'm turning in. Don't eat all the chicken,"

Richard pats his father on his shoulder and starts to walk off.

"Richard," Jacob says.

Richard turns around.

"Sit down, son, talk to me,"

The timer on the microwave goes off. Richard attempts to get Jacob's plate, but Jacob stops him.

"Sit down, son; I'll get it." Jacob gets up to grab his plate. Richard sits down.

"So, what caused you guys to elope?" Jacob asks.

"Ah, don't know, one night over her place and I thought about it,"

Jacob nods his head.

"Rich, everything all right,"

"Yeah,"

"You sure," Jacob questions.

"Yeah, why,"

"Well, you're up at two in the morning, drinking some kind of antacid," Jacob replies.

"Dad, I'm just a little stressed out, that is all," Richard says.

"Okay, so talk to me. What are you so stressed out about?"

The DeMarco children cannot hide anything from their parents. Both Jacob and Carolyn are able to see when something is wrong. Richard looks over at his father as he devours the barbeque chicken breast

"Emmy's mad at me," Richard says.

Jacob chuckles,

"Trouble in paradise. That's newlyweds for you. You fight, make love, fight some more,"

"There's no love-making," Richard admits.

"What?"

Richard takes in a deep breath.

"I blew it."

"You blew what?" Jacob asks.

126

"Sex," He says.

Jacob doesn't respond. Richard continues.

"We get married; she's excited and happy. Then for our wedding night, I make sure I have everything set out for her. I had her favorite song; I had candles everywhere, then we make love and-,"

"And what," Jacob asks.

"She was a virgin. She didn't like it." Richard says.

Jacob nods his head and then bits into the chicken.

"Did you guys talk?"

"Somewhat,"

"Somewhat," Jacob asks, shocked, "What's somewhat?"

"She said that she needs some space."

"Space, what is that?" Jacob asks, confused.

Richard shrugs his shoulders.

"I tried to talk to her, but she avoids me like the plague. Look around; my wife is not here." Richard said. "Every time I get near her, she runs. Makes up some excuse why she has to leave. Tells me she is working on her thesis or writing. She's not writing, and I know she's done with her thesis." "So she is lying to you?" Jacob asks.

Richard nods.

"Where is she?" Jacob questions.

"She goes to her apartment." Richard answers. "I'm dropping hints; she not stupid, she knows that I'm trying to talk to her, but she runs. I'm willing to be patient, I am willing to do whatever she wants, but I just want her to talk to me. Dad, I wanted that night to be perfect. I wanted her to be happy, and I blew it."

"No, you didn't blow it." Jacob comforts. "Tell me, why is she so shy? I mean, did something happen in her childhood, something traumatic?"

"She was just sheltered. She never really dated. She focused on her schooling. She's about to be a doctor, and she is only twenty-seven. Her parents died tragically in a car accident. She's just shy. She likes to hide."

"What about the other times you made love?"

"What other times?" Richard says sardonically.

"You have to be kidding me?" Jacob comments.

Richard shrugs his shoulders.

"You're married, you're newlyweds, making love is expected."

"What am I supposed to do, have sex with her knowing that she doesn't like it?"

"No, but this situation needs to be addressed. Bring her out of hiding and address it. You have to talk to her and soon." Jacob said.

THE NEXT NIGHT, AFTER tedious wedding planning everyone is exhausted. Carolyn and Jacob turn in and go to bed. David lounges the Sports Room, and Laura and Elizabeth stayed up late watching old classic movies. Richard waits for Emerald in their bedroom. As he stares out of the window looking at the stars, he decides that tonight he is going to take his father's advice and talk to Emerald. Emerald doesn't know that Richard is waiting for her. She thinks that he is with David in the Sports Room. She takes a long hot and soothing shower exhausting from the day. After the shower, she wraps herself in her lavender terrycloth bathrobe and walks into their bedroom. She is surprised to see Richard waiting for her.

"I thought you were with David," she says.

"No," Richard says as he turns to face her.

He smiles at her. She looks so sweet and vulnerable. He wants to take her in his arms and get lost in her. The smell from the shea butter and warm vanilla dove soap is intoxicating.

"I thought we spend some time together." He suggests.

"Oh," she says.

"You've been busy lately; we haven't had time to talk or whatever."

Richard slowly approaches her. He holds his hands out. Emerald hesitates to respond.

"Come here, baby," he says softly.

Emerald slowly walks to him and takes his hands. Richard pulls her in, wrapping his arms around her, and he holds her for a while. "I love you," he whispers.

He kisses her neck. Emerald's body tenses up. She pulls back from Richard's hold.

"What's the matter?" Richard asks noticing that Emerald is uncomfortable.

"Nothing, just a little stiff," she answers, rubbing her neck.

"Here," Richard said, attempting to massage her neck.

"No, it's okay, I got it," Emerald refusing Richard's help.

"No, Em, come on, let me." Richard pleads.

Emerald gives in. Richard leads her to the bed. She sits down. He climbs behind her and sits down. He starts to massage Emerald's neck. He notices how tense she was.

"Why are you so tense?" Richards asks.

Emerald shrugs her shoulders.

"Just relax." He says.

Emerald takes in a deep breath.

"I hope my mother and sisters didn't bombard you with wedding details," Richard says with a chuckle. "They can go over the top. Laura's wedding was like a ball,"

"Um, no," Emerald says with a chuckle and takes in another deep breath.

Richard notices that Emerald is having a hard time trying to relax.

"Em,"

"Hmm,"

"What's the matter, baby?" Richard asks softly, "You haven't been yourself."

"Overworked, I guess." She said. "You know, preparing for graduation, getting settled here,"

Richard wraps his arms around her and rests his head on her shoulders.

"Is there anything you need me to do?" he offers.

"No," Emerald says.

She attempts to moves away from Richard, but he holds on to her.

"Emerald, let me hold you please?" Richard pleads.

Emerald remains still. Richard gently tightens his hold and kisses her on her neck.

"You came home late last night." Richard states. "Where were you?"

"I was at my apartment writing; I lost track of time." Emerald answers, "I'm sorry."

"It's okay," Richard says. "I missed you that's all. Um, Emmy, why are you still using your apartment?"

"No reason," Emerald answers.

"Do you still need it? Are you thinking about subletting until the end of your lease?"

"No," Emerald answered, "Um, I just," she trails off.

"Em, what the matter," Richard asks as he kisses her neck again.

He continues to kiss her slowly and softly. He desires her so much right now. Emerald slowly tries to pull away, but Richard tightens his hold.

"Emerald, please," Richard pleads softly. "Em, we need to talk,

Emerald turns around to face Richard. His eyes are intense, as if he's in pain. She looks away.

"Emerald," Richard says.

Reluctantly she looks back at him.

"You been avoiding me," Richard says.

Emerald looks away and shakes her head.

"I'm not," she says softly, "I've just been busy."

"Busy doing what?"

Emerald doesn't respond.

"Em," Richard says.

Emerald looks up at Richard.

"We have to talk," he says.

Richard waits for her to speak. They sit quietly for a minute.

"I know that at first, I couldn't wait to be with you," Emerald begins. She looks up at Richard then shyly looks away.

"Did I hurt you," Richard asks.

Emerald shakes her head slowly.

"Then talk to me baby, what happened?" Richard asks.

She doesn't respond. She takes in a deep breath.

"I can't explain it," she said softly.

"Try," he orders in a cool tone.

Another minute passes.

"I think we made a mistake," she says as tears form in her eyes

"What?"

"We moved too fast," Emerald said.

Richard takes in a deep breath.

"Moved too fast," he says.

"Everything was just so rushed. One minute we were on the verge of having sex, and then we get married so you can have sex with me the proper way-,"

"No," Richard cut her off. "I wanted to marry you. You know this."

"So why did we rush to get married? We could have waited a few months."

Emerald stands up. She walks to the window.

"I wanted to be with you." Richard stands up.

"You wanted to have sex with me and not feel guilty about it!" Emerald cries.

He is offended by Emerald's comment. Richard walks to her.

"How can you say that?!" Richard questions. "Emerald I love you,"

Emerald turns away from Richard. Richard feels rejected. Emerald never turned away from him. He walks to her and places his hands on her shoulders.

"Is that what you think? All I wanted was sex?"

Emerald doesn't respond.

"Baby, I love you," Richard said. "We didn't make a mistake. We rushed into getting married; yes, but it was not for sex. I want to be with you, all of you. Marrying you wasn't a mistake."

"It didn't feel right," Emerald said.

"What didn't feel right?" Richard asks.

"Everything," she cries. "This was my dream; with you,"

Emerald stops talking. She takes a deep breath.

A moment of silence passes.

"Who were you with that night? Me or the movie star?"

"What?" Emerald asks, confused.

"You were expecting your fantasy with your movie star-,"

"No," Emerald said quickly.

She turns to face him.

"I was expecting my fairy tale with someone who loves me. I know you love me, but I couldn't feel you. Whenever you look at me, I feel your love; here," she touches her heart. "That night, I couldn't-,"

Emerald stops talking to keep from crying. Richard sighs.

"Come here," Richard says, reaching her.

Emerald approaches Richard. He wraps his arms around her. She cries into his chest.

"I'm sorry," she says.

"I'm sorry too," he says.

"How do we fix this?" she asks.

"Like this," he says, gently rocking her. "Just like this,"

A Period of Time

CAROLYN, ELIZABETH, AND LAURA assists Emerald as she puts on her wedding dress. Today is the wedding day, and after two hectic and sleepless weeks of planning, arranging, canceling, and organizing, finally, the wedding of Carolyn's dreams has arrived. Emerald's gown is strapless white silk with tiny diamond-like rhinestone scatted aimless around the bottom of the dress. The gown is flowing, like a waterfall. Emerald wore white silk gloves, and Laura managed to find a terrier for her head. Emerald's hair is worn down, pulled back out of her face. Laura places the terrier on Emerald. She looks like a graceful princess. Emerald wears Carolyn's white pearls around her neck. Laura insists on doing's Emerald's makeup, but as Laura studies Emerald's face, she sees that her beauty is natural, very little cosmetics are needed.

Together the three DeMarco women stand and stare at Emerald.

"Emerald," Carolyn whispered as tears formed in her eyes, "You look beautiful."

Emerald takes a deep breath,

"Do you think Richard would like my dress?" Emerald asks hopefully.

"No," Elizabeth says. "He'll love it."

Emerald smiles, takes a deep breath, and then sips a glass of ginger-ale. Carolyn notices Emerald's tensions.

"Girls, let me have a moment with Emerald," Carolyn says.

Elizabeth and Laura grin and each one hugs and kiss Emerald.

"Em, we are so glad that we have you for our sister-in-law," Elizabeth says to Emerald.

"Yeah," Laura says, smiling. "We're more than in-laws, Em, we're sisters,"

Emerald is touch by Laura and Elizabeth's affection.

"Wow, I never had sisters." She says, smiling.

"Well, now you do," Laura tells her.

They hug and kiss one another again and then leave Carolyn and Emerald alone. Slowly, Carolyn walked around the room, trying to find the right words to say.

"Are you nervous?" Carolyn asks.

"Very," Emerald admits. "I mean, I shouldn't be. Richard and I are already married. I just get nervous when there are a lot of people,"

"Richard said that you're very shy." Carolyn said smiling, "I'm glad that you allowed Jacob and me to throw this wedding for you,"

"Thank you for doing so," Emerald tells her and then takes in a deep breath.

"With planning the wedding, we haven't really talked," Carolyn said.

"About what," Emerald questions wide-eyed.

"About anything you want to talk about," Carolyn says. "Emerald, sit down, please."

Careful not to wrinkle her dress, Emerald sits down on the love seat. Carolyn sits down beside her.

"Like you, Emerald, I lost my mother when I was young and when Jacob and I started dating, his mother took me under her wing. She taught me everything. Maria was more of a mother to me than just a mother-in-law. I'd like for us to be that."

"I'd like that too," Emerald says, smiling.

"Richard is so happy with you in his life." Carolyn says, smiling, "I remember when he first told us about you, 'I found her, Ma, she was right under my nose, and I almost let her get away, I could tell by the tone in his voice that he was in love, and when we finally met you, I could see the way he would smile at you, it was if you were the only one around."

"I just hope that he doesn't stop smiling," Emerald says.

"Why would he stop?"

"So far, I haven't been a very good wife," Emerald confesses.

"What makes you say that?"

A Period of Time

"I don't know how to satisfy him," Emerald says, looking away ashamed.

"Satisfy him?" Carolyn asks.

"Yeah, you know, *satisfy*." Emerald replies.

Carolyn puts two and two together and then smiles, "Oh, satisfy." Carolyn says.

Emerald nods.

"What makes you think that?" Carolyn asks.

Emerald lets out a sigh and then looks away.

"Emerald, what's the matter, honey?"

"I didn't-." She confesses as tears filled her eyes. "I tried, but I-," Emerald hesitates.

She looks at Carolyn. Her eyes are trusting.

"I was a virgin on our wedding night. Can you believe that, a twenty-seven-year-old virgin?" Emerald replies.

"I think that's beautiful," Carolyn tells her. "I waited until I was married."

"Back then, it was expected," Emerald comments.

"Back in the stone ages," Carolyn says with a laugh.

"I didn't mean that." Emerald replies. "I mean, in those days, it was expected of a woman. It's was honorable for women to be a virgin."

"It still is, honey," Carolyn says to her.

Carolyn moves closer to Emerald and puts her right arm around her, and then holds Emerald's hand with her left arm.

"Well, what's it like now?"

"There is no now. We only did it once."

"Once," Carolyn asks, shocked.

Emerald looks away, embarrassed at Carolyn's reaction. Realizing she embarrassed Emerald, Carolyn softly called out her name.

"Emerald,"

Emerald looks back at Carolyn and immediately is hit by that spell bounding innocence that has captured her son. Where did all this innocence come from? Here is a twenty-seven-year-old woman with the heart of a child.

"Why are you so shy?" Carolyn asks.

"I don't know." Emerald says, "I don't mean to be. I try not to, but I don't do new well. When I am pushed into something new, I get really nervous and have panic attacks. It's best that I say away, hidden."

"Where did all this shyness come from?" Carolyn asked. "Were your parents shy?"

"No, they weren't shy. I'm the only child. Neither of my parents came from big families. I wasn't the prettiest girl in school, so no one talked to me."

"So you were simply passed over all your life," Carolyn says. "And now you're receiving attention, and you just don't know how to handle it."

"I suppose," Emerald says. "Who would have thought that I be here. I am married to the world's most handsome man, and I don't know what to do with him."

"Yes, you do, sweetie. What did you guys do before you guys got married?"

"We talk, go to the movies, and take walks through his garden."

"He fell in love with you, Emerald," Carolyn said. "You already had him satisfied,"

"Yeah, that's with the heart, not physically,"

"Did your parents ever talk to you about sex?"

"Yeah, just the basics; they were more fixated on my education or my writing. I'm so shy my parents didn't think that I would get married. No one came up to me asking me out, so I kept to myself. I would hear the girls talk in school about their first time and how awkward things were, and I thought to myself that if I get a first time, things would be different because he would love me."

"What was it like with Richard?" Carolyn asks.

"Not good," Emerald confesses.

"Your first time being that it wasn't what you expect, did you think that Richard stopped loving you?"

"No, pacifying his guilt. He didn't want to make love to me unless we were married. And it was only a matter of time that he couldn't wait anymore." Emerald says as tears filled her eyes.

"Were you mad at him?"

"A little," Emerald says. "Everything seemed rush. One moment we were talking, and then I look up, and we're having sex." Emerald says. "He tried to talk about it, but I was so overwhelmed and tired, mentally and physically, and I couldn't bring myself to talk about it; I just wanted to go hide somewhere. We finally talked when you guys first came out."

"Then what,"

"Then he felt bad, and then I felt bad because I know that he loves me. Richard will do anything for me, and the one thing he wants I don't know how to give. As a matter of fact, I wanted to have sex, but he kept telling me no, and that he was waiting for the right time. That was our wedding night." Emerald's face is stained with tears.

"So here I am on my wedding day, not knowing what to do on my wedding night,"

"Do whatever comes natural," Carolyn says to her, "But whatever happens, just relax and let it happen."

Emerald nods her head. Carolyn grabs a tissue from a box and dries Emerald's tears.

"You are so innocent and pure, and the last thing Richard wants is to take that innocence from you. The last thing he wants is to hurt you, and if he means that he's willing to wait for you, then knowing my son, that's what it means."

Emerald nods her head and then grins. Together both women hug each other.

EMERALD AGREED TO HONEYMOON in Rome. To Emerald, the hotel suit, is like an enchanting castle hidden behind the forest resting upon the hills. The hotel suite has four large rooms with a balcony overlooking a small beach with white sand. Richard smiles as he watches Emerald's face light up as they look around. She runs from room to room, amazed at how beautiful everything looks.

"You planned all this?" she asks.

Richard nods his head.

"And to think you didn't want a honeymoon," Richard says, wrapping his arms around her.

He leans forward to kiss her on the cheek.

"I can't wait to go shopping and buy Italian clothes and shoes, and-,"

"Just can't wait to spend my money, huh, woman?" Richard asks in a joking way, "I knew I should have made you sign that prenup."

Laughing, Emerald playfully punches Richard on the arm.

"It's nice to see you smile; I've missed it,"

"I'm sorry," Emerald says. "I haven't been very nice-,"

"Shh," Richard says, putting his fingers on her lips. "As long as you smile,"

"I guess I should go and unpack," Emerald says.

"You go on ahead," Richard tells her. "I'm going to check out the view on the balcony, and I have to make a few phone calls."

He takes Emerald by the hands and kissed them.

RICHARD SITS ON THE BALCONY as Emerald unpacks for their week in Rome. As she looks around the master bedroom, she smiles. She is far away from her small apartment in Pittsburgh. Just two years ago, she was just an eleventh-grade English teacher who had a book series published. She was now Emerald DeMarco, a successful author and movie producer. She was now married to actor Richard DeMarco. Her man sits on the balcony taking in the beautiful splendor of Rome. Her man, Richard. He loves her probably more than she loves herself. Richard has taken her to Hawaii and now taken her to Rome. Emerald never dreamed in a million years that she would be in Rome with her husband, with a husband. She closes her eyes and wonders why did she doubt his love? Why did she not enjoy their first night together? She knows that Richard would kill himself before he deliberately hurt Emerald. Suddenly she feels foolish. How could she not spend the past few weeks enjoying the touch of the man that loves her? How could she avoid his tender contact? She waited for this day, that day. She smiles and finishes unpacking.

"EM," SHE HEARS RICHARD call her name.

She takes in a deep breath.

"In here," she says.

She waits for Richard to enter the bedroom. To his surprise, he sees the romantic setting that Emerald had made. The room is dark, with the exception of the candlelight. She looks beyond enticing with the lavender lingerie on.

"What's all this?" he asks with a grin.

"Just a little something for the evening," She answers. "I put some wine on ice." "Sounds

nice," he says.

"Would you like me to fix you a glass?" Emerald offers.

"In a minute," He says, smiling at her.

He just wants to look at her.

Emerald nervously begins to fiddle with her hands. Richard slowly approaches her.

"Baby, we don't have to do anything tonight." He says her taking her hands into his.

"I want to." She quickly says.

"Are you sure?" he asks.

"Yes, unless you don't-,"

"You know I do," Richard says, smiling.

Emerald smiles back. Taking in a deep breath, she nervously begins to look around the room.

"What?" Richard asks.

"I'm not sure on how to move forward," she says softly.

"It's okay." He grins. "Tell me what you want,"
Emerald takes in a deep breath.

"I want you to kiss me," she says, still in her soft tone.

Richard moves closer and leans in to kiss her Emerald softly on the lips. Still close to her, he looks into her eyes. She nods her head, slowly encouraging him to continue. Richard passionately kisses her. Emerald takes her hands and holds Richard's face, taking his kiss. Richard takes his arms and pulls her into him. His hands begin to explore her body. With each touch, Emerald's body responded positively. Richard picks her up in his arms and carries her to the bed. He gently places her down.

"I love you," He whispers as their eyes lock.

"I love you too." She says back.

Richard slowly removes the lingerie, allowing it to fall to the floor. As they kiss, Emerald unbuttons Richard's shirt; her hands rub along his chest. Slowly, they climb into the bed together, and within moments, they unite as one.

This time, Emerald feels a connection. She could feel him physically and emotionally. Emerald can feel Richard's heart; she can feel his love. As he makes love to her, he kisses her passionately. She moans softly with delight as she begins to remember that deep-sea that she had once visited the first time that Richard kissed her. The sea doesn't seem so foreign. She is used to some levels of the deep, but she desires to seek out the levels further. The waves begin to carry her moving her from side to side. The more she submerges in the deep, the better she feels, and before long, her body explodes into tiny pieces.

Her body trembles beneath Richard's. He kisses her on the cheek and chuckles softly in her ear.

"I love you," He says to her as she exhales a satisfying sigh. "Are you okay?"

"Hmm," she responds.

THE NEXT MORNING, EMERALD rises early to look at the sunrise. She is surprised to see Richard on the balcony.

"Hi," she says to him, smiling.

"Good morning, baby," Richard says.

He reaches his arms out to Emerald and pulls her into him, wrapping his arms around her. Together they watch the heavens waiting for the sun to slowly merge up from the horizon.

"I wanted to see what you see," he told her. "Why sunrises are so beautiful to you,"

"Because they are beautiful and new," Emerald said. "They are beautiful and new each day,"

Richard leans down and into kiss Emerald on her neck.

"You," he says to her.

"Me," Emerald asks. She turns around to face him.

"You are my sunrise," Richard says to her. "You are beautiful and new each day,"

Emerald smiles bashfully and rests her head on Richard's chest.

"Last night was amazing," she says. "I mean really, really, amazing."

She looks up at him; he smiles at her and then picks her up in his arms and carries her back into the suite, leaving the sun to rise.

When it Rains.... it pours

THE SOFT BREEZE GLIDES its way through the window, slowly tickling Richard's cheek waking him up. He is not ready to wake up. He wants more time to lounge around in his Sports Room. The easy chair that he lounges in is soft and comfortable, making his lazy attitude justified. Richard had a busy six months. He just finished up another movie, the sequel to *The Topaz Chronicle*, called *Ride Another Day*. Emerald wrote the screenplay and, this time, took full control as director and producer. The movie was filmed in Antarctica and for six months in the cold. Richard transformed himself into an action hero trying to stop the evil villain from taking over the world. Richard had fun reliving the character that put him back on Hollywood's Most Wanted List. It was also interesting for Richard to watch his shy, timid wife become this strong, powerful woman who was in control. Emerald was amazing. Now, however, it is time to rest, time to enjoy the cool air that barely came through California.

Richard had woken up early in the morning to exercise. At forty, he is still handsome. His dark brown eyes are still smoldering. His body is still well-sculpted like a Greek god. After his work out he went to his favorite room in the house, his Sports Room, to relax and watch a little ESPN Classic, and he eventually fell asleep. This was a good little power nap. Richard doesn't want to wake up just yet.

He hears this soft sound, a pleasant sound coming from the outside. It's someone singing. It isn't loud singing, but a soft and sweet melody. The wind carries an intoxicating fragrance through the window; the scent is perfume, Emerald's perfume. She is outside singing in the rose garden. As if he is in a trance, he slowly gets up from his chair and walks to the window. They have been married for two years, and for two years, she has kept him in her spell.

The gate to the rose garden is too high for Richard to see Emerald, but he can hear and smell her. Richard hasn't seen his Emmy in two days. He was finishing up the minor scenes in the movie; by the time he gets home, Emerald was asleep. Emerald is a morning person; she wakes up before dawn just to watch the sunrise, and then it was off to the editing room to put the last-minute touches on the movie. So for two days, they haven't kissed each other or gazed into one another's eyes. For two days, they haven't held each other. However, that is going to change. This weekend they don't have anything to do, now it is time to make up for the lost kisses. Richard goes to find her.

Emerald sees Richard approaching her. She greets him with a warm, friendly smile; that smile melts his heart every time. Richard wraps his arms around her and gives her a big, passionate kiss. As he kisses her, he wants her right here and right now. Richard then places his hands on her belly; inside lives a tiny being that develops daily. Emerald is five months pregnant. Her stomach is round and firm. She is pregnant and beautiful. She has that mother-to-be glow. Richard can't wait for his baby to be born. A baby, a little person, is growing inside her belly, living, breathing, and kicking. Richard makes sure that Emerald has everything that she needs, from the crazy midnight cravings to a soothing back rub.

"Hey there, sleepy head," She says to him.

"Hey, how long have I been sleeping?"

"All day,"

"You mean all morning."

"No, all day, I heard you get up this morning to work out, but then you went straight to the Sports Room; I went off the studio came home to check on you; you were still asleep. Then I did some writing, and here you are."

"How's my baby?" Richard asks, rubbing her stomach.

"Baby is fine."

Just then, the baby kicks, responding to the sound of its father's voice. Richard takes Emerald's hands, and together they walk in the garden.

"Richard, Paul Garland called again," Emerald informs him.

Richard doesn't respond.

"He left four messages and called three more times when I was home." Emerald continues.

Still, Richard doesn't say anything. Emerald looks up at Richard.

"Are you going to call him back?" she asks.

"I don't know, Em," Richard says with a sigh, then runs his fingers through his hair.

"Are you still thinking about it, or are you avoiding him?" Emerald asks.

Richard lets out another sigh.

"Emerald, I don't know what to do. Why would he pick me?"

Richard has been offered a role in a new, very controversial movie. The character's name is Clayton Buchanan, a man running for governor under the Democratic Party, but the difference is he is very conservative, very frugal when it came to money. He was against any type of rights for women and minorities, whether African American, Latin American, or Asian American. If anything, it would not be surprising if this character was a member of the Ku Klux Kan, and for some reason, this director wanted Richard DeMarco for the role. Although the role sounds interesting and the money that is being offered is enticing, Richard doesn't know what to do. This movie is a satire to poke fun at all the politicians who claim that they are for the people, that they wanted to help bring in different types of plans for the country that will benefit the poor. This is controversial indeed, and this movie might make him or break him as an actor for the good or the bad. Richard feels that if he takes the part, then he is slapping his wife in the face to play a bigot while at the same time married to a black woman. To Richard, that seems hypocritical, but if he is to take the part, he is also showing that just because he is married to a black woman he is not a bigot although he may

144

play one. What if he plays the part too well and offends the black communities. Richard is stuck between a rock and a hard place.

"Richard, it's a good part," Emerald said. Again Richard is silent. "Do you want the role?"

"I don't know what I want." Richard answers. "I'm hoping that maybe, just maybe, there will be another role lined up somewhere that can distract me from this one."

"Do you want my advice?" she offered. "What?"

"Take the part," Emerald tells him.

Richard looks at Emerald as if she has lost her mind.

"Don't look at me like that; I am serious."

"Do you realize what you're telling me to do?"

"Yes," Emerald told him, "Listen, this part may be controversial, but it's good, and Paul Garland wants you because you're good, and you can bring serious life to this character."

"Yeah, but I would be playing a racist, something that I am not. Do you know how many times the N-word is in the script?"

"Yes, I counted. The character also says derogatory comments about Latin Americans and women. The perfect jerk! You've played parts before that were far from who you are as a person. I remember once you played a rapist, you're not a rapist."

"No, I'm not that but I-,"

"What?" Emerald says. "Are you worried because you would be playing a racist, and you're married to me?"

Richard is silent.

"Would you consider the part if you were married to a white woman,"

"Emerald-," Richard admonished sternly.

"Come on, work with me." Emerald encouraged. "You're married to a white woman; would you consider the part?"

"No," Richard snaps. "I'm a minority. I'm Italian."

"Okay, okay, but seriously, Richard, this role is far from the action hero; this is Golden Globe material. You can do this."

"What about the black communities?"

"What about them?" Emerald asks in a cool manner.

"What if I play this part and do well that black people won't want to see my movies anymore?" Richard explains. "Danny Glover played Mr. in *The Color Purple*, and he did such a good job that the world almost hated him. I don't want that."

"Yeah, but Danny got the population to accept him again. He's a wonderful actor. Gary Sinise played a bigot when he played George Wallace, and that was a good movie."

Richard looks at Emerald. He knows that whatever decision he choices, she will stand by him.

"Besides Richard, this is a satire; you never know people may see the art of in it. Like the television show*, All in the Family*, Archie Bunker was a racist, a simple-minded racist, and the population loved him."

Richard nods his head, and then together, Emerald, and he walks back into the house and in to Emerald's study. Two months after they got married, Richard built her a study. An eighteen-foot by thirty-foot room with three book shelves full of books from her favorite classic authors like J.D. Salinger, Toni Morrison, and F Scott Fitzgerald, to modern authors like James Patterson, John Grisham. There is a soft gray-colored couch with a matching love seat and chair. The coffee and end tables are an oak color. There is a desk with a laptop computer and a printer. Also, there is a small refrigerator that stayed stock with goodies, especially now that she is pregnant. In the very front of the room was a twenty-five-inch plasma television. The windows are basic yet just large enough for Emerald to look out at the rose garden. Just like Richard loved his Sports Room, Emerald loved her study.

Together they sit down on the couch. Richard begins to rub on Emerald's belly. The baby moves as if it's playing with its daddy. Emerald smiles; she is so happy to be pregnant.

"So take the script?" Richard says.

"Yep,"

Richard sighs and then leans over to kiss Emerald,

"Okay,"

RICHARD WALKS INTO EMERALD's study early Monday morning. Emerald is watching the television. On the screen is Allen Sampson, an African-American political leader who has been known for his outrageous comments about the ongoing oppression of African-Americans. He is being interviewed on the morning show called *Wake Up America*. He is also a lawyer known to take the most controversial cases and make the defendant look like an underdog and then make him come out on top. Ever since Richard decided to take this part as Clayton Buchanan, the media has been having a good time questioning why an Italian American man who is married to an African-American woman wants to play the part of a bigot. Many top journalists are requesting interviews, but both of them declined. One tabloid newspaper after another is saying all sorts of things about Richard and Emerald. Since all this began, Richard added new security equipment to the estate.

"Here is a woman who not only writes movies for the white man, but she is married to him too." Allen Sampson said on the television. "This woman has going on record saying that it was her husband that saved her, that he made her beautiful. Maybe this woman didn't give the black man a chance to tell her she was beautiful. I think she's lovely."

"Emerald DeMarco is a shy person. Not many know about her," The reporter said.

"Black women have no business being shy! Black women are supposed to be strong, independent, not shy, and oppress. We, as a black community, have struggled for too long to be held down. Dr. Emerald DeMarco does not represent the black woman. She represents the passive woman who lets a man walk over her. What strong black woman do you know who is going to stand by her man while he plays a disrespectful character that is in disregard to her race?" Allen questions.

"The DeMarcos seem to be a happy couple. Maybe Emerald does not see it as disrespectful?" the reporter said.

"Happy in the eyes of the public, but how do we know that she is shy by nature or he has her on lock down. As far as we know, he can call her a nigger!" Allen states firmly.

Richard immediately turns the television off.

"Why are you watching this?" he asks her.

"Because," she starts to say, "I just wanted to see what he has to say about this,"

"He doesn't have anything to say." Richard snaps. "He just wants to hear himself speak."

"Don't be mad at him." She says sweetly.

"Listen, Em; if this part is too much, I won't take it," Richard says. "We don't start filming for another month by the time the baby will be here."

"Don't worry about it. I don't care what people say. What matters is us, you and me."

Richard helps her stand to her feet. She is now seven months pregnant and as big as a house, yet she loves every minute of it. The baby constantly moves and kicks. It is a nice sweet feeling inside of her. At times, pregnancy can be hard. Sometimes her back aches, and sometimes in the middle of the night, Emerald would have a muscles spasm in her legs, and every now and then, the baby would hit a nerve in Emerald's upper left thigh, causing her to double over in pain, yet to Emerald, it is worth it for this tiny little baby that she is going to meet.

"Well, I gotta run. I have to meet with my editor, and then I have a doctor's appointment. What are you doing today?"

"Just wardrobe fitting," Richard answers with a solemn look on his face.

"So I'll meet you at the doctor's?" Emerald asks.

"Yeah,"

She smiles at him, hoping that he would stop looking so serious, and smiles. He manages to give her a grin. He leans forward to kiss her.

RICHARD ARRIVE AT THE doctor's office; the nurse quickly approaches him.

"Mr. DeMarco," she says, "We've been trying to reach you."

"What's going on, and where is Emerald?"

"During the sonogram, we found some unusual activity," The nurse begins.

"What unusual activity?" Richard asks. "Where is Emerald?

"The baby had wrapped itself around the umbilical cord. There wasn't a heartbeat-,"

"My wife!" Richard snaps. "Where is my wife?"

"At the emergency room!"

Immediately Richard races out of the doctor's office; he is accosted by a crowd of paparazzi and reporters, all questioning him about the comments made by Allen Simpson.

"Richard!" they call out his name.

He is blinded by the flashing lights from the cameras.

"Richard, what do you make of what Allen Sampson said today?" they ask.

"Not now!" he says. "No comment."

He walks quickly to get in his car, but he is cut off by a cameraman. He stands in front of Richard, quickly snapping his picture.

"Move!" Richard says sternly.

"Richard, are you a racist!" the cameraman asks.

Richard grabs the camera and smashes it on the ground, and then punches the man in his face. He bellied over in pain, blood rushing from his nose.

"Son of-," he cries out.

Many of the other cameramen rush towards him.

"I told you to back off!?" Richard snaps.

Quickly he gets into the car and races to the emergency room.

Richard doesn't have time to think about what he has just done. Emerald and his baby is his main concern, but he does hope the police don't come after him.

RICHARD PACES THE HOSPITAL floor nervously. The doctors have told him nothing. Emerald has been in surgery for nearly two hours. Now is not the time to lose his wife; never is the time to lose a wife. Richard has waited too long for a woman like Emerald. He has waited too long to be happy and completely content, and he was not about to give this life up, not now, not ever.

Richard begins to regret taking the part of Clayton Buchanan. What was he thinking? He didn't need this kind of role to make a name for himself; he already had a name for himself.

Richard DeMarco is a household name, thanks to Emerald. Now he might lose her all on account of his greed. Yes, the money he is going to receive will be nice, but not at the risk of losing his Emmy. He doesn't even know if the baby was a boy or girl or if it even survived.

Doctor McIntyre disturbs his thought when he taps Richard on the shoulder.

"Mr. DeMarco." He begins.

"Doctor," Richard says.

"Emerald is fine, but the baby-,"

"Oh, no," Richard says.

"I'm sorry." Dr. McIntyre says with sad eyes. "She was born dead."

Richard sits down and buries his head in his head. Dr. McIntyre sits down beside Richard. As a doctor, he has seen many situations like these, a young couple expecting their first child hoping and waiting for the little bundle of joy to fill their lives when suddenly their happiness is ripped from them. Sometimes, in these cases, Dr. McIntyre has had to tell the young couple that they can never have children again, that it is not safe for the mother. There have been times that the mother doesn't make it, leaving the baby to survive without its mother and with a discouraged father. However, this is not the case with Richard and Emerald.

"What caused the baby's death?" Richard asks, finally lifting up his head.

"From previous sonograms, the baby was very active. Unfortunately, the baby was so active that she got herself wrapped around the umbilical cord, and she strangled herself. This was no one's fault. Listen, Mr. DeMarco, despite the circumstances, Emerald is healthy, and she is able to have more children. Mr. DeMarco, if you need anything, anything at all, please do not hesitate to call."

Richard nods his head and then shakes the doctor's hands, and immediately he winces with pain. Richard was so consumed with Emerald that he didn't notice that he hurt it when he punched the cameraman.

"You all right?" Dr. McIntyre asks.

"I hurt my hand," Richard admits.

"How did you do that?" Dr. McIntyre asks as he examines Richard's hand.

"I really want to see Emerald," Richard says.

"Mr. DeMarco, let me set your hand." Dr. McIntyre said. "Then I can take you to Emerald," Richard hesitates.

"Let me see her, please,"

Fortunately, Dr. McIntyre is able to talk Richard into getting his hand ex-rayed and set for a cast. He broke his pinky finger.

RICHARD WALKS SLOWLY DOWN the hall towards Emerald's room. His heart breaks with each step. He can't bear to see the pain in Emerald's eyes. His baby, his child, his little girl has died. Richard hasn't gotten the chance to spoil her.

He didn't get a chance to meet her. Richard and Emerald decided to wait until the baby was born to see what if it's a boy or girl, and they didn't pick out names yet. He like the name Angela or Kelly, maybe even Ruby or Jasmine. He wondered who she would look like. Would she have Emerald's smile and quiet personality, or will she have his eyes? He would hold and kiss all over her, expressing his love for his little girl, his little angel. This baby would have defiantly been Daddy's Little Girl. When she turned sixteen, he would get her that pony.

When it was time to date, he would forbid it. When she meets Mr. Right, and after Richard's approval, he would walk his baby girl down the aisle to marry the man of her dreams, and Emerald and he would sit back and wait for grandchildren. But now, this will never come because his baby has died.

HE LOOKS THROUGH THE small glass window and sees Emerald sleeping. She lies perfectly still. She looks different. Just earlier today, she had a large round belly, now her stomach is flat. Richard opens the door and slowly walks inside. Quietly, he approaches her. Tears run down his cheeks. His throat is tight, and his stomach is in knots. He leans down to kiss her on the forehead. Emerald slowly begins to wake up.

She looks up and sees Richard, and immediately their eyes lock. He doesn't have to say a word.

Although Emerald knows that she is alive, she feels like her heart has stopped beating. The inside of her body is cold, and she could no longer feel the being that was once growing inside of her. All she feels is the hollowness of her womb.

"I'm sorry," she says in a whisper.

Tears fill her eyes.

Emerald looks away from Richard's eyes. It pains her to look at him.

Who would have thought that she will have to bury her child? Emerald isn't thirty years old yet, and she has to bury the third person in her life. Mothers don't bury their children. Parents died so their children can bury them. She blames herself. She should have taken better care of herself, working while pregnant. She should have stayed home and had her editor come to see her.

"No, I'm sorry," Richard cries to her. "Emmy, the doctor said that you can have more."

More pain? No, thank you! She thinks to herself.

Tears just stream down the sides of her face.

"Please don't cry," he pleads with her. "What can I do? Anything you want, I'll do."

"Just hold me." She cries.

Richard climbs into bed and puts his arms around his wife, and together they cry.

CAROLYN DEMARCO KNOCKS GENTLY on the door and then slowly walks into the hospital room. The knock wakes Emerald up from her sleep. Although surprised to see her mother-in-law, Emerald is grateful to see her. Emerald sits up in the bed and gives a small, weak grin.

"Hi," Emerald says bashfully.

"Emerald honey," Carolyn comforts. "We came as soon as Richard called." Emerald bashfully looks away. "Let me hold you."

Carolyn sits down on the edge of the bed and wraps her arms around her daughter-in-law. Emerald begins to cry softly in her arms.

"Shh, yes, it's okay, it's all right," Carolyn whispers.

After some time, Emerald breaks from Carolyn's hold.

"Where is Richard?" Emerald asks.

"He's in the cafeteria talking with Jacob, David, and the girls."

"Everyone is here?"

"Oh, yes," Carolyn says. Emerald lets out a sigh as Carolyn pushes Emerald's bangs from her eyes. "Do you want to talk about it?"

"What's to talk about? My baby is dead."

"What happened?"

"She strangled herself with the umbilical cord. She was born dead," Emerald says. "But what confuses me is that I felt her kicking all this morning,"

"She must have trying to break free," Carolyn says.

"I couldn't even save my child!"

"Emerald, you didn't know." Carolyn tries to comfort her. "But it's going to be okay; you can still have more babies."

"I don't want anymore."

"Honey, don't let the pain decide,"

Emerald doesn't say anything. Richard enters the room. Emerald notices the splint on his hand.

"Richard, what happened to your hand?" Emerald asks.

"I punched a reporter," Richard confesses.

"What?" Carolyn asks, shocked, "Have you lost your mind?"

"Ma," Richard complains. "I don't want to talk about it,"

"It was about that movie, wasn't it? Carolyn questions. Richard looks away.

"That movie!" Carolyn exclaims with frustration.

She gets up and begins to pace the room.

"Sometimes, I wonder what goes on in your mind. Why would you do a movie like that?"

"Don't blame Richard," Emerald defends. "It's not his fault; if I didn't want him taking part, he would have turned it down."

"That's not the point," Carolyn says. "It's the principle. You got actors and actresses who would take any kind of part simply for the fame or the money. Then their image gets ruin,"

"Ma, this is not the time!" Richard warns.

"No, it's not, your wife needs you, and now you might be facing a lawsuit for assault!"

"Ma, he won't press charges as long as I pay his medical." Richard replies.

"Why did you hit him, Richard?" Emerald asks.

"Emmy, baby, lie down," Richard say, approaching Emerald. "Everything is okay."

She lay down in the bed and closed her eyes. At this point, right now, she wishes that she was in Pittsburgh, alone in her world where no one can hurt her, no one can bother her, and no one can harm her. Emerald begins to wonder what life would be like if she had never come out to California. At twenty-nine, what would she be doing? Would she still be painfully shy, hiding in her house, only to come out to teach her classes or go to the market? Right now, this seemed like the good life because there would be no one to harm her. Richard would still be a figment of her imagination; he wouldn't be her Richard, but Richard DeMarco. She would watch him on television only to hope and dream, and the baby would just be an image, not a painful reminder.

EMERALD DID NOT REALIZE she had fallen asleep. She wakes up her room to a room full of flowers. She sees the nurse checking over her hospital chart.

"I'm glad you're awake, Mrs. DeMarco." The nurse says, "I can check your pulse."

As the nurse begins to check Emerald's pulse, Richard comes in with a bouquet of flowers.

"Hi." He says, smiling at her.

"Hi Richard," She says as Richard leans down to kiss her. "Where did all these flowers come from?"

"From everyone," He says, "my parents, my brother, and sisters. Your job, your editor, the publishing company, the studio, a few of my co-stars."

"Wow."

"And these came from Allen Sampson." The nurse says, holding a large floral arrangement.

Richard and Emerald are stunned that Allen Sampson would send flowers. Emerald rolls her eyes.

"Get rid of them," Emerald says.

"Get rid of them?" the nurse questions looking at Richard.

"Yes, get rid of them; I don't need his hypocrisy stinking up my room!" Emerald snaps.

Confuse about what to do; the nurse looks at Richard as if to get his approval.

"What are you looking at him for?" Emerald snaps. "I said get rid of them!"

"I beg your pardon, Mrs. DeMarco, I just-,"

"Are you still here with those weeds?" Emerald yells.

Quickly the nurse leaves the room with the flowers. Richard is shocked at Emerald's attitude.

"Em,"

"What?" she snaps again.

"Calm down, baby." He says softly. "What's the matter?"

"What's the matter?" she asked as if he asked a dumb question. "I lost my baby, I got a tacky civil rights leader sending me a bunch of weeds, you punching people out, and I got Nurse Hatchet giving me a hard time."

"Okay," Richard says, trying to calm her down.

He is sensing that Emerald is about to have a panic attack. She hasn't had one in two years, but he knows her too well that he can feel in his body when they are about to come.

"Baby, we got rid of the flowers." He comforts.

Emerald lets out a sigh.

"I'm sorry," She says; Richard caressed her face. "Tell that nurse that I'm sorry, I'm just-,"

"It's okay, Emmy." Richard coddles.

"I've been here for three days, and I am ready to go home," Emerald says.

"Dr. McIntyre said that you could go home tomorrow," Richard tells her. "You can relax and unwind at home, in the rose garden,"

Emerald nods her head.

"Emmy, about the baby," Richard begins. "I thought we name her Rhena."

"Fine," Emerald says coolly.

"We can have a real nice memorial for her," Richard suggests smiling at Emerald.

"Whatever." She says coldly. "I just want to be alone right now, please."

Richard feels rejected. He wants so much to be with Emerald right now, but she is pushing him away.

"Um, okay, can I get you anything?"

"No, but make sure you tell the nurse I'm sorry,"

"Okay."

"Emerald, I love you,"

Emerald give Richard a small grin then said;

"I love you too,"

Richard leans in to kiss her and then slowly walks out of the hospital room.

Confrontation

RICHARD CANNOT BELIEVE THAT he allowed Emerald to talk him into leaving. Emerald had basically pleaded with him to leave, to get out of the house. For the past two weeks, Richard has been hovering over Emerald, tending to her every need, giving her no reason to want to lift a finger. It has been two weeks that Richard and Emerald lost their baby girl. She begged her in-laws to leave. She didn't need them around anymore. What she really needs is time to herself; no one to bother her and no one to pester her.

It has been a rough two weeks for Emerald. The medicine that she needs the most is alone time. In the eyes of Richard and his family, it seemed like she was avoiding everything; she was. Emerald didn't want to see the world outside of her home. She would take quiet walks in the rose garden or hide in her study where she can write. Emerald is physically sore from having the baby. She is emotional from the loss of the baby. She has gained weight instead of losing it. Her skin is breaking out as if she is a teenager plagued with acne. The doctors said that her body would act out of sort. He put her on hormone pills to keep things under control, and within six weeks, she should be back to normal.

This is the kind of situation that made Richard wonder about Emerald's state of mind. Instead of fighting, it is like she is hiding. He has worked so hard to keep her from hiding. He blames himself for the loss of his daughter. It was his movie that made the media go crazy. That movie caused such a composition among the black community by triggering off the civil rights activist like Allen Sampson to say degrading remarks about Richard and Emerald. Richard decided to quit the movie. Even if he was acting like a bigot, he didn't want the world to see him as such. He hasn't told Emerald about his decision, but he will. Right now, his main concern was his wife and getting her back.

Emerald doesn't blame Richard for the loss of their child. She looks at his movie as just another movie, just another box office smash, just another paycheck. So what if he is playing a bigot? The world alone plays the part of bigots. They will smile in someone's face and talk about them behind their backs, and the real controversy about the movie is that it exposes the ugliness of society. If anyone is to blame, Emerald blames herself.

The real blame lies with the acts of Mother Nature because it was no one's fault; the baby was so active that she got herself wrapped around the umbilical cord and died. So no one is to blame.

Before Richard leaves the house for the morning, he goes to the rose garden and finds Emerald with his dog Bugsy by her side.

"Okay, I am going out for a couple of hours." Richard said as if he announcing it to the world, "I don't know where I am going, but I am leaving."

"Go shopping, go to the library, just go," Emerald said.

"You in such a rush to get rid of me?" Richard asks with a small grin.

"I'm not trying to get rid of you, Richard. I just need to be alone."

"Emmy, you are always alone. In times like this, you don't need to be alone. It's time to spend with family and loved ones."

"Family and love ones have been driving me crazy." Emerald snaps. "I need some space."

"Emmy, it's a fifteen-room house. How much space do you need?"

"The rooms won't matter if ever time I go to one, and there is someone hovering over me."

Richard looks away. Emerald sees that she had hurt Richard's feelings.

"You don't have to do this alone," Richard replied softly, looking back at Emerald. "This is my baby too."

"I know, but I carried her," Emerald said. "For seven months, she lived inside me,"

"So that makes me less of a parent?"

"No, but the bond is different between. I felt her kick first, not you. Richard, I know that this is just as painful for you. But I can't think straight with everyone bugging me, and you know how I get when there are too many people around. If it's not your mom, it's your sisters; if it's not them, then it's your father, and then you. When do I get some time?"

Richard didn't say reply. Again he looks away.

"Richard, what are you afraid of?" Emerald asks.

"I just don't want those walls of defense to come up. I want you to talk to me,"

"We're talking now!" Emerald exclaims. "Afraid of me becoming a recluse, new flash Rich, I am already one!"

"Okay, okay, Emerald, you made your point," Richard said, frustrated.

Emerald looks at Richard. She can see his frustration. She doesn't want him to be frustrated with her.

"Richard," her soft voice sounds almost like music.

Richard looks at her. She extends her hand out to Richard. He takes her hands and walks to her and takes her hands and then wraps her arms around his back.

"I'm okay, really. Trust me enough to be okay." Emerald said.

Richard leans forward to kiss her, and then he hugs her.

"I love you." He said.

"I love you." She says.

"I'm leaving, but if you need anything-,"

"I know; call you on your cell phone."

Richard kisses Emerald again and then backs away.

"Okay, I am leaving." He informs.

"Bye,"

Richard slowly walks out of the garden. Emerald lets out a sigh of relief, and she then looks at Bugsy.

"Peace and quiet, huh, girl?" Emerald said as Bugsy stands up on her legs.

Emerald rubs her behind the ears.

"You're my baby, aren't you, girl?"

Bugsy and Emerald begin their walk through the garden. The breeze is so welcoming. In spite of the California heat, there is always a soft subtle breeze that flows through the rose garden. No one can bother Emerald when she is in here. No nosy neighbors, pestering in-laws, overbearing husbands; no one.

This is her safe place, her hiding place. Emerald would have quiet times in her office where she can read or write. This garden is where she mostly at ease. Emerald can never forget about the baby.

Bugsy stops walking. She senses something unfamiliar. Her ears perked up, trying to listen to every detailed noise. Then she begins sniffing for a fragrance that is unknown to her, and then she begins to growl softly.

"What, Bugsy?" Emerald asks.

Within' moments, a shadow of a person slowly emerges, causing Bugsy to barks loudly and viciously. Emerald holds tight to her collar.

"Who's there?" she questions.

Slowly the person comes into view. Emerald is surprised to see who is standing before her, but she doesn't show emotion. Bugsy stops barking and shows off her sharp, piercing, white teeth. She's an old dog, but she is still tough. Allen Sampson stands nervously before Emerald and her companion holding a bouquet of roses.

"I saw the gate left open." Allen said humbly, "I knocked on the door, but no one answered,"

"Then you should have left," Emerald replies coolly.

"I'm sorry, I needed to see you," Allen said.

He attempts to approach Emerald, but Bugsy starts growling. She is ready for Allen to be stupid enough to come closer.

"Does it bite?" Allen asks nervously, already knowing the answer.

"Chews," Emerald informs, giving him a cold stare.

Allen grins slightly at Emerald's remark pretending that it is cute yet not doubting her whatsoever.

"Well, believe it or not, I don't want any trouble," He says.

Emerald doesn't respond.

"I come in peace. I brought some flowers, but I guess you don't need any." Allen looks at his surroundings. "May I," he asks, attempting to approach Emerald again.

Curious about why Allen Sampson is here at her home, Emerald tells Bugsy to sit. Although she sits, Bugsy's guard is still up. Carefully not trying to trigger the wrath of the dog, Allen approaches and immediately is struck by Emerald's beauty. Her dark brown eyes are captivating. Although there are a few minor pimples on Emerald's face, her skin is beautiful, her beauty nearly distracting his train of thought.

"I um, I come to apologize," Allen said. "Your baby, I can't help but feel responsible. My mouth is raising such a reaction with the media causing that kind of stress; I'm sorry."

"Apology accepted." She says with no emotion.

Allen smiles, wondering what to do next.

"Is that it?"

"Um, yes,"

"Then leave!" Emerald snaps.

Bugsy stands up, ready to attack when given the word. Allen looks at Bugsy and then looks back at Emerald. He grins, nods his head, and then begins to walk away. As Emerald watches Allen leave, immediately, she is hit with compassion. Emerald takes a deep breath and calls out for him.

"Mr. Sampson." She says.

Allen stops walking. He turns around to face Emerald. "Yes,"

"May I ask you a question?"

"Yes,"

"Why do you say those things?"

"I was only expressing how I feel, Mrs. DeMarco," He answers her.

"Then why do you feel that way?"

"Because no matter what we as African Americans do or accomplish, we will never be equal. The white man will see us as just a bunch of niggers."

"That's where you're wrong, Mr. Sampson." Emerald Said, "My husband loves and respects me,"

"Love and respect? Your husband agreed to be in a movie like that! Have we come thus far?"

"It's a movie; get over yourself! Where do you get your logic of thinking?" Emerald asks, disgusted at Allen's comment.

"You are an African-American woman. How can you live comfortable in this place without the support from fellow African-Americans? In your book, I don't see any influential African-American characters. Your book made your white husband famous."

Emerald wants to slap him.

"My book isn't about black or white. It's about adventure. For someone so educated, you speak like a foolish person who thinks they have a clue. My success comes from everyone, black, white, Chinese. *The Topaz Chronicle* series is still a top ten besting books not because white people read, not because black people read it, but because everybody bought it. You know what your problem is? I am your worst nightmare. I am an educated black woman who you cannot control, but let me explain something to you, Mr. Sampson. I have not one but two masters in English and one in education, and I have my doctorate. So if anyone is in control, it is me because I am teaching your children."

Allen stands frozen for a moment. He is shocked at Emerald's response. He tries to find some witty political comeback to what she said, but instead, Allen looks at his surroundings observing the rose garden that looks like a tropical forest. Emerald feels sorry that she just insulted Allen. Together they stand in silence.

"When Richard and I first started dating, of course, I wondered what people would say, not just because of our interracial relationship, but because here was Hollywood ladies man dating an average no-name from Pittsburgh. My whole world suddenly changed. I was very shy, insecure, and afraid of my own shadow, but Richard allowed me to be me. He never forced me to do anything I wanted to do."

"But you're beautiful; why would someone with your beauty, your intelligence, be insecure?"

"No one thought I was beautiful but Richard," Emerald told him. "No one paid any attention to me. I can get all the attention I want now. I'm a bestselling author; I am also married to the world's most handsome man, but nothing else matters as long as I have Richard's attention. Richard didn't make me who I am. I was already an established writer; my book series was ten years old when we began to film it. I was fifteen years old when I wrote it. Richard just taught me how to handle the pressure of success. Mr. Sampson, my husband, worships the ground I walk on. He tends to every need, grants every wish, and supplies ever demand. In our world, there is no black; there is no white, there is just love." Allen grins.

"I see you are beautiful inside as well as out,"

Emerald smiles bashfully, revealing that soul-catching innocence that has captivated the world. Allen didn't know if he had falling in love or what just caught up in her spell.

"What is going on here?" said a voice startling both Emerald and Allen.

Both of them stand frozen as they see Richard.

"Richard," Emerald said, smiling.

She approaches her husband. Richard stands firm and tall keeping his eyes on Allen.

"Mr. Sampson came to apologize."

"Apologize," Richard asks in shock.

"Yes," Allen said. "My comments were uncalled for, and the first thing I am going to do is make a public apology."

"That's not necessary," Emerald says with a polite grin.

"Oh, but it is," Allen said. "Mr. DeMarco, I am very sorry for the disrespect I have given you and your wife."

Allen walks to Richard with his hand extended to shake. Richard shakes his hand.

"It is nice meeting you both," Allen said.

"I'll see you out." Emerald offers.

"No, thank you, Mrs. DeMarco," Allen said. "I'll find my way."

Allen leaves. Richard walks over to Emerald.

"Are you okay?"

"Yes," Emerald says, smiling.

"How did he get here?"

"He said that the gate was left open." Emerald answers with a casual shrug of the shoulders. "Why are you back so soon?"

"I forgot my cell phone," Richard told her. "Now, I am defiantly not leaving you here; who knows who is going to show up. I am going to tighten up the security."

"Richard, I can take care of myself," Emerald says with a grin.

"I know," Richard says to her.

Richard holds out his arm, Emerald takes it, and together they walked through the garden.

"I love walking in here with you," Richard says. "I remember when I first showed you the rose garden. It was our second date. I watched you study everything with your eyes. You seemed so relaxed here."

"I was maybe because no one could see me," Emerald said with a chuckle.

"So shy," Richard said smiling at her. "You would hide your smile avoid eye contact with me, but when you would smiled at me, you took control of everyone ounce of my soul. Sometimes I would question how I almost let you slip away, but when you came to the premier party. I was not letting you slip away this time. I was going to win you over."

"You already won. I was in love with you from the moment I met you."

Richard wraps his arms around her.

"Richard, don't quit the movie." Emerald said.

Richard is stunned that Emerald knew what his decision about that movie.

"Em," he began.

"Listen don't let this situation make you want to quit something." She said, "Especially now,"

"Emmy, I can't do that movie, I don't want to be seen in that way."

"I know you feel responsible for our lost, but by you doing that movie, you're showing the world that you won't let anything hold you down, not Allen Sampson, not our situation, nothing. And it wasn't the movie that cause this, it was just bad luck, so don't quit."

Richard looks at Emerald.

"Are you sure?"

"I'm positive." Emerald said.

"Okay," Richard said to her. "but as for right now, I am not letting you out of my sight.

Emerald smiles and together they walk into their house.

The Crush pt1

IT IS A BRAND new semester. Emerald is excited because she is going to teach at one of the best colleges in the country. She is going to teach two types of English classes. One is a Creative Writing course, where she can teach this class how to explore the depths of their mind and create whatever their soul would allow them. The other one is her favorite, a Literature course. In this class, she can teach her students how to expound on a particular phrase that the writer has said.

At thirty-two, Emerald DeMarco is a household name, not only because she is married to Richard DeMarco, but she has established herself to the world as one of the bestselling authors. At this college, Emerald will receive her own office with her name on the door: "Dr. Emerald DeMarco." She cannot be more excited.

Before the sun decided to emerge and give the clouds their morning kiss, Emerald has been trying on different types of pantsuits. She loves pantsuits, and she has plenty to choose from, some that she hasn't been worn. It is very important to her that she makes a good impression on the faculty and on the students. Emerald doesn't want to be overdressed because then, in the mind of the faculty and the students, she would be dressed this nice because she is rich, and she doesn't want to look to plan because she doesn't have to. Emerald wants to look perfect.

Richard enters the room with two cups of coffee in his hands, one for Emerald and one for himself. She is still in her bathrobe, holding up two suits in the mirror.

"Em, what are you doing?" Richard asks, sitting the one cup of coffee down on the nightstand, "You're going to be late."

Ignoring Richard words, she holds up the suits. "Which one, the cream or the navy?"

"The navy," He answers.

"Are you sure?" she asks.

"Why do you ask me for if you're going to doubt me?"
He asks.

He set his cup of coffee down then wrapped his arms
around her. "What are you so nervous for, this isn't your first
time teaching?"

"No, but this is my first time teaching at a university; I
am teaching two classes, two advance classes, I'm teaching
smart intelligent students,"

"So you were teaching dumb kids before?" Richard
jokes.

"No," she said, laughing at Richard's joke.

Emerald is so excited that she is glowing. Richard
cannot be more proud of her.

"Em puts the navy suit on," Richard says to her,
smiling.

"Okay," She tells him.

Emerald hands Richard the cream-colored suit, and he
puts it back into the closet.

"Emmy, your students will love you. You're a great
teacher."

"Thank you, Mr. DeMarco," Emerald said,
smiling,

"You're welcome, Dr. DeMarco." Richard kisses
Emerald.

"Okay, lunch, we got out to Maretti's," he suggests.
"Sounds nice,"

"Okay, get dress," Richard tells her, then leaves.

EMERALD DRIVES HER CAR into her designated parking
lot at Sylier University. Butterflies are swarming around in her
stomach. She takes in a deep breath and tries to relax.

I can do this. She says to herself as she parks her car.

Slowly she gets out of the car and walks to the front of
the school. This is exciting, a new school to teach new faces.

Everything will be okay.

Emerald walks into the college and heads to her office; greeting her with a warm and friendly smile is the Dean of The School, Phillip Winset, and Emerald's secretary Rae Smith.

"Good morning, Dr. DeMarco," Phillip and Rae said.

"Good morning," Emerald said, smiling back,

"I have everything all in order for you in your office," Rae informs.

"Thank you."

"Are you ready for an exciting semester?" Phillip asks. Emerald smiled bashfully. "Again, I must say that it is an honor it is to have you teaching at our school."

"And again, I must say that the honor is mine, Mr. Winset. I'm honored to be teaching here."

Emerald and Phillip shake hands. Ever since she accepted the position, Dean Winset has been excited that *The Emerald DeMarco* is teaching at Sylier. Emerald and Rae walk to Emerald's office. Emerald's office is nice and big. She had decorated everything herself. There is an oak desk with a window facing the furnished lawn. Emerald has light gray blinds put in at the windows. A small coffee table sits in the center of the office, surrounded by a light blue couch and a love seat. This room is warm and cozy. Emerald wants her students to feel at home when they come in.

As Emerald sits down at her desk, Rae hands her a list of files for her to go through concerning her classes.

"Okay, here are the course syllabus and reference handouts."

"Okay," Emerald said.

"I am so happy to be working with you," Rae said, smiling.

"Yeah,"

"I am a big fan of yours." "Mine?"

Emerald asked.

"Yes, I got the whole *The Topaz Chronicle* series, the book, and DVD; I also have all of your other books," Rae said.

Emerald smiles bashfully.

"You're my role model. You are talented, intelligent, beautiful, and rich and on top of that, you are married to the most handsome man in the world."

"Thank you," Emerald said. "But I'm just your average person."

"You're more than average," Rae told her. "Anyway, get ready for your classes."

"These classes are huge, a hundred students per class," Emerald comments.

"That is only because the girls in your class want to meet you, and the boys want to *meet* you," Rae tells her.

Emerald grins.

"Can I get you anything else?" Rae asks.

"Ah, no, I am just going to get a mocha and then go over my lecture." Emerald replies. "Thanks, Rae." "I can get your mocha." Rae offered.

"No-," Emerald kinds protest.

"Really, Emerald, let me," Rae says with a smile.

"Um, okay," Emerald reaches into her purse to pull out some money. "I'll have a peppermint mocha."

Emerald hands Rae the money; Rae grins then leaves. Emerald sits down and looks over her notes.

EMERALD STANDS IN THE classroom waiting for her class. First-class is English Literature, and the story that she is going to prepare them to study is *The Wedding*, by Dorothy West. To Emerald, *The Wedding* is a classic. Dorothy West was the last surviving writer of the Harlem Renaissance. *The Wedding*, a beautiful tale about a well-to-do family that vacations in Martha's Vineyard, The family is preparing the wedding of their youngest daughter, who could have chosen any eligible man, given the right race and social class. Yet, she falls in love and is about to marry a white jazz musician. Set in the 1950s. This engagement stirs up mixed emotions. However, Dorothy West brings elegance to this story that breaks the shackles of race and class. Emerald cannot be more excited about teaching this class and studying this book.

After about ten minutes, Emerald sees that her class is seated in their seats and ready to listen as she expounds on one of her favorite books. She smiles as they look at her; some smile back, others stare. Emerald takes in a deep breath. "I'm Dr. Emerald DeMarco, and this is English Literature. For the next two weeks, we will be studying *The Wedding* by Dorothy West. Now, I am going to briefly take roll and then pass out the course syllabus."

Emerald takes roll and then passes out the course syllabus. Afterward, she looks at her class.

"Keep in mind that I am a pretty fair teacher. Show up to class, participate in class discussion, turn in your homework, and you should pass with no problems."

Her eyes scan the room.

"Okay, if there are no questions, let discuss *The Wedding*. Dorothy West, anyone knows anything about her?"

A student raised their hand.

"Yes, Mallory, is it?"

"Yes," she said and smiling, "I know that she wrote during the Harlem Renaissance."

"Yes, as a matter of fact, she was the last surviving writer," Emerald informs with a grin.

"Dr. DeMarco," a student called out as he slightly raises his hand. Emerald nods, permitting him to speak. "Do you think you would have written during the Harlem Renaissance?"

"What do you mean?" Emerald asks.

"Well, you're a writer. If you have lived during those times, would you have been a Harlem Renaissance writer?"

"I don't know." Emerald answers thinking. "If any of you lived during the Harlem Renaissance, what would you have done?"

"Looked for you," He answered and then blushed.

He put his head down. Various chuckles and giggles go throughout the room. Emerald smiles.

RAE FINDS EMERALD IN her office. She has survived her first class, and now she is preparing for her next class, Advance Composition.

"How was your class?" Rae asks.

"It went well." Emerald answers. "Except they really weren't interested in discussing the material. I got asked more questions about me, the writer, movie producer instead of me their teacher,"

"Well, Emerald, you are a celebrity," Rae says with a chuckle.

Rae's comment made Emerald feel ridiculous.

"I'm not a celebrity. I happened to be married to one." Emerald corrected.

"Emerald, half of your students are those who want to meet you."

"What do you mean?"

"What do I mean?" Rae questions. "Look at you; who wouldn't want to meet you." Emerald doesn't respond.

Rae cannot believe Emerald's humility. Rae has heard that Emerald DeMarco is a shy and modest person but never thought to be so. Why would someone in Emerald's shoes be so shy and modest?

"Emerald, you're a star; everyone knows you by name, face, and credibility. The majority of your students are required to take this course; they probably never read your book, but why not get taught by Emerald DeMarco? The other half because they are fans of yours, read your books, see the movies, and want you. The rest are English majors and find it an honor to be taught by you. You are a modern-day Jackie Kennedy, you're sweet, elegant, and very classy, and the funny thing is you don't even know the impact you have on people. I just met you, and I'm ready to kiss your feet. Face it, Emerald, why do you think the world loves you because you're Richard DeMarco's wife?"

"I never knew that the world loved me. I knew I had some status, but you make me feel like some icon."

"In some people's eyes, you are," Rae told her. "Anyway, you have some time before class, is there anything I can do for you?"

"No, I'm okay," Emerald tells her.

Rae smiles and leaves the office. A knot begins to form in Emerald's stomach, causing her pain. She sits down, trying to regain her focus. Emerald then gets up and walks to the door and sees many students walking around.

Which one of these students is in my class? She asked herself.

Suddenly Emerald is having a hard time breathing. Emerald cannot believe that she is about to have a panic attack.

"No, no, not now,"

She hasn't had one in years, and now all of a sudden, they're back right before class starts. Emerald cannot go before her students like this. However, now knowing what she knows, she couldn't go before them at all. She decides to call Richard and have him come pick her. She is going to give Mr. Winset her resignation. Then she is going to go home, hide in the rose garden and never come out again. All this will be okay because Richard will say that it's all right. Richard is always there for her.

At several movie premiers, they went to; he would hold her hand as they waved to the fans. It is only when she is with Richard that Emerald can handle situations, but now Richard is not here, and she needs him.

RICHARD IS NOT ANSWERING his phone. Emerald knows exactly where he is. He is in his sports room and has falling asleep watching some classic sports highlights.

Emerald decides to go to the cafeteria to get some ginger ale. She grabs her wallet and leaves her office. Her cute well-furnished office with her name on the door means nothing to her now. She has a well-furnished office at home she can

live at home and teach. No one will ever know who she is.
She can even have Richard put a nameplate on the door that
said Dr. Emerald DeMarcos' office.

As Emerald enters the lounge, she sees several students
talking and laughing among themselves over coffee, muffins;
and candy. She wonders if any of them are in her next class.
Emerald walks up to the checkout counter.

"May I help you?" the cashier asks politely.

"Yes, a large ginger ale, no ice," Emerald answers.

The cashier nods her head and grins. She gets
Emerald's ginger ale. Emerald again looks around the lounge,
wondering if anyone knows who she is. Of course, they know.
She is Emerald DeMarco, a famous, writer, movie director, and
wife of the famous Richard DeMarco.

"Here you go, Dr. DeMarco," says the cashier. "That
will be a dollar-seventy-five."

Emerald stomach twists when the cashier calls her
name. Emerald has never seen this woman in her life. As
Emerald gets money from her wallet, a voice from behind
speaks up.

"I got that." He said.

Emerald turns around to see who the stranger is.
Standing behind her is a tall, handsome African-American man
smiling at her. There is something familiar about him, but
Emerald can't put her finger on it.

"Um, no, thank you." She says politely.

"No, it's okay." He insists and quickly hands the cashier
two one-dollar bills.

"Um, thank you," Emerald said bashfully.

He grins.

"You don't remember me do you?" he asks.

"No, I'm sorry, I don't," she said to him.

He chuckles at Emerald.

"You're still the same shy girl from high school."

"High school,"

"Yeah, I'm Christian Williams." He informs.

Then it registers. Christian Williams was only the cutest boy in school. Christian had looks and brains. He was captain of the basketball team and senior class president. All the girls, including Emerald, had a crush on him. All the girls except Emerald pursued him. Looking at him now, he is still handsome, and he still has that winning smile.

"Wow, it's been a long time." She says, smiling.

"Yep,"

"What are you doing out here in California?" Emerald asks.

"I'm a teacher here," Christian told her. "I teach English."

"I'm an English teacher here too." She says.

"I know." He says to her. "You're more than an English teacher. Pittsburgh is real proud of Emerald Dixon." Emerald smiles bashfully.

"Do you have a few moments to sit down?" he asks.

"Yes,"

Of course, she has time to sit down. As a matter of fact, she has all the time in the world. She is getting ready to resign. Christian leads Emerald to an empty table.

"I just knew Schenley was going to be graced with your presence at the class reunion," Christian said. Emerald grins bashfully. "Other than your success, how has life been treating you?"

"Good," Emerald responds. "What's going on with you?"

"Well, I was married, but now I'm divorced. I came out here to California for a fresh start about two years ago."

"Wow," Emerald says, sipping her ginger ale.

"Nervous?" Christian asks.

"Excuse me?"

"You got the ginger ale for your nerves."

"How did you know?" Emerald asks suspiciously.

Christian hesitates to answer. He gives a coy grin.

"Emerald, this may sound forward, but I used to have the biggest crush on you in high school,"

"Me?" Emerald asks in shock.

"Yes," Christian says, smiling at her.

"Me!" Emerald asks again.

"Yes, what is that so hard to believe?" Christian asks with a chuckle.

"Because I was shy and awkward, and no one talked to me." Emerald wants to sink into her chair.

"No one talked to you? Emerald, you didn't talk to anyone," Christian said with a chuckle. "We thought you were a snob."

"A snob," Emerald is shocked.

"Yep,"

"We all thought that you thought that you were too good to talk to us. But I knew that you were shy. Most of the boys liked you but were intimidated by you,"

"Me?" Emerald asks again in disbelief.

"Yes, a smart and pretty girl like you. You were something in high school." Christian said. "Like I said, Pittsburgh is real proud of you."

"Well, Pittsburgh wouldn't be so proud of me right now."

"Why not,"

"Because I'm afraid to go to my class," Emerald confessed.

"What?" Christian asked with a chuckle.

"I'm afraid to go to my class."

"Why?" Christian asked, confused.

"Because they know who I am." She said in a whisper.

Christian nods his head, but he is still confused.

"Why shouldn't they know who you are? You're the teacher."

"They're not going to know me as the teacher, but as a famous person." She explained. "I mean, the kid in my last class said that he would look for me if we lived during the 1920's."

Christian understands now. He smiles at Emerald. Christian had Emerald figured out wrong; she was defiantly not a snob, just an extremely shy and humble person.

"What do you expect? You are a famous person," He told her smiling,

"I'm not famous! Besides, I'm still me!" Emerald says, taking in a deep breath. "I went into a class not thinking about being famous, just teaching. Now my secretary has me all nervous because half the class is my class because a famous person is teaching it."

"I got news for you." Christian began. "Since you started teaching, the students you taught chose you because you're famous. Now your job is to show them that you're a good teacher. When they leave your class, they can leave knowing that they were taught by Dr. Emerald DeMarco, not a good, but a great teacher. When you first came out here to work on that movie, did you want to work with some no name?"

"No,"

"No, but you wanted to work with someone who had a name for himself because he is a good director, right?"

"Right,"

"Okay, that is you, now you have a name, use it. Like Johnny Cochran, when he was living, who did not want him to represent them? What writer doesn't want Oprah to read their book? Emerald, I read all your books, seen the movies, and girl, you got it. Enjoy this. It is an honor that these kids chose you and want you to teach them,"

What Christian is saying makes sense.

"So what you're saying is, it's okay to be wanted because of who I am."

"It is more than okay," Christian said. "It is wonderful. Emerald, if you weren't a great teacher, do you think you would be here? No, Sylier does not just hire anyone. This school has a reputation to keep. Only the best teaches here, only the best attend here. My mom, okay, has her Ph.D., and she was trying to call the jail to see about her brother. The people were not letting her get through, so I told her, 'Ma, you are a doctor, don't just tell them that you're Miles' sister, tell them that you are Dr. Elise Williams and you need to see about the conditions of Miles Baker. Use what you got. You are Dr. Emerald DeMarco, a professional writer; you have books on the best sellers list right now, so it is evident that you know what you're talking about when it comes to writing. You are an educated teacher; go for it, babe."

Emerald takes in a deep breath.

"Thank you, Christian." Emerald said, "I feel so much better."

"What are classmates for?" Christian said with a grin.

"Richard is usually the one who calms me down. He always knows the right thing to say."

"Wow," Christian said. "You're glowing. You smile as if you're still newlyweds. How long you two been married?"

"Five years."

"Five years, he is a lucky man."

"I'm the lucky one," Emerald says, smiling. "Richard is so wonderful. He knows what to say to make me feel better. He's a dream come true. I went from this frumpy girl to Emerald DeMarco and the funny thing is, I am still me."

"Yes, you are," Christian said. "It's amazing how our paths crossed,"

"Yes, coincidence," Emerald said, smiling.

"Have you been back to Pittsburgh?"

"For what? There is no need for me to go back."

"Your family,"

"I have no family. My parents died ten years ago."

"What about your fans?" Christian asked.

"Fans, what fans? Richard is the movie star; he has the fans."

"Emerald, you're the bestselling author in the world; you have fans," Christian said.

"Writers don't have fans,"

"Who keeps buying your books?"

"People,"

"People who are fans of your work Emerald," Christian said with a chuckle.

"I don't need to go to Pittsburgh for that. I have fans here."

"Pittsburgh is your home, your roots. You can't deny that,"

"I don't deny where I am from," Emerald said. "But my life is here, in California with my husband."

"A devoted wife," Christian said. "I should have married you."

"What do you say that?" Emerald asks.

Christian looks deep into Emerald's eyes, and immediately he is taken by those dark brown hypnotizing eyes.

"Emerald, you are an amazing woman. You are sweet, humble, and beautiful. You are the ideal wife."

"Was your marriage that bad?"

"Yep, I couldn't get my wife to look at me. She was a work-a-holic."

Emerald gives Christian a sad grin. Both Richard and she are work-a-holic, but they learned to compromise with their schedule. Richard does one movie a year, and if the film is on location, he makes arrangements for Emerald to be with him. Whether she is on the movie set observing or in the luxurious hotel suite relaxing or writing a book, she is with him. The times when Richard is not working, he is home to greet Emerald when she comes home from work.

"So you're an English teacher," Emerald asks, changing the subject.

"Yep, I teach college writing, advance comp, effective speech, and grammar."

"The works," Emerald said with a bright smile.

Man, is she pretty—Christian thought.

"Yeah, I do it all; I have my Ph.D.," he tells her.

"That is wonderful, so you're Dr. Christian!" Emerald said smiling,

"Yeah, that is me."

"So what do you go by, Dr. Williams?"

"Nope, call me Chris or Christian," He said humbly, "No, being a doctor has its benefits; the money is real good."

"I'm not pressed for money," Emerald says, shaking her head.

"I guess not," Christian said sarcastically.

He looks at the diamond ring on her finger, the diamond tennis bracelet around her wrist, and the diamond earrings. Emerald sees Christian looking at the jewelry.

"Richard takes good care of you."

"Jewelry is material. Just things that can be replaced, but what really matters is how one treats each other. Richard can buy me all the jewelry in the world, but it's all ashes if he doesn't treat me right."

"If I ever decide to get married again, I hope she is like you," Christian compliments.

"That is very sweet," Emerald says bashfully. "I am looking forward to working with you in the English Department, Dr. Williams."

"I'm looking forwards to working with you, Dr DeMarco."

"Well, I am going to my class," Emerald said, standing up.

Christian stands up as well.

"Knock them dead. Show them why you're their teacher."

Christian watches as Emerald walks out of the lounge. She is still beautiful. Who would have ever thought that after all this time, he would be working alongside her? Christian was always particular of Emerald. He would watch her in the hallways at school, wondering about this shy girl. Wondering what was to become of her, and now here she is.

CHRISTIAN KNOCKS SOFTLY ON Emerald's office. Thinking that person knocking is Rae, Emerald replies: "Come on in, Rae."

Emerald is surprised to see Christian walking into her office. She stands up from her desk and walks towards him, smiling.

"Hey, what are you doing here?" she asks.

"I just came by to see how your class went."

"You're checking up on me?" Emerald asks with a grin.

"Yeah, that's what classmates do."

Emerald chuckles,

"Everything went well,"

"Yeah," Christian asks.

"Yeah, at first, it was a bit uncomfortable, but I took everything step by step."

"Did anyone ask you any questions about you?"

"Some did, about my book, but considering that this class was a Creative Writing class, they asked me more on the composing of my book, you know like advice."

"See, you did well." Christian smiles. "Next time you get nervous, just pretend that they're in their underwear,"

"Christian, that trick is so old," Emerald said, laughing. Emerald is too involved with Christian to notices Richard entering her office.

"Hello," Richard says.

"Richard," Emerald said cheerfully, "Hi."

"Hi." He said, looking over at Christian.

"I'm sorry Richard, this is Christian Williams, one of the English teachers here, Christian, this is-,"

"Already know, enjoy your work," Christian says, extending his hand to shake.

"Thank you," Richard says, shaking Christian's hand.

"Rich, Christian, and I went to high school together, and now we're working together."

"Wow, what a coincidence," Richard says.

"Yeah," Emerald smiles at Christian.

"Pittsburgh is real proud of Emerald,"

"Yeah, she is amazing," Richard said, looking at his wife. "I came by to take you to lunch."

"Oh, right," Emerald remembers.

"Emerald, I'll see you later, Rich; it was nice meeting you.

"The same," Richard said.

Emerald watches as Christian left the office. Richard watches Emerald.

"Em,"

"Hmm,"

"Emerald!" Richard said.

"What," Emerald answers, finally looking at Richard.

"Lunch,"

"Yeah, I'm starving."

"How was your day?" Richard asks.

"Very good,"

"Yeah,"

"Yes, I got nervous at first; my secretary Rae told me that the whole class was here to see me." Emerald began.

"Isn't that the point?" Richard says with a chuckle.

"No, imagine that you're the teacher, and the class wants you because of who you are. Anyway; so I got so nervous, and I tried to call you, but you didn't pick up,"

"I was home."

"You were probably in the Sports Room sleeping. Anyway, so I go to the cafeteria to get a large ginger ale, and right when I'm about to pay for it, some man offers to pay. I look at him really good and realize who he is, and it was Christian. And get this Richard, he said that he and along with most of the guys in our class has a crush on me."

"On you,"

"Yes, I was so shocked because no one talked to me in high school. He said that everyone thought that I was a snob. Can you believe that?"

"I thought you were a snob when I first met you," Richard said, joking.

"No, you didn't!" Emerald laughs. "But really, can you believe that Richard, I was popular in high school and didn't even know it."

"Yeah, I can believe it," Richard says, putting his arms around her. "You're popular now,"

"Yeah, well, all that has to do with chance," Emerald tells him. "That is not the same,"

"Anyway, Christian was there to calm me down."

"Calm you down?" Richard asked.

"Yes, I was a nervous wreck about my class, and he made it okay to be famous. And it was okay for my class to want Dr. Emerald DeMarco. He said that I should be honored that I am a requested teacher,"

Richard chuckled at his innocent wife. After five years of marriage, she is still naïve. He loved to watch her experience new things and new situations. However, he is beginning to feel insecure about this new man in her life. Should he feel insecure?

"So tell me more about the man who has a crush on my wife."

Noticing the tension in his voice, Emerald looks at Richard and wonders what he is thinking.

"He doesn't have a crush on me now; he is just a colleague." She tells him.

"Did you have a crush on him?"

"Yeah, every girl did." She told him. "Richard, are you jealous?"

"No," Richard said, backing away. "Just teasing you," However, Richard is jealous. He noticed the way Emerald was looking at Christian when she talked and laughed with him.

Richard also noticed how Emerald watched him leave and now they're working together. He begins to wonder if this is more than just a simple high school crush and that had faded away after graduation or is there something still there. Richard shakes his head trying to shake off the silly accusations.

"So you survived your first day of school." Richard comments.

"Yep, with Christian's help." She tells him.

Richard smiles and pretends that her comment doesn't bother him.

The Crush Pt2

RICHARD AND EMERALD WALK through the airport hand and hand. Everything around her seems to be moving still, almost as if things are unreal. Richard looks over at Emerald and sees the tension on her face. He chuckles.

"Emmy, want me to get you a ginger ale?" he asks.

Emerald shakes her head no.

"No?" Richard asks, surprised by her answer.

"No, I have to do this without ginger ale." She says, taking in a deep breath.

"I am so proud of you," He said, kissing her, "I wish I could be there your opening night-,"

"Richard, don't worry about it." She tells him, smiling. "I'll see you tomorrow morning."

Emerald still cannot believe that she has agreed to speak at the University of Pittsburgh for a Literature Conference. She was hand-selected by Christian Williams, a friend, and colleague who chose her. At first, she hesitated; she would be going back to her hometown and speaking in front of hundreds of teachers who taught literature and students who studied literature, and many writers who were considered genius when it comes to literature. But, just the thought is an honor. Christian's good friend Patrick Dean, a fellow teacher, is head of the English Literature program at the University of Pittsburgh. While organizing the conference, Patrick suggested that Christian should ask if Emerald would attend. After a half-hour of convincing her, Emerald discussed the idea with Richard, and he was more excited about the whole ordeal than Emerald.

Richard always knew that Emerald was special. He always knew that once she relaxed and let go, she can embrace the fact that she is an excellent writer as much as the world sees the fact. However, the date of the conference conflicted with Richard's work schedule.

◆

"Then I won't go," Emerald said to Richard while they were eating dinner.

"Emerald, don't be silly," Richard told her smiling, "Pass the bread, baby."

Emerald passed the plate of garlic bread.

"I can't go without you." Emerald proclaimed.

"Yes, you can." Richard said, "This is your hometown; they can't wait to see Emerald Dixon."

"No, no," Emerald said. "It's been too long,"

"Everything will be okay," Richard said as he sipped his beer. "I'll be there the next day,"

Emerald remained quiet for a moment, and then she took in a deep breath,

"Okay." She finally said."Plus, Christian will be there."

"Hmm, you mean the man who has a crush on my wife?" he asked sardonically.

"Richard, don't start," Emerald said, rolling her eyes.

"What?" Richard asked with an impish grin. "I'm just stating the obvious. The man has a crush on you."

"Had, Richard, he *had* a crush on me, and that was high school. He doesn't feel the same anymore." "If you say so," Richard replied.

"Why are you so jealous?"

"I am not jealous," Richard told her.

"Yes, you are?"

"No, I am not. Look, Emmy, I know that there are going to be some men who find my wife attractive that's okay because you are. You are a beautiful woman, even more so now than you were before. You also have established your place in society. Before me, it was Emerald Dixon, the teacher, the writer. Now it's Emerald DeMarco, the teacher, the writer, producer. What man in his right mind is not attracted to an intelligent woman, especially an intelligent black woman."

"That's it!" Emerald said. "You're worried about him because he's black!"

"What?"

"Richard, Christian is an intelligent man who is black," Emerald stated.

"Emerald, why are you making this about race?" Richard asks, offended.

"Because it is," Emerald replies.

"Excuse me?" Richard asks, shocked.

"Christian is not only my colleague, but he's my age, we go back to high school, and he's black."

"Em, don't be silly,"

Richard knew the point Emerald was making. There may be a strong possibility that she would be attractive to Christian. They have a lot in common. Richard is not worried about Emerald leaving him for Christian. Richard's issue is with Christian. Richard can tell how he looks at his wife that he has feelings for her.

"Wow, my husband intimidated by the big black man." Emerald joked.

"Emerald," Richard admonished, not finding the joke funny.

Emerald looked at him with her soft eyes that were trying to understand the root of his intimidation.

"Emmy, okay, yes, I am a little jealous. I mean you two are colleagues, you work together all the time, you have a lot in common, and you two are the same age. I am forty-six years old. So yeah, I get a little jealous,"

"It's okay to be jealous, but realize that you have nothing to be jealous about. Yes, Christian and I have a lot in common; that is only because we do work in the same field. But he was Mr. Popularity in high school; I was not. So other than work, there is nothing else. Rich, you work with beautiful white women all the time, women close to your age, mature women, not women like me who are simple-minded and have panic attacks."

"Emmy, you're not simple-minded," Richard told her. "I love you, baby. You are innocent, pure, and that's what makes you, you. Any man, black, white, purple, would love you," Emerald grinned.

They both leaned forward to kiss each other, and the magic was still there. Whenever they would kiss, that same emotion tingled through them, and still, they were able to quench each other's desires. There has never been a day when Richard hasn't desired Emerald. From those dark brown doe eyes that melts his heart to the curves of her body. Richard's desires for his wife were more than just physical; it was emotional.

Every time he would make love to her, it was like making love for the first time. It was still like a new adventure exploring the curves of her hips, tasting the sweetness of her thighs, caressing the stomach that was soft like silk.

◆

"I'm going to miss you," Emerald said at the airport as she and Richard sit down.

"Normally, it's you that is going away, and I see you off."

"Now, it's the other way around." He said, smiling at her as he kisses her hand.

"It's going to be nice going back to Pittsburgh." Emerald replies.

"When I come up, maybe you can show me around."

"Yeah, okay." Emerald chuckles as she takes in a deep breath.

"You sure you don't want that ginger ale?"

"No, Emerald will be fine." said a voice from behind them.

Richard and Emerald turn around and sees Christian standing behind them, smiling.

"Christian, you made it!" Emerald said happily.

"Of course I made it," Christian said, smiling at her. Christian looks at Richard, and he extends his hand. "Rich, how you doin'?"

"I can't complain," Richard said, shaking Christian's hand.

"Our flight will be leaving in ten minutes," Emerald informs Christian. Christian nods his head in response.

"So tell me about this conference," Richard asked as everyone sat down.

"Well, we met every year to discuss the top ten literature books of the year. Every speaker gives their opinion on the book, the characters and sees where it reflects on today's society,"

"In other words, a bunch of stiffs having an annual book club meeting?" Richard asks jokingly.

"Basically," Christian said, laughing at Richard's joke. "I did Emerald's *The Topaz Chronicle* five years ago."

"Really?" Emerald asks.

"Yep," Christian said, "So your appearance will be a big honor as if royalty was coming. Pittsburgh's own stopping in."

"Stop making this more than what it really is," Emerald replied shyly.

"It's true," Christian said. "Rich, Pittsburgh is very proud of Emerald Dixon,"

"I'm proud of Emmy too," Richard told her. "This conference is a big step for her,"

"She'll be fine." Christian replies.

Soon the announcement over the airport announces the flight to Pittsburgh, Pennsylvania, is now boarding. As Christian stands up, Emerald takes a deep breath, and then together, she and Richard stand.

"Okay, baby." He said, smiling; he takes both of Emerald's hands and kisses them, and then he kisses her. "I'll see you tomorrow, okay."

"Okay," She said, smiling.

Emerald gives Richard one more hug and kiss, and then she joins Christian and heads towards the plane.

CHRISTIAN AND EMERALD ARE seated on the plane. He looks over at Emerald as she stares out of the window.

"Can I ask you a question?" Christian asks.

"What?" she asks, facing him.

"You and Richard, why does he baby you so much?"

"What do you mean?"

"I mean, he treats you as if you can't do anything for yourself."

"No, he takes care of me." Emerald corrects Christian.

"Emerald, you're a grown woman. You can take care of yourself,"

"It is nice to have someone pampering me." She said with a smile. "Wouldn't you like someone to take care of you?" Christian shrugs his shoulders. Emerald continues.

"Wouldn't you like someone to massage your shoulders after a long day, have a hot bath waiting for you, and at the end of the night, make love and wake up in each other's arms?"

"Sounds nice," Christian said, "But how realistic is that?"

"Very," She told him, "My husband does it for me all the time. Can I ask you a question?"

"Sure."

"You and your ex-wife, what happened?"

"She didn't appreciate the hot baths."

Emerald understands. Some women don't appreciate the good man when they have one. After three years of working together, Emerald and Christian have become good friends. Together they have lunch and talk about books or discuss other writers. Christian would give Emerald teaching tips. Christian has high respect for Emerald. In his eyes, she was a real lady. From the way she would talk, never using profane or obscene language.

In Emerald's eyes, it seems as if Christian's heart has been scared from his divorce. His ex-wife broke more than his heart. She damaged his soul, leaving him to die in the world, never to trust or love again.

"Christian, do you think that you'll ever get married again?"

Christian let out a sigh,

"Maybe," he answers. "If I find the right woman, kids will be nice. You and Richard, are you two going have more children?"

Emerald shrugs her shoulders and then quickly looks away. Just thinking about children made her sad. It is a constant reminder of the baby she lost six years ago. It is a subject that she never talked about.

"Kids, just not our time yet, I guess," Emerald answers softly.

"Will you ever have them?" he asks. "I read about the baby-,"

"So tell me about this conference," she said, changing the subject.

"Okay, Emerald, I get the hint." Christian said smiling, "I got a feeling that this conference is going to be really good."

"I am looking forward to it," Emerald said.

She leans her head back on the seat and closes her eyes.

PARTICIPANTS OF THE CONFERENCE is staying at the Fairmont Hotel in Downtown Pittsburgh. The bell boy takes Emerald's bags and escorted her to her suite. Christian informs Emerald for opening night, there will be a catered dinner party for many of the speakers held in the hotel's ballroom. As Emerald gets settled in her suite, she calls Richard, but there is no answer. Then she remembers the three-hour time zone difference, it was five-thirty in Pittsburgh, it is three-thirty in California. Richard isn't home.

Emerald begins to get ready for the dinner party. Christian said that he would pick her up at eight o'clock.

THE DINNER PARTY IS a classy affair. Everyone is either in a black-tie or black evening gown. Emerald takes the mold when she enters the dining hall wearing a silk backless coral evening gown. In her ears are six karat diamonds, and she wears a matching tennis bracelet. Her long hair is pulled back in a bun. She's not wearing her trademark wire-rim glasses. Her brown eyes catches everyone one's attention. Of course, everyone heads turn when she walks into the room.

"Everyone is staring at us." She whispers nervously to Christian.

"Can you blame them? You got the finest man in the world escorting you tonight." He jokes.

Emerald laughs.

"I wonder if there is any ginger-ale?" she murmurs.

"No, Em," Christian encourages. "Come on, relax, everyone here is just like you, a writer or teacher, okay."

Emerald takes in a deep breath and nods her head.

"Come on; I'll introduce you to Pat Dean."

Christian leads Emerald through the crowd of people to meet his friend Pat Dean. Pat is a mild-mannered laid back individual. He stands at five foot eight, and he has soft red hair and piercing green eyes.

"Christian, glad you made it," Pat says, smiling as he and Christian shake hands.

"How's it going? Pat, I like you to meet-,"

"Emerald Dixon," Pat said, shaking Emerald's hand. "It is a pleasure meeting you and an honor having you at the seminar."

"It's Emerald DeMarco." She corrects him politely, "and the honor is mine, Mr. Dean."

"I'm Pat; Mr. Dean was my father," Pat says, smiling. "Everyone here is looking forward to your analysis, Mrs. DeMarco."

"Please, call me Emerald. And I am looking forward to hear from the others." Emerald said smiling.

Pat smiles at the beautiful yet humble writer.

"Is Richard here?" Pat asks.

"No, but he will be here tomorrow,"

"Wow, Christian, not only are you escorting a beautiful woman, but a beautiful married woman at that."

"Well, what can I say? The ladies love me," Christian jokes.

Together everyone laughs. Pat shakes Emerald's hand and then excuses himself and leaves. As a waiter pass by with a tray full of Champaign, Christian takes two glasses off the tray and hands one to Emerald.

"No, thank you." She said

"Come on, Emerald, relax," Christian said. "Loosen up."

Emerald thought for a moment, then took the drink,

"Well, one won't hurt."

"To a wonderful conference," Christian said, holding up his glass.

"To a wonderful conference," Emerald said smiling.

THROUGHOUT THE NIGHT, CHRISTIAN leads Emerald through the crowd to meet other teachers and writers. Everyone is pleased to meet Emerald DeMarco, and Emerald is pleased to meet everyone. Tonight reminded her of *The Topaz Chronicles* premiere party when Richard escorted her around meeting other actors and directors. Emerald remembered how sweet Richard was guiding her through the crowd. Emerald is missing Richard. She is missing holding his hand and hearing his voice.

Why did I come out here without him? She asks herself. *I am not going to make it.*

WHILE CHRISTIAN ENGAGES IN conversation, Emerald manages to sneak away and escape outside of the ballroom to sit in the lobby. She begins to take in deep breaths. She can feel a panic attack coming on. Emerald reaches into her purse to get her cell phone out, and she tries to get in touch with Richard, but like before, there is no answer. She checks her watch it reads nine-thirty; where could he be? After so many rings she sighs and then hangs up the phone.

"Emerald!" the voice startles her.

She turns around and sees Christian standing behind her.

"Christian, you scared me." She says, beginning to catch her breath.

"Sorry." He replies, sitting down beside her. "What are you doing out here?"

"Getting some fresh air," She tells him.

Christian sees that she is flushed and a bit antsy.

"Are you all right?" he asks her.

"Yeah," she said, shrugging her shoulders. "It just that I'm not one for crowds."

"Still?"

"What do you mean still?" Emerald asks.

"Well, you teach in front of fifty to a hundred students, and you go on movie premiers with Richard, and you're still shy?"

"Teaching doesn't really bother me, but the movie premiers do. But right now, I guess right now; I'm homesick."

"How are you homesick? This is your home town?"

"I know, but this place is foreign to me now. I made a life in California. I miss my husband, the rose garden, my office-,"

"Your mansion," Christian jokes.

"No, I guess, I've grown to the California life, hot weather all year long."

"Well, your husband will be here tomorrow."

"Yep," Emerald says with a grin.

"Come on back in," Christian says, standing up.

"I think I had enough of the dinner party." Emerald replies.

"You just don't go and make an appearance then leave.

People will think you're a diva."

"Diva?" Emerald asks with a laugh.

"Yeah, a snob,"

"Don't start with that snob thing," Emerald says, laughing. "I noticed a convenience store a block away. I'm going to grabs some junk food and ginger ale and then back to my room."

Emerald starts to walk outside of the hotel. Christian quickly follows up behind her.

"Wait, I can't let you go by yourself."

"It's a lovely night," Emerald said. "Plus, this is my hometown, remember. I know the way back to the hotel."

"Yeah, I know, but if anything happens to you, Richard would have my head. Let's get your junk food; then we can come back and eat in the hotel lounge. They have good hot wings, a change of scenery."

Christian holds out his arm to her. She takes his arm, and together they walked down the walkway of the hotel. They walk alone in silence. Emerald begins to observe the scenery around her, from the lights of the buildings to the cars going and coming.

"Look at the sky," Emerald said, gazing up at the heavens. "Have you ever seen such a beautiful night?"
Together they look up at the sky. The silver moon highlighted the navy blue sky as the stars twinkled like diamonds. As they continue to walk on, Emerald takes in a deep breath as if she is absorbing the magnificent beauty.

"I love looking at the horizon, especially when the sun sets and rises. It is so amazing. Have you ever seen such beauty?"

"Yeah, you," Christian said.

Emerald looks away bashfully.

"I'm sorry, Emerald, but you are gorgeous under the moon,"

Emerald grins.

"The sunset is like being in love; it's unpredictable like you don't know what the outcome of the horizon, you don't know anything about the colors until your see it, just like you don't' expect to fall in love. But when you fall in love, it's like that sunrise or sunset; it's beautiful."

"Until it fades away," Christian said.

"The beauty does fade into the night or into the morning, but you can always look forward to seeing it again the next day. There will always be a new sunset, a new sunrise. And that is just like love, you may fall out of love, but there will be new loves."

"You are so deep," Christian said with a chuckle.

"Christian, do you feel that you wasted your time getting married."

"No, I take it as a learning experience. I loved my wife, she was beautiful, intelligent, but she was extremely independent. She wouldn't even take my name when we got married. It was Shannon Moore, not Shannon Williams or even Shannon Moore-Williams. Everything we had was separate, nothing was equal, and nothing was shared. Her car was brought with her money, the bills that she made she paid for; there were even separate bank accounts. Now I can tolerate a woman having her own money, but I couldn't do anything for her. Like Richard will get you anything you ask for, not Shannon; the only time it seemed normal for her to take gifts from me was when it was on anniversaries, Christmas, and birthdays.

"Why was she so independent?"

"Who knows, Emerald, one day I went and filed for a divorce and told her that she was wasting her time and to go live her life. Without even blinking, she signed," "Then she wasn't yours," Emerald said.

Christian just shrugs his shoulders.

TOGETHER THEY ENTER THE hotel lounge. Emerald and Christian sit down at an empty table.

"Sometimes I feel bad for you." She says.

"Why?"

"Well, because you loved your wife." Emerald began, "and she didn't love you back. It's heartbreaking. I don't know what I do if Richard stopped loving me."

A waitress approaches. Immediately Christian orders food.

"Get us some hot wings, and get me whatever you have on tap."

"Just water for me," Emerald said.

"Water?"

"Don't start!" Emerald said, smiling.

"Get her a wine cooler or something," Christian said to the waitress.

The waitress nods then walk away.

"Christian, why did you do that?"

"Because Emerald, I want you to loosen up. You are in your hometown. Have a little fun. Besides baby, one wine cooler is not going to make you a lush. Anyway, enough of my sad love song of a life. Tell me, was it love at first sight with Richard?"

"For me, yeah, I loved Richard since I was in the tenth grade'"

"The tenth grade?" Christian said. "No wonder why you didn't pay us guys any attention, your eyes were set on a movie star."

"Yeah, I suppose."

"So, what did you do to get him?"

"Nothing, one day he just starting to have feelings for me, and we've been together ever since."

"I don't know if I could ever marry a movie star," Christian said. "Her doing those sex scenes with handsome men."

"You know what, at first it was weird, but you kind of gets used to it. It's him on the screen, but he's such a good actor that you see the character. Plus, he hasn't done that many since we been together." Emerald said.

"Why haven't you ever taken up acting?"

"You don't know me by now to know the answer to that?"

"Right, Miss. Shy." Christian says with a chuckle.

The waitress brings out the drinks.

"You hot wings will be right out," She informs.

"Thank you," Christian and Emerald reply.

Christian watches Emerald pour her wine cooler in the glass and takes a sip.

"I know that it is not the upscale Champaign that you are used to drinking, but it's all right." Emerald shrugs.

"Christian, I don't drink Champaign," Emerald says. "I'm not much of a drinker."

EMERALD AND CHRISTIAN DID not realize that three hours have passed.

Emerald also did not realize how many wine coolers she had drunk. However, Christian can see that she was a bit intoxicated. He laughs at her.

"What is so funny?" she asks, smiling.

"You, you're drunk." He teases her.

"I am not drunk." She says, shaking her head. "But I feel really overdressed with this ball gown and me in this lounge. This is a teacher's conference, not the Golden Globes." Christian chuckles.

"You should be used to getting dressed for those award shows and other red carpet events," Christian said.

"Whatever, I'm going up to my room."

Emerald stands up but almost loses her balance.

"Oops." She says.

"Okay, come on." Christian stands up.

He leaves enough money on the table to cover their bill and for a tip and he escorts Emerald to the elevators. Emerald head is spinning.

"I'm a bit dizzy," she says.

"That is because you're drunk,"

"I'm not drunk," Emerald says. "Those wine coolers are not enough to get me drunk." "You're not a drinker,"

Once they get into the elevator, Christian pushes the button that leads them to their floor.

"Wow, I can't believe I got Emerald DeMarco drunk." Christian jokes laughing. "You know, you're kind of cute, drunk."

"I am not drunk." Emerald defends. "I may be a bit buzzed but drunk, no, no, no."

Emerald tries to break free from Christian arms, but she loses her balance again and falls in to Christian's arms. "What's going on with me?" Emerald asks.

"You're drunk in your ball gown trying to balance yourself in those four inch heels." Christian answers laughing. "I'm not drunk," she says.

Emerald tries to pull free again, but Christian tightens his holds.

"Em, let me hold you and walk you to your suite," he orders in a cool sweet tone.

Emerald looks up at him smiling. Whatever she is feeling, she is appreciative to have Christian with her.

"I'm drunk, huh?" Emerald asks with chuckle.

Christian nods his head. Emerald laughs as she buries her head in Christian's chest.

"Oh boy," she says. "I am going to feel this in the morning,"

She looks up at him and smile. He smiles at her and laughs to himself.

How in the world did I get you tossed from wine coolers, Christian asks himself.

Christian looks Emerald in her eyes. She is so pretty.
"You are so beautiful." He said.

Emerald smiles as she looks up at him. Christian has strong arms like Richard. The way he is holding her is making her feel good. Christian is handsome. His dark brown eyes are captivating like Richard's. He has a goat tee he had made him look mysterious. Emerald loves a goat-tee. Richard has a goatee. Without realizing what is happening, Christian and Emerald lean in closer to each other and start to kiss each other. This kiss feels nice. It's been a long time since Christian has kissed a woman. Emerald is comfortable. Is it the alcohol that is in her or the fact that she is enjoying being held?

What am I doing, -she asks herself. *I am kissing another man. I am married!*

Quickly Emerald pulls away. She is horrified at what just happened.

"Emerald, wait!" he said. "I'm sorry."

"Me too! I am a married woman, a happily married woman!"

"Listen, it's no big deal; we're both a bit drunk."

"A big deal, of course, it's a big deal!"

The elevator finally arrives to the designated floor. The doors open, and Emerald jumps off the elevator. She begins to run quickly toward her suite, Christian reaches for her.

"Em,"

"Stay away from me!" she snaps and quickly run down the hall towards her suite.

Emerald cannot breathe. She has a panic attack. What was she going to do? Why did she kiss Christian? What in the world was she thinking? Was she that drunk? Once she enters into the suite, she is hit with a surprise.

"Surprise!" Richard exclaims, sitting on the couch. He stands up and walks to her. "Surprise, baby!"

"Richard!" she says, almost falling back against the door. She runs into his arms and wraps her arms around him, and then she kisses him passionately.

"Hmm, what a greeting!" he said smiling.

Richard kisses her again.

"You been drinking?" he asks.

"I've been calling you all day!" she exclaimed.

"I know, baby, but I was making arrangements on coming here; I really didn't want you to be alone on your first night home."

"I love you." She said as tears fill her eyes.

Richard notices that she is trembling.

"What's the matter?"

"I just missed you." She said as tears fell down her cheeks.

She seems tense.

"Was things too overwhelming?" Richards asks.

"Tonight was just a dinner party." Emerald shakes her head. "Like a meet and greet."

Richard can tell that something is bothering Emerald. He cups her face in his palms.

"Emmy baby, you're trembling. What the matter?"

"Nothing," she answers, trying not to cry. "I just missed you. I am homesick in my hometown." Tears stream down her face. "I kept calling you just so I can hear your voice, and I kept getting that stupid voice mail."

"Okay, okay, baby, I'm here," Richard said as he wraps his arms around her.

Richard can feel her heart racing. She has a panic attack. "Breath, baby,"

"I can't do anything," She said, crying. "I can't do anything without panicking."

"Baby shh," he said, slowly rocking her in his arm. "It's okay,"

He waits for her to settle down. Together they sit down on the couch. Emerald places her legs across Richard's lap, and he gently stroked them.

"What happened tonight?" Richard asked.

Richard looks Emerald in the eyes, and their eyes locked.

Emerald leans forward and begins to kiss her husband. She pulls up her dress and straddles herself on Richard's lap. "Unzip me," she says.

Richard unzips Emerald's dress. Quickly she pulls the dress over her head. She sits on his lap wearing lacy black panties and a matching bra.

"Em, what happened tonight," Richard asks.

Emerald leans forward to kiss Richard. For a moment, they kiss each other passionately. With Emerald's advances, it is clear to Richard that Emerald is not up to talking, but he wants to know what set her off to have a panic attack.

"Emmy-," he said in between the kissing, "Baby, what happened-,"

"Rich, please," she says. "I don't want to talk."

Richard looks Emerald in her eyes and clearly sees that she is not in the mood to talk. Emerald leans in to kiss him again. Richard rubs her back.

"You're tense," he comments.

Emerald nods slowly. Richard reads the look in her eyes that is telling him to make love to her all night long.

"Take the tension away, please," she begs softly as she kisses him.

"Okay," Richard said softly.

"Don't let go," she whispers.

Richard and Emerald kiss each other passionately. Richard leans forward to lay Emerald on the couch. She watches him undress, and within minutes they unite. Emerald can breathe again. As they make love, Richard can feel the tension leaving Emerald's body.

THEY STAY ON THE couch, entangled in each other's arms. Emerald looks over at Richard and sees that he is asleep. Slowly she gets up from the couch, carefully trying not to wake up Richard. She walks to the mini-refrigerator and grabs a ginger ale, and drinks it quickly. She starts to cry. She hates herself at this moment. Richard did not deserve her, and she is not worth anything. Emerald wonders if she should stay at the conference or should she go home and just tell Richard that it was too much for her to handle. However, knowing Richard, he would make her do it, and that fact that she has a name in society, her abruptly leaving would not look good. What was she going to do?

Emerald takes a shower. She hopes a shower will make her think clearly. As the hot waterfalls upon her body, she wonders if she overreacted. After all, she was drunk, and she is not much of a drinker. She was emotional, and she was also experiencing jet lag. Emerald looks at her hands and sees that she was in the shower long enough. She turns the water off, gets out of the shower, and puts her robe on. Emerald feels somewhat better, but this situation is still on her mind. If in the event that she stays, Emerald decides to work on her presentation. She orders room service, asking for a pot of coffee. As she waits, she sits at the dining table to begin to work. Yet despite her efforts, she still is thinking about Christian. He is an intriguing and intelligent man. Emerald feels that she can talk to him about anything. They have been friends for three years, and they do have a lot in common. Both are English teachers, both of them enjoy reading the same books. In fact, they both joined a book club together. They would laugh at the same things as if they are sharing a secret joke.

Will this simple kiss ruin their friendship? Emerald never had any friends. As of now, Richard has been her only friend. What is confusing is that Emerald liked the kiss. Does this mean that she wants Christian?

Emerald doesn't understand what she is feeling. She never thought that she would desire another man. Why would she? Richard has and does satisfy all of her needs. She can talk to Richard about anything. Richard makes her smile. He comforts her when she is sad. Richard is the only man she has known. What would it be like knowing another man? Would Christian satisfy her like Richard does, or would he be better? Should she tell Richard what happened, or should she leave well enough alone? If she decides to say something to Richard, she is not going to say it during the conference.

If Emerald decides not to tell Richard, then she would be keeping something from him. Emerald has never kept a secret from Richard. Plus, Richard seems to be intimidated by Christian, and if she tells him, then this would only confirm his jealousy. What if Richard gets so upset that he divorces her?

Just the thought of Richard leaving her made her stomach tie into knots. He is the air that she breaths. He is the reason why she exists.

Emerald looks over at Richard while he sleeps. She can never love another man.

No matter how hard she tries to put it out of her mind, she kept feeling Christian's lips on hers.

Room service brings her the coffee. Emerald tries to drink it to sober up. She attempts to get some work done, but she sits at the table, she eventually falls asleep.

THE NEXT MORNING, RICHARD watches as Emerald examines herself in the mirror. She wants to make sure that she looks perfect. She wears a charcoal-colored pantsuit, and she wears her hair down and curls.

"Em," Richard said as he walks up behind her. He puts his arms around her. "You look fine."

Emerald looks at him through the mirror and smiles at him. Richard then looks at her through the mirror.

"What." She asks, smiling.

"We make a good-looking couple," He tells her.

"Yes, we do." She says, smiling.

Richard leans down and kisses her on the cheek.

"Okay, come on, Dr. DeMarco."

Richard backs away as she put on her glasses then grabs her briefcase.

"Okay, I'm ready," She says.

Together Richard and Emerald leave the hotel room.

Fall

Richard's Grace

THEY HAD DECIDED TO meet at an old abandoned park where Christian is certain that no one would come through to interrupt them. A lot needs to be discussed between the two friends before they can continue with their lives because they cannot leave this situation unresolved.

Christian skips rocks as he waits for Emerald. It is an extremely hot day which is typical for the California summer. Christian wears a pair of khaki pants with a white T-shirt and black sandals. He is nervous. Christian has never felt this nervous about meeting anyone, and although he could understand why he is nervous, he wishes there is something he could do to ease his tension. At this point, he could see why Emerald drinks ginger ale.

Slowly Emerald walks through the park. She doesn't want to meet Christian, but she knows that she has to. Who is to know how this meeting is going to turn out. Will they stay friends and go on as nothing happened? Will they be distant, just associates at work being civil to one another? Never to be good friends again, or worst, not being friends ever at all. Despite had what happened, Emerald does not want that.

Christian looks up and sees Emerald slowly approaching. She looks good in her dark blue jean Capri pants and white sneakers white tank top. Her hair is pinned up in a bun.

Richard is a lucky man, Christian thinks to himself.
"Hi," she says shyly.
"Hey Emerald," Christian said. "how you doin'?"
"I'm okay." She says, "You?"
"I'm good."
The small talk is painful; it is too informal. Emerald takes in a deep breath and then aimlessly looks around the park. Christian shoves his hands in his pockets.

"I'm sorry!" they both said.

They chuckle. There, the tension is broken. It feels as if a cool breeze has come to remove them from the summer's humidity.

"Emerald, I didn't mean to offend you in any way. You are a wonderful person, a beautiful person, a real lady, and most importantly, a friend. I don't want to lose our friendship."

"I don't want to lose our friendship either, and I really sorry that I ignored you back in Pittsburgh." "It's okay." He said with a grin.

He extends his hand.

"Friends?" Christian says.

"Friends," Emerald says as she shakes Christian's hand. "So now what?"

"Now what?" Christian asks.

"Do we go on as nothing happened?" Emerald asks.

"What do you mean?"

"Richard doesn't know." She confessed. "Are you going to tell him?"

"I don't know," Emerald admits.

"I would tell him."

"You would?" Emerald said, shocked by his response.

"Yeah," Christian said. "Yeah, think about it, does Richard, have any secrets from you?"

"No."

"Then you don't keep things from him. Besides, you two are famous, people like you defiantly should not have secrets because if the wrong information gets out to the wrong person then-,"

"He might leave me."

"Naw," Christian said, tossing a rock in the pond. "Not over a kiss. Besides, he kisses girls all the time,"

"That's his job."

"So," Christian said. "Go home, talk to your husband. Will he get upset? Yes. Would he want to bash my brains in, maybe, but in time you two will be okay."

"Why did this happen?" Emerald asks.

"Because we were both drunk and lonely, you were a nervous wreck missing your husband. I'm not over my divorce, and there is a slight attraction between you and me,"

"What?"

"Emerald, if you weren't married-,"

"But I am happily married!"

"And I can honestly say that I respect that. I'm not into breaking up marriages; that's why I feel so bad."

"I am happy in my marriage; I love my husband. How in the world can I be attracted to you?"

"Because we have a common bond, we work together, we're friends, and we went to high school together."

"Yeah, but Richard is the only one I've known; I never thought that I would want another man,"

"There is another reason; it's almost intriguing to want something new."

"But I love Richard." Emerald defends herself.

"It doesn't matter; my favorite meal is steak and potatoes; it doesn't mean I don't want chicken or fish every now and then. What you're feeling is natural, but it's how you respond to those feelings. So you might like me, big deal, do you commit adultery, no. You stay mature and faithful to your husband. I might like you. Do I make passes at you, no? I respect your marriage and move on. You and I worked it out; now, what you need to do is work it out with your husband."

Just the thought of telling Richard makes Emerald want to cry. This would hurt him so much because Emerald knows that Richard thought the world of her.

"This would break his heart," Emerald says.

"It would hurt even more if you don't tell him and he finds out from someone else," Christian told her. "If I was your husband and you told me that you kissed another man, I would very upset but considering the circumstances, how drunk and lonely we were, and knowing that this is not what you do, I'd forgive you. It might not happen overnight, but I'm not going to throw our marriage out the window. I tried with my wife;

she wouldn't let me in. She wanted to be married so she could simply say, 'I am married, but she didn't love me. So why waste each other's time."

Emerald sighs as she nods her head.

"You said that Richard is the only man you ever known. Richard was your first?"

"Yeah, we waited until we were married."

"That is real beautiful. Richard got a real gem. He's not going to give you up that easy, I guarantee." Again, Emerald sighs.

"Well, okay, I am going to go now; I'll see you at work tomorrow,"

"See ya tomorrow," Christian said.

As slowly as she arrived, Emerald walks just as slow out of the park.

EMERALD FINDS RICHARD IN his favorite place in the mansion, the Sports Room. Richard is playing pool at the pool table when he sees Emerald standing in the doorway. He smiles at her.

"Hey, baby." He said. "Come see this."

Emerald walks over to Richard and greets him with a kiss.

"Okay, now watch, yellow ball in the blue four, then corner pocket, okay, you watching?"

Emerald nods her head and watches as Richard makes the shot. Emerald claps her hands.

"Very nice! I knew that you could do it!" She said, smiling at him,

"You always did have faith in your old man," Richard said, then kisses her on the cheek.

"Where you been?"

As Richard takes another shot on the pool table, Emerald takes in a deep breath.

"I had to talk to Christian."

"Not another Conference." Richard jokes.

"Um, no," Emerald said, "Richard, I have to tell you something." Richard doesn't look up from the pool table.

"What I have to say-well, um, first of all, I am really sorry, and if you never want to forgive me again, I'll completely understand."

This gets Richard's full attention. He looks up at Emerald.

"What's going on?"

Emerald takes in a deep breath and decides in her heart to accept whatever might happen. The knot in her stomach begins to tighten.

"I kissed another man." She confesses as tears welled up in her eyes.

Waiting for Emerald to say something more, Richard stands still, looking at her.

"When?"

"In Pittsburgh,"

"Christian?" Richard asks, knowing the answer.

Emerald nods her head,

Why?" he inquired.

"I was drunk,"

"You were drunk?" he questioned.

"Yeah, we went to the dinner party, and I was really nervous, so I had a couple of drinks, then we left and went to the lounge and had more drinks. Then Christian takes me back to the suite, and while in the elevator, it happened."

"Then what,"

"I backed away and ran into the suite."

"That's it?" Richard asked.

Emerald nods her head. Richard continued to look at her, wondering if there is something behind that kiss.

"Why did you kiss him?" Richard asked. "You were *that* drunk?"

"I guess." She said as if there is no hope.

"You guess?" Richard asked as if her answer was too vague. "So, what was this morning about?"

"He wanted to apologize."

"Apologize," Richard mumbled. "I'll give him something to apologize for," Richard walked over to the window.

He is upset. There are no words right now to explain what is going on in his mind or even in his heart. Of all people, she kissed Christian Williams, the man who is in love with his wife. Richard knew that if given the right moment that Christian would try to push up on his wife. "Richard," Emerald said softly, "Say something." "What do you want me to say?" Richard asked.

"I don't know, yell, scream, anything."

"I never yelled at you before, and I am not going to do it now," Richard told her.

At this point, Richard doesn't know if he should be mad at Emerald or mad at Christian. Should he feel intimidated by Christian? What does Christian have that Richard does not? Richard is rich, a multimillionaire, he is a movie star, grossing in twenty-five million per movie. Richard can have anything he wants, so why does he feel threatened by Christian, an English teacher from Pittsburgh. He is on Emerald's level. They are both English teachers, scholars of knowledge. As one individual would see diamonds and gold and valuable treasure, Christian and Emerald see books as valuable treasures. Richard had heard several of their conversations, and he listened to the intellectual talk that they share; it was nothing like what Richard and Emerald talk about. Yes, they talk about deep, intellectual things, but it seems like when Emerald talks to Christian, their conversation is a bit deep and more profound. Richard has seen the way Emerald's face lights up when Christian is around. Her face used to light up for him. Does his wife desire another man?

After all, Richard is forty-six years old. He is still handsome, and he still has the muscular body that he is known for. The entertainment magazines still consider him one of the country's most handsome men, but what does Emerald see?

"Do you have feelings for him?" Richard asked, turning back to face Emerald.

"What?" Emerald asked, shocked about the question.

"Do you have feelings for him?"

"What kind of question is that?" Emerald asked, offended.

"A question that needs an answer," Richard snaps. He takes a deep breath to regain his composer.

"I mean of all the men in the world; you had to kiss Christian."

"Excuse me?" Emerald questions his accusation. "I didn't plan on kissing him. I was really lonely in Pittsburgh and nervous. I couldn't reach you and-,"

"That does not give you an excuse to kiss another man!" Richard states sternly.

He turns his face from Emerald. Her heart is breaking. He had never turned away from her.

"I am sorry." Emerald pleads.

"Why him?" Richard questions again. "Why not some other man, I mean, if you kissed some total stranger, then you can blame it on the alcohol, but see Christian, is just not some man, he is someone who you knew-,"

"No, I didn't know him in high school; I knew of him. He didn't know me; he knew of me."

"What about now, I see how you two are now?"

"Other then you, he is my only friend, and that is only because we work together in the same field."

Richard turns around to face Emerald.

"So you have no feelings for him other than friendship?" Richard interrogated.

"Yes, it's you who I love. I loved you since the tenth grade, since I was fifteen, for twenty years I have loved you, no one else."

"No, you loved me the actor since you were fifteen; you love me the man since we have been dating."

"No, Richard," Emerald said, shaking her head. "From the moment I saw you in your first movie, I looked into your eyes then. I saw this gentleness; even on the screen, I could see that you were a wonderful man; I fell in love. And when I finally met you, I was crazy in love with you. Then that night at the premiere party, when we looked into each other's eyes, I saw the same gentleness in your eyes that I saw when I was fifteen years old and knew in my soul that I loved you. And the look in your eyes, I saw a possibility that you just might love me too. Then when we kissed, I wanted to melt all over the floor. I could never love another man. I could never desire anyone else. You are my existence, Richard. You are the reason why I am who I am today. So what I had a crush on Christian when I was in high school, a crush is nothing to being in love."

"When I kiss you now, do you still melt?"

"Every time," She told him as tears fall from her eyes.

"That kiss with Christian, it happened that night I came into town," Richard asks.

Emerald nods.

"Was that why you were so shaken up?"

Emerald nods her head again.

"Why didn't you tell me?"

"I don't know," she said. "Everything happened so fast, I couldn't think straight. Richard, I'm sorry, I betrayed you, Richard."

"You didn't betray me," Richard said. "You made a mistake, a bad mistake, but it was just a mistake."

He holds his hand out to her; she quickly walks to him and takes his hand. He pulls her into him and holds her. Emerald begins to cry in his arms.

"I'm so sorry, Richard." She cries.

"It's okay." He said softly in her ear.

"I'll do anything you want, anything! If you want me to quit working at Sylier University, I will; anything to make this up to you-,"

"Emmy, you don't have to quit your job," Richard said.

Richard takes his hands and cups her face in his palms, and then dries her tears.

"Don't beat yourself up over this. It was just a kiss. It's not the end of the world. We can get through this." Emerald nods as tears roll down her face.

"Baby, don't cry; you know I can't take it when you cry." He whispers. "We're okay."

Richard hugs Emerald again. He could see that she is more shaken up by this than he. He knows in his heart that Emerald loves him. He knows in his soul that she is his for life, that she can and will never love another man, and that he is all of the men that she needs.

Richard looks at her in the eyes, and their eyes lock. She is truly repentant for what she has done. Richard knows that when she goes back to work, whatever emotion there is between her and Christian is now no more. They will continue to work together as colleagues and go on with their lives as if nothing happened.

Richard leans in to kiss Emerald softly on the lips. His kisses tell her that everything will be okay, he forgives her. Emerald kisses tell Richard that she truly appreciates his forgiveness and knows that this will never ever happen again. They continue to kiss each other, softly touching one another, and before then, they soon begin to make love ending the pain that is just caused, and this time, a special type of covenant was made.

<u>Two Hearts</u>

MUCH PANDEMONIUM FILLS THE hospital room,
nurses coming and going in and out of the room checking
Emerald's vital signs and checking Emerald's heartbeat.
Richard is by her side, holding her hand, taking a damp cloth,
whipping her forehead, and drying her tears.
Occasionally he would whisper softly in her ears.

"Everything will be okay, I promise." He says.

Emerald doesn't believe his encouraging words. She
knows that he didn't believe them himself.

At this point, Richard doesn't know what to believe. He
is afraid. Emerald does not want to be in this situation again.
She has vowed secretly in her heart that she would never
experience such pain in her life again, but somehow she
managed to allow this thing to happen. How did she let this
happen? Where did she lose control? She closes her eyes and
begins to remember when it all started.

◆

It was an extremely hot summer day, hotter than any
usual summer day in California, and it seemed like the heat had
gotten the best of Emerald. All she wanted to do was lounge
on the couch in her office and sleep forever. She had the
summer planned. She was going to take the summer off from
teaching and spend time with Richard before he starts a new
movie at the beginning of September. However, at this
moment, she just wanted to be lazy and let the heat have its
way with her.

As usual, Emerald woke up early at the crack of dawn
to observe the sunrise, but fell asleep before it peaked from the
heavens. When she woke up, she went to her office to watch
the morning news and again fell asleep. When she finally woke
up again, it was past noon.

"Wow," she said. "I didn't mean to be this lazy!"

Emerald got up and went to find Richard. She saw him coming from his gym. He greeted her with a smile.

"You just waking up?" he asked.

"Yeah," She said. "I've must have been tired."

Together they entered the kitchen. Emerald poured herself a cup of coffee while Richard grabbed a bottle of water from the refrigerator.

"This summer is going to be wicked," She said, stirring in a teaspoon of sugar.

"Yep," Richard said as he sipped his water.

"I think we should go away to somewhere really cool," Emerald said. "Like Poland or something. It is hot. Is the A.C. on?"

"Yeah," Richard said with a chuckle. "Are you okay?"

"Yes, it is just hot in here," Emerald told him, tugging at her shirt to make herself cool. "I'm going to take a shower."

As Emerald walked away, Richard just shook his head and laughed.

Women, he thought to himself.

Later on that day, Emerald was asleep in bed when she was awakened by light, and Richard is shaking her awake.

"Em, Em, Emmy," Richard said, waking her. "Emmy, come on, get up."

"What?" she asked, whining.

"Are you up?"

"Yes, what do you want?" she snapped.

"I can't find my dark green silk shirt."

Emerald looked at Richard as if he lost his mind.

"Richard, you have a closet full of shirts."

"Yeah, I know, but this shirt has short sleeves and low button-anyway, remember the last time I had it on, you took advantage of me, took my shirt off, and seduced me'"

Emerald started laughing,

"Seduced you?"

"Yeah, you seduced me." Richard teased. "And now I can't find my shirt." Richard looked under the bed.

It was comical to Emerald as she watched a forty-six-year-old man crawl around aimlessly on the floor like a baby.

As Emerald attempted to roll over in bed, Richard crawled to the bed and sat upon his knees, and addressed Emerald.

"Don't go back to sleep." He said. "You slept all day, and we have somewhere to go."

"We,"

"Yes, we. Lance Perkins' movie premiere is tonight."

"Your point?"

"My point is he has invited us, and we are going."

"I don't want to go," Emerald whined and lay back down in bed.

Richard didn't play Emerald any attention. He stood up and walked into her closet, pulled out an ice blue dress, and laid it across the bed.

"Put this on." He told her and then left the room.

Emerald sighed; the last thing she wanted was to go to a party full of people.

At the premiere party, Richard and Emerald joined many famous celebrities in supporting their friend Lance Perkins. A longtime friend of Richard's who had directed his first movie. Although it was nighttime, the weather did not allow any form of cool breeze to relax the humid atmosphere. Instead, it remained hot and humid inside the club and outside of the club.

As usual, Emerald was on Richard's arm, mingling with their Hollywood friends. Many of them were giving out their cards telling each other, "Call me, we'll do lunch," or "Call me; I got some things that might interest you."

To Emerald, this was the same thing over and over. Some might call, some might not. At this point, Emerald could care less. She was never big on the premier party scene anyway. If Richard makes a movie, okay, fine, she will make an appearance showing that she is supporting her husband, and then after shaking a few hands and smiling in a few faces, it was time for her departure and back to her quiet, cozy home on top of the Hollywood Hills.

After so long, Emerald managed to sneak away and go into the restroom. She thought maybe, just maybe, she can get some peace and quiet. As she approached the bathroom, her stomach began to turn, and before she knew it, she was in the stall vomiting.

While Emerald was vomiting, someone in the restroom heard her; a woman in the bathroom knew of Emerald. She ran to Emerald with concern.

"Emerald, are you okay?"

"Yeah," Emerald said, trying to regain her composer.

The woman assisted Emerald as she walked to the sink to wash her face.

"You are extremely pale!" the woman said.

"I am extremely hot," Emerald said, adjusting the water on the sink

Emerald grabbed a towel and damped her face with it in an attempt to put the cool off.

"It is warm in here." Emerald cried.

Emerald continued to take the cloth and dabbed her face with it trying to cool down. As she took a deep breath, all of a sudden, the room seemed to be spinning, and everything appeared to be foggy. Before she was able to stand up straight, Emerald collapsed on the floor.

"Woo," Emerald said, dazed and confused. "What in the world?"

"Emerald!" the woman said, kneeling down.

"I'm okay, just lost my balance, that's all," Emerald explained.

The woman placed her hands on Emerald's face.

"You're not okay, and you're burning up!"

"That explains why I am so hot," Emerald said, nodding her head.

"I'm going to get Richard!"

"No, don't worry-," said softly.

Before Emerald could object, the woman was out of the bathroom. Emerald made no attempt of getting off the floor. The floor was cool, and that is all that matters to Emerald. Moments passed by until Richard stormed into the ladies' room.

"Richard, you can't come in here," Emerald said. "It's for girls."

"Baby, what's going on?" Richard said, kneeling down to Emerald.

He cupped her face into his palms. He can feel that she was hot.

"I just lost my balance," Emerald said. "I'm okay. Rich, I don't want to get up; it's really cool down here."

Richard looks up at the woman.

"Rich, she threw up, then tried to wash her face, then collapsed on the floor."

"Em," Richard said, looking at her.

"It feels so good on the floor," Emerald said, tears welled up in her eyes. "I'm really hot,"

Richard looked into her bleary eyes and saw that his wife was not well.

"We're going home, baby, okay," Richard said to Emerald.

Richard gently lifted Emerald off the floor.

"Go through the side door," said the woman. "Less media out,"

"Thanks," Richard said to her.

Richard and Emerald waited nervously at the doctor's office the next day. Richard wanted to know why his wife was feeling so sick.

"I could be going through menopause," Emerald suggests.

"What?" Richard asked with a chuckle.

"I've been really hot, and I am thirty-five years old."
She said.

"Emerald, menopause his late forties, early fifties,"
Richard told her.

Emerald just shrugged her shoulders. The doctor came
in and took his seat at the desk. He looked at them both and
took a deep breath; Richard took Emerald's hands.

"Relax," the doctor encourages. "Richard, Emerald,
your test results show you are healthy." He said.

"It's menopause!" Emerald said. "I told you, Richard,
I'm going through the change."

"Oh no," the doctor said, laughing. "Emerald, you're six
weeks pregnant."

Stunned at the news, both Richard and Emerald stared
at the doctor as if he fell off of the planet Mars and was talking
in his Martian language.

"How?" Emerald asked.

"How?" the doctor asked Emerald wondering if she
really needed to know how she conceived.

"No, I know how, but what happened?" Emerald asked.

The doctor laughed again at Richard and Emerald's
reaction. Emerald shook her head in disbelief. "No, this
can't be right," Emerald said.

"Oh, it's right." The doctor said in a confirming way.

Richard looked over at Emerald; she was not happy
with the news. She showed no signs of joy to be carrying a
child. Although Richard was shocked at the news, he was
excited about having a child.

"Do another test?" Emerald demanded. "I can't be
pregnant; maybe it's some malignant lump or tumor,"
"Emerald!" Richard admonishes.

"Emerald, I ran the test three times. It doesn't get any
more accurate." The doctor told her. "I thought you two would
be happy."

"Doctor, let me have a moment alone with Emerald."
Richard requested.

The doctor nodded his head and then left his office. Richard took Emerald's hands and kneeled down on the floor at her feet. He looked deep in her eyes, searching for the reasons that she had against children.

"Em," he asked softly, "What's the matter?"

"I can't do this." She told him. "I can't do this."

"Why?"

"I don't want any children." She said softly.

Those words cut sharp into Richard's heart. No children? His wife doesn't want to bear his child?

"Why?"

Tears formed in Emerald's eyes. She took in a deep breath and then looked at Richard.

"I can't go through that again."

"What? Being pregnant?"

"Richard, we came so close to having our first child, and-,"

"Okay," he said softly. "But Em, that was a different pregnancy."

"Yeah, I am older, well into my thirties, and at high risk. What if-,"

"Listen, whatever concerns you have, I am sure the doctors and I will see to them."

"What if we lose this one like we did the last one?"

"Then we'll try again, and if it comes to the point where we can't, then we can adopt or have a surrogate child!"

"Surrogate! I don't want another woman carrying your child!"

"It will be your child too! Your eggs and my sperm-,"

"A woman carrying your baby; something that I can't do?"

"Emerald, you're carrying my baby now."

"What if it I lose this baby?"

"We won't talk like that. We'll take one day at a time, and like I said, whatever concerns you have, baby, the doctor and I will see to them."

Emerald took in a deep breath and then quietly said:
"Okay,"

"Okay." He told her, smiling. "I love you."

Richard leaned into her and kissed her,

"We'll be okay, I promise,"

Emerald was still doubtful and uncertain, yet she remained quiet. Richard took her hands and kissed them, and went to get the doctor.

The doctor nervously entered into his office and sat back down.

"I'm sorry, Doctor," Emerald humbly said.

"No need to apologize, Emerald." The doctors said in a comforting way. "You suffered a great deal with your first pregnancy, and any woman in her shoes would feel and even react the same way. But Emerald, you are in good shape, and I can't see why you shouldn't have a healthy pregnancy,"

"That's what you said before," Emerald said to the doctor.

The doctor nodded his head.

"I did, but unfortunately, things do happen,"

"Are there any concerns that Emerald and I need to be aware of?" Richard asked.

"Just schedule for an amniocentesis; we'll go from there. But I see nothing to be concerned about." The doctor ensured them. "Just schedule an appointment with the receptionist. Are there any other questions or concerns?"

Richard looked at Emerald; she shyly looked away and then shook her head.

"Ah, no, that will be all, Doctor," Richard said.

Richard and Emerald drove home in silence. Richard wanted to jump around and shout to the world his good news, but Emerald wanted to hide behind her walls. As they entered the house, Emerald began to walk up the stairs towards the bedroom.

"Em, you want something to eat?"

"No,"

"Em, you need to eat."

"Maybe later,"

Emerald went to lie down. Although Emerald believes in Pro-Life, right now, this pregnancy was something that she did not want, yet terminating the pregnancy was not an option. Besides, she didn't have to think of abortions or anything of that sort because it was only a matter of time when she would lose this one like she lost the last one. So Emerald decided to just stay prepared for this to end because it wouldn't hurt as much when it happens.

Within the next five months, Emerald lived as if she was superstitious. She didn't really acknowledge the baby that was growing inside of her. In her mind, it was easier to lose someone that you didn't know than to lose someone you did know. Emerald wouldn't allow Richard to build a nursery.

Emerald didn't tell many that she was expecting because it was only a matter of time when she wouldn't have anything to show for her expectation except more heartache. When some people would see her round belly and question, she didn't deny the fact that she was pregnant; she just nonchalantly tell them that yes, she is with child, and no, she doesn't know what she is having. Emerald refused to allow her co-workers and family members to throw her a baby shower.

◆

Now, just like she thought, she is in premature labor eight months into her pregnancy, just like before, and just like before, this is not supposed to happen. All of this is simply too much for one's lifetime because not only did Emerald bury her parents, but her first child, and now she is going to have to bury another child. What more can one asks for in life but a break.

The doctor enters the hospital room.

"How you doin' Emerald?" the doctor asks.

"Let's get this over with," Emerald snaps.

Used to Emerald's pessimistic attitude, the doctor gave her a grin,

"Okay, based on your ultrasounds, the baby's heartbeat is extremely strong, and now we see why,"

"What's going on?" Richard asks, confused.

"Instead of one strong heart, there are two weak but steady heartbeats," the doctor informs.

"Two? Two heartbeats," Richard shakes head, trying to comprehend.

The doctor nods his head with a grin. Emerald grabs Richard's arms once she caught on to what the doctor was saying. Two hearts beats means two babies.

"Two babies," Emerald exclaims.

"Yes, Emerald, Richard, you're having twins." The doctor said, smiling. "And it is very normal for you to go into premature labor with twins."

"How did we not know?" Emerald asks.

"There were two sacks, which mean that Emerald released two eggs when she was ovulating. Both eggs were fertilized, and the reason why they went unnoticed because one was on top of the other."

"So fraternal twins," Richard asks.

"Yes," The doctor said. "We were not able to tell the sex, but congratulations."

"So they're alive!" Emerald said with excitement. "My babies are alive!"

"That's right." The doctor says, smiling. "Look at the monitor. See that; their heartbeats are beating, and soon, you two can enjoy not one, but two babies."

Richard wraps his arms around Emerald and holds her tight.

"I am going to check on a few things, but I will be back to see about you in a little bit." The doctor tells them then leaves.

Richard and Emerald cheer loudly and hug each other tightly.

"Everything is okay," Emerald said, crying. "Everything is going to be okay."

"Yes, everything is fine," Richard says, smiling.

"THEY'RE BEAUTIFUL," THE NURSE said to Richard and Emerald. "Congratulations again, Mr. and Mrs. DeMarco." After eight and half hours of labor, Richard and Emerald are looking at their newborn twins, a boy, and a girl. Considering that the twins are premature, there are in the incubators.

The babies seem fragile and weak, but the doctors assured Richard and Emerald that they were doing well and responding positively. Both of them are healthy, with a full head full of hair. Emerald and Richard cannot be happier.

"Thank you," Both Richard and Emerald said to the nurses.

The nurses leave the room leaving Richard and Emerald alone with their children. Richard looks at his baby girl. Finally, he has that baby girl where he can shower her with kisses and presents and maybe even a pony. She already has a special place in his heart, and she is only two hours old.

"Daddy is going to spoil you," Richard says to the sleeping baby girl.

As far as their son, Emerald has her eyes glued on him. A male child to carry on his father's name, that male child whom she can teach how to love and respect women like his father loves and respects her. Her son is going to be special in her eyes. He is going to be Mommy's, Little Man.

To think she didn't want this child, these children. To think that she rather live the rest of her life not caring if she had any children because of fear. She almost closed her heart,

226

forever. But if it wasn't for the man in her life who is her everything, constantly convincing her that everything will be okay, these babies might not have been.

"Thank you, Richard," Emerald said to her husband.

"Thank you; you did all the work," Richard said smiling.

"But if it wasn't for you encouraging me, there would be no work to do," Emerald said to him. "I don't know what I would do if the results were different. What if the doctor told us to prepare for worst?"

"Don't think about that, Emmy," Richard told her. "At first, I was worried so, but we're okay."

"We don't have a nursery," Emerald said. "I was so worried about losing the baby-,"

"We'll get a nursery, don't worry about it," Richard told her with a grin. He leaned forward to kiss her, "What do you want to name them?"

"For our son, let's name him Joseph William."

"Joseph William DeMarco," Richard said, thinking. "I like that, Joey DeMarco,"

"Not Joey," Emerald said sternly, "Not Joe, but Joseph,"

"Yeah, okay." Richard chuckles at Emerald. "For our little lady, let name her Jacqueline Maria DeMarco."

"Maria," Emerald said smiling, thinking of Richard's grandmother, "Jacqueline and Joseph DeMarco, the DeMarco twins."

Richard and Emerald laugh at the thought of their twins.

"Do twins run in your family?" Emerald asked.

"No, yours?"

"No."

"Oh, well." Richard said, "They do now, huh."

Emerald smiles,

"I wonder what is to become of them."

"Maybe some acting," Richard suggests.

"Or writing," Emerald said. "Or law, one of them might become a lawyer, and the other a doctor. We can put Jacqueline in dance classes, and then she won't be so shy."
"Who said that she is going to be shy?" Richard asks.

"If she is anything like me," Emerald replies.

"If she is anything like you, she will be beautiful, intelligent, and extremely kind. And if she is shy, there is nothing wrong with being shy."

"It hindered me for years, and I still get-," she trails off.
Emerald is still embarrassed by the handicap.

"But you have grown so much." Richard encourages her.

Emerald smiles.

"Thank you for helping me to grow."

Richard and Emerald continue to sit and look at their babies. They have so many reasons to celebrate but tonight, they will celebrate the two.

got kids?

THE FRENCH RIVERA IS beautiful, especially at night. It seems like every star has decorated the sky as the moon highlights the clouds. There have been film parties after film parties. Only the elite of Hollywood are at the Cannes Film Festival this time of year promoting their independent films. Actors, directors, and producers all have come out to see one of the world's most romantic and beautiful countries. This was the summer event, Cannes Films Festival. No one who is someone dared to miss this event.

Although this festival is simply for the filmmakers and their actors, it didn't stop others from attending. The city is packed with fashion designers and musicians. All have come to celebrate the independent films. However, despite the spectacular event, none of this would be observed through the eyes of the DeMarco twins because they are grounded.

Joseph and Jacqueline DeMarco, the twins of Richard and Emerald DeMarco, are the joy of their parent's life. Joseph DeMarco is his mother's pride and joy. He is everything his mother wants in a son. Joseph looks like his father with the same dark brown eyes that make all the young girls take notice. What is most intriguing about him is he has his mother's demeanor. Joseph is shy and quiet. He hides behind his glasses and his books. Jacqueline, on the other hand, is the total opposite. She resembles Emerald having that same striking beauty. She has the same subtle eyes that speak of innocence. Jacqueline has long black curly hair, and her figure makes her look older than her sixteen years. Unlike her brother, Jacqueline commands attention whenever she enters a room. She wants to be seen; after all, she is the daughter of a film legend.

For sixteen years, Emerald and Richard have tried to raise their children away from the media's eyes, but the whole world wants to know everything about the DeMarco twins. What school they're attending, who are their best friends?

Now being in Paris at a film festival and not being able to see the magnificent sights and not be able to live in the spotlight has been torture for Jacqueline. She is grounded because she had borrowed her parents' car without their permission or having a license. Joseph is grounded simply because he was an accomplice. The DeMarco twins never go solo when it came to any of their schemes. However, his punishment didn't faze Joseph because he is a homebody anyway.

Jacqueline watches her mother get dressed for the evening. At fifty-one, Emerald DeMarco is still amazingly beautiful. Like most girls, Jacqueline looks up to her mother.

Emerald cannot decide which of the two dresses that she is going to wear. Along with her stylist, they weigh the option of a basic black evening gown with an open back or lavender haute couture dress.

"Which one," Emerald asks her daughter.

Jacqueline looks over at her mother, shrugs her shoulders, and then turns her attention towards the balcony.

"You know, Jackie, pouting won't help your punishment." Emerald scolds gently.

"The black," Jacqueline says, approaching Emerald.

The stylist places the lavender gown in the garment bag, while Emerald takes the black one. Emerald holds the dress up to her and stands in front of the mirror. Jacqueline joins her. Together they look in the mirror.

"Pin your hair up, do a natural face and red lips," Jacqueline suggests. "Can I pick out your jewelry?"

Without waiting for her mother's answer, Jacqueline begins to go through her Emerald's jewelry box and pulls out a diamond necklace, and holds it up towards Emerald

"Daddy buy this for you?"

"Who else?" Emerald asks with a chuckle.

"I am going to marry someone rich, so I can have tons of diamonds." Jacqueline states.

"That's not why you get married, Jackie." Emerald replies.

"I know, but Daddy is devoted to you. He buys you diamonds simply because he wants to, not just for birthdays, anniversaries, and stuff like that."

Emerald chuckles at Jacqueline. Only their features tell that they are mother and daughter. Richard enters in the room. At sixty-two years old, his handsome looks have become distinguished. No longer sporting the goatee, he now has a groomed beard. Richard still has those dark brown eyes that are dangerous, but those dangerous eyes became soft and gentle when it comes down to Emerald.

"You're not dressed?" Richard asks, almost complaining. "The car is here,"

"I'm sorry," Emerald said, walking up to him. "I couldn't decide on which dress,"

Emerald smiles sweetly at Richard. He smiles back and caresses her face.

Richard leaves the room and returns to the living room of their suite.

Richard paces the living room while his son lounges on the couch. He looks at Joseph, his young son, who is nothing like him. The two may enjoy a good football game and basketball game, but Joseph is defiantly a Mama's Boy.

"Mom still not ready yet?" Joseph asks, not looking at his father.

"Nope," Richard answered with a sigh.

"Pacing is not going to speed things up," Joseph said, climbing off the couch.

He goes into the refrigerator and grabs a bottle of soda.

"You know how women are," Joseph said.

"Tell me about it." Richard agreed.

"I hope when I get married, my wife doesn't take forever getting ready," He said, sitting back down on the couch.

Richard smiles as he sits beside to his son.

"So how are things with-,"

"Deanna, okay, I guess, but we're just friends," Joseph said.

"Friends huh," Richard asks suspiciously.

"Yeah, she and I enjoy hangin' out together."

Richard nods his head with a grin and then looks at Joseph. Nervously Joseph looks at his father.

"What?" Joseph asks defensively.

"I didn't say anything." Richard chuckles.

Joseph knew what his father is implying about his lady friend.

"We're just friends," Joseph stressed.

"Okay, okay." Richard chuckles. "So you don't like her in that way."

Richard can see his son has romantic feelings for the young girl that they are discussing. It's just like Joseph to be evasive about the situation or to be too shy to do anything about it.

"Just remember what we talked about it." Richard reminds him.

"Yeah, I know use protection," Joseph said sarcastically.

"No more than that!" Richard snaps, appalled at Joseph's remark.

"Respect, if you don't think much of her, then don't do anything with her."

"I know, Dad, I'm teasing," Joseph said, laughing.

Richard has taught his son to value women, just like his father has taught him and his brother David. Don't lead a woman on into thinking there is more in their relationship if there isn't. If they are just friends, then be friendly. If there are no feelings there; then don't bother with her. And if you love her, honor, and respect her, and give into every command. Richard taught Joseph to always be a gentleman. Pull out a lady's chair when she is about to sit down. Open a door for a woman. Stand up when a woman enters a room. Richard told

Joseph that women are gifts and should be treated as such, to be treated with the utmost respect. Richard also taught his son to never put his hands on a woman in the act of violence. Richard told his son to protect his sister, be the best brother that a sister could have, never let a man disrespect his sister. Therefore Joseph received the formal DeMarco's Instructions on women.

Emerald and Jacqueline finally come from the room wearing the lavender haute couture gown, and she wore her hair in a bun. The stylist was behind Emerald.

"How do I look?" Emerald asks Richard.

As always, Richard is mesmerized by Emerald. Joseph watches as his father is drawn to his mother as if he is hypnotized. Richard grabs Emerald's hands and kisses them. Emerald smiles at her stylist. The stylist blows kisses to both Richard and Emerald and then leaves.

"You look wonderful, Mrs. DeMarco," Richard says to her as he attempts to lean down and kiss her, but Jacqueline intervenes.

"Don't Daddy, you'll mess mom's makeup." Jacqueline scolds.

Emerald grins bashfully.

Richard looks at Jacqueline.

"Well, you will, Daddy. Besides, aren't you two too old to be making out?"

Emerald giggles. Richard just shakes his head at his daughter.

"Let's go," Emerald said laughing, "Miss. Jacqueline-,"

"I know, I know, I'm grounded, don't leave the hotel suite," Jacqueline said.

"Joseph," Emerald said.

"I know; I'm grounded too, and make sure that she doesn't leave the hotel," Joseph said.

"Very good," Emerald said.

She kisses both of her children goodbye. Richard kisses Jacqueline on the cheek, and Emerald and he leaves the hotel suite.

Only the rich stayed at this grand hotel, a luxurious inn that was once owned by kings and queens.

As Richard and Emerald leave out of the front door, Derrick Arrington, a bell boy from America who is in France for the summer, watches as Mr. and Mrs. DeMarco leaves. He picks up the phone and dials the DeMarco's suite.

"Hello," Jacqueline said, picking up the phone.

"Bonjour Madam," Derrick said smiling. Jacqueline giggles.

"Bonjour Derrick,"

"I just saw your parents leave." He informs.

"Yeah," she said.

"I get off in a half-hour, want to hit the town."

"Sure, but I have to be back by two," Jacqueline replies.

"Of course," Derrick told her, "I'll see you soon."

"Jackie, what are you up to?" Joseph asked her as she hangs up the phone.

"Nothing that you know about?" she teases.

"You're going out without that guy?" Joseph asks. Jacqueline nods.

"He thinks I'm mature for my age," she says, smiling.

"Why would he think that," he teases.

"Shut up." She said, walking to her room.

"Jackie, Mom, said not to leave the suite," Joseph said, following her. "Now, for the past week, you been out with this guy, and I been covering for you."

"And you're doing a very good job." She teases as she pulls out an outfit.

Joseph just shakes his head. No one would ever guess that Jacqueline and Joseph are related. In Joseph eyes, Jacqueline is loose, wild, not the kind of girl he would consider dating if she was not his sister. Although she is nice and giving, and she is always willing to share, Jacqueline is too much for him. However, at the same time, he wishes that he could be as free-spirited as his twin. The world is fascinating to her.

"Where are you going?" Joseph asks.

"Just around," Jacqueline answers nonchalantly.

"Around where?"

"A few spots here and there," She replies. "You know, Joey, if you learn to relax and live a little, we just might let you tag along. Think about it, The DeMarco twins, in ole gay Cannes!"

"No, thank you."

Jacqueline just shakes her head at her reserved brother. She wishes for once that he would loosen up and have fun.

Jacqueline loves the French atmosphere. She loves the country, loves the food, and is not about to let her parents or her up-tight brother stop her from enjoying her summer break.

JACQUELINE IS DRESSED TO meet Derrick. She wears a brown low cut shirt revealing her natural tan stomach, and she wears cream-colored tight pants, and her long hair she wears down. Like Emerald, Jacqueline needs very little makeup.

"How do I look?" she asks her brother.

"Like a hooker." He said, smiling.

"Shut up." She said, smiling back at him. "Joey, are you sure you don't want to go? I'm sure Derrick knows a few nice girls for,"

"No, thank you," Joseph says to his sister.

Jacqueline sighs.

"You know, we have the advantage to live life to the complete fullest, and you want to be here in a hotel suite with nothing to do."

"I have plenty to do." Joseph defends himself. "There is a Steven Spielberg movie marathon on tonight! All of his classics,"

"Spielberg?" Jacqueline says. "I wouldn't doubt he is at Daddy's premier."

"Well, I am the good twin, so I am staying put," Joseph tells her.

THE KNOCK AT THE door causes Jacqueline to get excited. Quickly she walks to the door. She takes a deep breath then answers the door. Standing before her is Derrick. He is tall, handsome, and twenty-one years old. Derrick is spending the summer in Europe deciding if he is going to study art. He is a fan of Richard DeMarco's and had read every one of Emerald's books. He thought he is the luckiest man in the world to be dating Jacqueline DeMarco. He knows that she is only sixteen, but it is intriguing to him to watch her play grown-up to impress people.

Within the past week, Derrick has been taking Jacqueline out, knowing that she is grounded. He would watch her parents leave, and then they would sneak out and tour the town and have her back long before Mr. and Mrs. DeMarco come back from their night. Derrick avoids taking Jacqueline to all the popular places in fear that they would run into their parents. Instead, he takes her to the alleys, where it is more of an adventure to go to the underground clubs.

There will be a little drinking; if drugs are around, Derrick keeps a close eye on her, not allowing her to get into too much alcohol.

"Ili, Derrick," Jacqueline says, smiling.

"Hello, Jacqueline, "Derrick said. "Hey, Joe,"

Joseph doesn't bother to look up at Derrick; he is too busy watching television, so he simply waves his hand in the air.

"Mr. Sociable," Jacqueline says sarcastically. "Let me get my jacket,"

Jacqueline goes to get her jacket and then winks at her brother, and then within moments, Derrick and she leave.

SHE THINKS SHE'S IN love. In her eyes, Derrick is very mature. He is not like the other boys she had a date with, who are silly and immature. Derrick has dreams and goals. Although she and her family are leaving in a couple of days, Jacqueline has sincere about her feelings for Derrick.

As she rides along the back alleys in his used Volts Wagon, Jacqueline feels like she is truly experiencing the adventures of life. The kind of adventures only one would dream about.

TOGETHER THEY ENTER INTO a dark, smoky club called LaRue's. LaRue's is run by LaRue, an eccentric woman with long red hair that hangs well past her back. She has bright, sparkling green eyes. Whenever Derrick brings Jacqueline to her lounge, LaRue would talk about Emerald's books. LaRue's boyfriend's name is Monte. He is just as eccentric as
LaRue. He writes and reads poetry on stage with jazz music playing in the background. Everyone listens, smoke marijuana and drink, and think that Monte is this great philosopher.

As Derrick and Jacqueline enters LaRue's everyone cheers. Enjoying the fan fair, Derrick holds Jacqueline's hand and waves at everyone. Watching her parents for years, Jacqueline knows how to work the crowd.

"Bonjour, Jacqueline, commet allez-vous?" *How are you?*

"Tre bien, merci et vous?" *Very well, thank you, and you?*

"Tre bien," LaRue said to her. *Very good.*

Jacqueline knows a little French, just enough for the pleasantries. Derrick is an expert in French.

"Merci," Jacqueline said. *Thank you*

The people in LaRue's lounge speak little English. Just enough to communicate with the American customers, but most of them would speak French. LaRue's and Monte's English is suitable.

"Comment Cava, Emerald?" LaRue asks.

"Ma mere est bien," *Mom is fine.*

"I am a fan, big fan," LaRue said in her broken English. "When is the new book coming?"

"Soon," Jacqueline said. "but in the states first. Give me your address, and I'll send you an autographed copy." "Oui," La'Rue asks, smiling brightly.

"Oui," Jacqueline said.

Derrick thanks LaRue for the drinks, and he and Jacqueline walk to a vacant table to sit down. He pulls some marijuana from his jacket pocket and lights it up; he takes a few puffs and then passes to Jacqueline, and she smokes it. To Jacqueline, this is life. It is her realm. Just being cool and being around those that love her.

THE HOURS PASS BY like minutes Derrick and Jacqueline talk with a few people, listen to Monte's poem, they dance, drink more, and get high, and before long, Derrick has become too intoxicated to pay attention to the amount of drugs and alcohol that Jacqueline has taken and neither of them notices that someone has slipped something into Jacqueline's drink. He thought nothing of her new overly hyper actions. As they dance, Derrick pulls Jacqueline closer to him feeling her body next to him causing him to get aroused. He begins to desire her with each moment they dance. Without thinking, Derrick leans forward to kiss Jacqueline, tasting her lips. Jacqueline's body trembles; she loves the way Derrick kisses her; she wants him to kiss her forever. She wraps her arms around his shoulders and begins to run her fingers through his hair, and now, even more so, Derrick is turned on. He begins to caress Jacqueline, rubbing her all over her body.

Then without asking Jacqueline if she wants to leave, Derrick leads Jacqueline to a small room with an old dingy couch. Together they fell on the couch kissing and fondling each other. Derrick wants more than just kissing and touching, and with Jacqueline's state of mind, she too wants more. Derrick sits up and takes his shirt off. He unbuckles the belt to Jacqueline's pants, exposing her lime green panties. Derrick then looks at her, and although Jacqueline's face is glistening with sweat, she is still beautiful.

"Is this your first time?" He asks as he pulls down his pants, revealing his plaid boxers.

Jacqueline nods her head.

"Don't worry; I won't hurt you,"

Derrick lies down on top of Jacqueline and slowly grinds his pelvis against her. He pulls her pants off, revealing her caramel-colored legs.

"You are so beautiful," He says, caressing her legs.

"I love you, Derrick," Jacqueline says.

"Yeah, okay," He said, pulling down her panties, and then he pulled his boxers down.

Derrick spreads her legs, and he positions himself to enter inside her. Before he does, Derrick looks at her. Jacqueline has her eyes closed, and she is not moving.

"Jackie," he said, but there is no response from her.

Derrick put his hands on her face and gently taps her.

"Jackie." Again she doesn't respond. "Jackie, stop playing with me."

Derrick puts his hands on her chest; her heart is pounding inside of her chest.

Immediately Derrick jumps up. He realizes that she has taken something that she wasn't supposed to. Quickly he puts his pants back on and then runs towards the door so he can go and get help. Realizing that she is lying there half-naked, he finds a dirty blanket lying in the corner of the floor; he grabs it, covers her up, and then goes to get help.

AT THE HOSPITAL IN THE emergency room, the doctors pump drugs out of Jacqueline's stomach. The DeMarcos: Richard, Emerald, and Joseph race through the hospital trying to get information on Jacqueline. It is difficult because most of the hospital staff speaks little English and the DeMarcos speaks little French. However, a woman doctor notices the DeMarcos and approaches them.

"Mr. and Mrs. DeMarco," She says in perfect English.

"Yes," both Richard and Emerald said.

"I am Dr. Amy Brown. I've been Jacqueline's doctor."

"Jackie, how is Jackie?" Emerald asks.

"Jacqueline is fine," Amy said.

Everyone let out a sigh of relief.

"There was acid in her bloodstream."

"Acid?" Emerald asked.

Richard and Emerald look at Joseph, who himself is just as a surprise to find out about Jacqueline.

"What?" Joseph asked in a defensive way.

"We need to keep her for a few days to detoxify her system, but Mr. and Mrs. DeMarco, you two are both very lucky that she was brought in when she was; if they had waited, Jacqueline would have died."

Horrified by what Dr. Brown's said, Emerald gasp for air Richard holds her.

"Jacqueline was brought in half-naked. So we ran a few tests, a rape test, and a pregnancy test," Dr. Brown told them.

"Rape! Pregnancy!" Emerald is beginning to have a panic attack.

"Yes, but both of them came back negative, there have been no signs of rape, and she's not pregnant; in fact, she is still a virgin."

"Who brought her in?" Richard asks.

"Her boyfriend," The doctor told him.

"What boyfriend?" Richard asks.

Amy points to Derrick, who is sitting alone in a far-off corner. In Richard's eyes, he sees a scrawny kid with no reason to exist. Immediately Richard charges for him. Emerald, Joseph, and Amy run after Richard.

"You little punk!" Richard said, snatching Derrick by the collar of his shirt and slamming him against the wall.

"Mr. DeMarco, I can explain!" Derrick manages to say.

"Richard, let him go," Emerald yells.

"I'm gonna call security!" Amy said and then quickly walks away.

"No!" Emerald said to Amy, "Richard, let him go!"

"Please, sir!" Derrick pleads.

Richard doesn't put Derrick down. He lifts him off the floor.

"Explain," Richard growled.

"All we did was go to a party, and someone must have slipped a mickey in her glass."

"Was that someone you?" Richard interrogated.

"No!"

"You gonna lie in my face!" Richard question as he tightened his grip." She was brought in half-naked. "What you plan on doin' boy?"

Derrick doesn't answer.

"You plan on raping her?" Richard asks.

Richard lets go of Derrick and begins to slap him.

"Mrs. DeMarco," Dr. Brown warns.

"Boy, don't you know I can have you killed!" Richard threatened.

"Richard!" Emerald exclaims.

Richard grabs Derrick again.

"No sir, she wanted to have sex," Derrick said.

Richard slams Derrick up against the wall. Joseph runs up and punches Derrick in the stomach; he falls over in pain.

"Joseph," Emerald exclaims.

"What do you mean she wanted to? Don't you know old she is?"

"Yes! She's sixteen," Derrick answers, trying to talk.

"And you planned on screwing her anyway?!"

Joseph heads to him again, but Richard holds up his arm to stop him. Derrick doesn't answer. Richard puts his arm down and allows Joseph to punches him in the nose.

"Richard, Joseph enough!" Emerald exclaimed.

"Beating the boy won't solve anything. He is somebody's child,"

"Jacqueline is my child!" Richard, he roared.

Emerald then turns towards Derrick.

"Listen, please," Derrick pleads. "I know how old she is. I usually watch her, so no one would try anything-,"

"Usually?" Richard asks. "You taken her out before?"

"I've been seeing her since you guys been in Cannes. I work at the hotel,"

"So you sneak her in and sneak her out?" Richard asks.

Richard then looks at Joseph.

"You knew about this?" Richard asks.

Joseph looks away.

"Joseph," Emerald says in a tone that told Joseph that she is disappointed in him.

"Mr. DeMarco," Derrick begins. "I'm a big fan-,"

Richard grabs Derrick again, but Joseph quickly intervenes.

"Dad, Dad, don't-," Joseph said. "It's my fault. I should have told you when she started going out. We weren't supposed to go out."

"A fan?" Richard asks, looking at Derrick. "You sneak behind my back by taking my daughter out and then take advantage of her?"

"Sir, please don't question my integrity," Derrick said as he wipes the blood from his nose.

Appalled at his statement, Richard shakes his head then walks away.

"Mr. and Mrs. DeMarco," Dr. Brown replies.

She looks at Derrick's face and then looks back at Richard. Richard doesn't seem apologetic. His posture dares her to call the police. She nods and tends to Derrick.

Joseph takes his mother by the hand and leads her to an empty chair. As they sit down, tears stream down Emerald's face.

"Mom, please don't cry." Joseph pleads softly. "I'm sorry, I should have told on her." Emerald looks at Joseph.

"How is your hand?"

Joseph held up the hand that he used to punch Derrick, "I'm okay." he said.

Emerald looks away. Joseph feels bad that his mother is hurting. He feels bad that he didn't tell his parents about what his sister was doing. Joseph looked at his mother and wiped her tears away. The last thing that Joseph DeMarco wants to do is to hurt his mother. Joseph loves honors and respects his mother. There is no doubt that he is a "Mama's Boy." When Joseph was younger, he would follow his mother everywhere, he would stay in her office with her while she would write, or he accompanied her when she would take walks in a garden. Just like Richard, Joseph can't stand it when a woman would cries. Emerald looks over at Joseph. He is her sweet, handsome baby boy who would light up with excitement when his mommy would come home from work. Joseph laid his head up Emerald's shoulder.

"What can I do, Mom?" Joseph asks softly.

"Don't change." She says to him and then kisses his nose. "I don't comprehend Jackie's free spirit,"

Dr. Brown comes back to Emerald with a grin. "Mrs. DeMarco, I can take you to see Jacqueline now,"

Emerald nods.

"Go find your father," Emerald told Joseph.

Emerald stands up and follows Dr. Brown to Jacqueline's room.

Before Emeralds walks in, she turns to face Dr. Brown.

"Thank you," Emerald says.

Dr. Brown smiles.

"My husband would have killed him too," Dr. Brown winks.

Emerald watches the doctor walk away. Slowly Emerald emerges in the room. Jacqueline lies helplessly on the bed. Although she wants to, Emerald tried not to cry.

"Jackie," Emerald says in a soft tone.

Jacqueline slowly turns towards her mother. The disappointed look in her mother's eyes causes Jacqueline to cry.

"I'm sorry, Mom," she said.

Emerald doesn't say anything.

"You and Daddy hate me?"

"No, we don't hate you, but we are very disappointed." "Don't say that," Jacqueline said.

"What else would you have me say?" "I don't know?" Jacqueline cries.

"Want me to say that it's all right?" Emerald asks. "Because it's not!"

"No, but you don't have to tell me that you're disappointed!"

"Jacqueline Maria DeMarco!" Emerald snaps. "You are so rebellious! Don't you know that you almost died?!"

"Yes."

"You were almost raped!" Emerald exclaims.

"No, I wanted to?" Jacqueline said.

"Wanted to?" Emerald questioned, horrified. "You were drugged; you had no clue of what you wanted. To lose your virginity in some club!"

Emerald almost has a panic attack. She started to breathe hard.

"You deliberately disobeyed your father and me!"

"Mom, you act as if you never did anything when you were my age!"

"I didn't!"

"Of course not; you were so perfect," Jacqueline said sarcastically.

"No, Jackie, I had a brain. I knew better than to go somewhere I had no business! My first date I was twenty-six years old, and it was with your father."

The room is silent for a long time. Both mother and daughter are frustrated. One is frustrated because she is tired of trying to live up to her mother's expectations. Who can please the most perfect woman in the world, the Great Emerald DeMarco? Emerald is tired and frustrated because she has a daughter whom she can't comprehend. She is a child that is not like her whatsoever. Where did this wild seed come from?

"Mom, why were you so shy?" Jacqueline finally asks. "You are so amazing, and everyone loves you."

Emerald looks away bashfully.

"Mom, are you still shy?"

"I still get nervous at times when it comes to a crowd." Emerald confesses her, "But as long as your father is around, I'm okay. In a strange way, your father made things easy. I can handle any crowd as long as I have him by my side. Jackie, that boy is not the kind of company you want to keep,"

"Mom, he treats me like an adult."

"He treats you like a whore!" Emerald snaps. "You were brought in half-naked! They gave you rape and a pregnancy test. No man who thinks something of you would put you in such a position. A man who cares wouldn't let your first time be in some club but in someplace special. Jackie, you only get one first time,"

Jacqueline ponders on her mother's words. In her eyes, her mother is the epitome of class.

"What was your first time like?" she asks her mother. "I mean, was it with Daddy?"

"Yes," She answered. "We waited until we were married. Now, there were times when things got heavy, and we came close, but your dad never pushed me into doing anything I didn't want to do."

"When you said you came close, what stopped you?"

"Your dad," Emerald said.

"Why?"

"Because he said something was missing?"

"What,"

"A ring on my finger," Emerald says to her. "See, Jackie, your dad always said that I was the rare gift, and he couldn't just have sex with me. Because in the event that we did, and your dad wouldn't have married me. He wanted me pure for the man who was to be my husband, whomever it may be, whether it is your father or someone else. Jacqueline, men value and respect ladies. That young man did not see you as a lady but an easy and loose girl."

Jacqueline sighs as tears fell down her face.

"Is that how you see me?" she asked her mother.

"Of course not," Emerald said, drying as she takes a tissue and dries Jacqueline's tears. "I see a beautiful young lady who is free-spirited, but the only thing you need to do is learn how to avoid certain situations."

"What does Daddy think of me?"

"You're his world," Emerald says, smiling.

"Other than you," Jacqueline teases. "Daddy says 'My Emerald is my emerald,'"

"I may be his emerald, but Jackie, you are his diamond." Emerald smiles down at Jacqueline, "I love you, baby."

"I love you too."

The two ladies hug each other.

"Want me to get you, father and brother?" Jacqueline grins, "Okay."

"Okay," Emerald said.

She leaves the room.

MOMENT LATER JOSEPH COMES in carrying a balloon and teddy bear that he brought from the hospital gift shop.

"Hey," he said, smiling.

"Hi, Joey," Jacqueline says as she sits up.

"I got these for you." He hands her the gifts.

"Thank you," she told him. "So you're not mad at me?"

"No." He said, sitting next to her on the bed. "Are you okay?"

Jacqueline nods her head then she notices Joseph's hand is bruised.

"What happened?"

"Me and Dad beat up your boyfriend."

"You did what?" she asks, shocked.

Joseph smiles with pride.

"How mad is Daddy?"

"Mad," Joseph says with a chuckle. "Dad was going to kill him."

"You guys really beat Derrick?" Jacqueline inquires.

"Yep," Joseph said, beaming. "Yep, slapped him around good. It was funny." Joseph said with a chuckle.

"Funny?" Jacqueline questions. "How was that funny?"

"I don't know; it just was?" Joseph answered in a blasé matter.

"Did I get you in trouble?" Jacqueline asks.

"Yeah, but what else is new with us?"

"I'm sorry."

Joseph just shrugs his shoulders.

"I'm glad you're okay," Joseph says to her. "I don't know what I would do without my other half."

Richard enters the room. He grins at both of his children, his beloved baby girl and his boy. Although Richard smiles, Jacqueline can see in his that he is disappointed. Joseph excuses himself and leaves his father and sister be alone. Richard sits on the bed next to Jacqueline, and he cups her face in his palms.

"I'm sorry, Daddy." She says as tears well up in her eyes.

Richard doesn't need to ask what was on Jacqueline's mind when she rebelled. He already knows. She is a rambunctious teenager, an average teenage boy-crazed girl. Richard remembered doing wild and crazy things as a teenager. He chased girls, partied all night, missing his assigned curfew. He remembers the wild and crazy days when he was in his twenties. He sits down on the bed.

"Have you learned a lesson in all of this? Richard asks.

"Yes." Jacqueline answers.

"And that is?"

"Don't be stupid." She answers.

"Well put," Richard says. "How long have you been doing drugs?"

"I don't do drugs, Daddy." Jacqueline defends. "I smoke weed every now and then; nothing serious." "Nothing serious?" Richard questions. "Your situation right now is not serious?"

"Yes, but Daddy, I'm only here because someone put something in my drink?"

"A drink, which you should not have been drinking because you are sixteen, and you are grounded, so you shouldn't been out of the hotel."

"I know," Jacqueline said, pouting.

"You know, as in you will never do it again, or you know not to get that high again?"

"Trust me, Daddy, I am never doing that again!"

"As for this Derrick character, dismiss him from your life, from your memories," Richard demands.

Jacqueline nods her head.

"I mean it, Jacqueline Maria. You won't be here next time; you'll be in a morgue."

"Okay, Daddy."

"Okay, baby, get some rest."

"Daddy, can Joey stay with me?" Jacqueline asks.

"Baby, we'll have to talk with the staff. You need your rest."

"Please, Daddy," Jacqueline pleads.

She looks at her father with those baby brown eyes. Richard doesn't know why he tries to resist his daughter. He lets out a sigh.

"I'll see what I can do."

Jacqueline smiles as Richard kisses her on the forehead.

"Lie down," he orders.

Jacqueline lies down, and Richard leaves.

JACQUELINE DOESN'T WANT TO be away from Joseph tonight. Although the twins are different in many ways, they can only be apart for so long. As she waits for her brother to appear in her room ready, an unexpected visitor appears in the doorway. He walks over to her, smiling.

"Derrick," She says, sitting up.

"I waited for everyone to leave. I wanted to see if you're okay,"

"I'm okay."

She looks at his face; his nose is swollen.

"My brother and dad-,"

"Don't worry about it." Derrick says with a cool demeanor, "Maybe when you get out,"

"Are you fooling me?" Jacqueline asks. "My brother and father just beat you up, and you're asking me out?"

"They didn't do anything that I can't handle," Derrick says, shrugging his shoulders. "I mean, I can sue, but what is that going to prove?"

"I cannot believe what I am hearing. You don't care about me? I almost slept with you,"

"But you didn't!" Derrick said coolly.

"Did you know I was that messed up?" she asks.

Derrick shrugs his shoulders.

"Figures, I wouldn't be surprised if you slipped me that drug."

"Come, Jackie, don't be stupid."

Suddenly Derrick isn't so cute or intriguing anymore. Suddenly he has become a typical guy who did not qualify to date the daughter of a Hollywood Legend.

"I want you to go," Jacqueline said.

"Jackie," Derrick begins. "We-,"

"Get out!" she says.

The look in Jacqueline's eyes is making Derrick feel low. He nods his head, accepting her rejection, and then leaves. Jacqueline lies back down in bed and takes in a deep breath. As she waits for Joseph, she realizes the true essence of her value. She is the daughter of Richard and Emerald DeMarco. The daughter of Hollywood royalty, and Emerald is the queen of literature. Jacqueline is a type of princess, and her brother is a prince. From this day forward, she vows in her heart to take on this new status with pride and grace, as a lady should. Does this new transformation mean that she is going to stop having fun and be a free-spirited individual? Absolutely not, yet this new Jacqueline is going to have limitations. As for the guys, they have to be a type of gentlemen like her father, and she will be that lady like her mother.

JOSEPH ENTERS HER ROOM smiling. She smiles back. He walks to Jacqueline. She sits up.

"Turn the television on," she says. "We can watch the Spielberg marathon."

WINTER

Richard's Season

IT IS UNUSUAL FOR EMERALD to be in Richard's Sports Room. This is his personal space where he can relax, unwind, and escape. Like Emerald has the rose garden, Richard has his Sports Room. Emerald has no need to go in there unless she needs to speak with Richard, such as this time where she is waiting for him. Richard had gone to an audition for a movie, a big action-adventure. Many people are skeptical about Richard taking this part because this year, he will be sixty-five. In this line of work, he is considered to be over the hill, yet Richard is still fit. Yes, sometimes the back might ache, and he has arthritis, yet he still in good shape. Richard wants this part more than anything. For several reasons, one because it is a good role, two he hasn't worked in three years, and the third reason is personal he feels he has proved to the world that although he is going to be sixty-five years old; he is not dead.

Although he is now considered a Hollywood legend, winning three Oscars, four Golden Globes, and several international awards. Hollywood does not see him as the same action hero that he was thirty years ago. They want to see him more in roles that pertain to more mature characters and that is okay with Richard, but the roles he is being offered are simple-minded old men, grumpy old men, nothing that a true legend would play.

His children, Joseph and Jacqueline, admire and adore their father. They love Richard DeMarco, the actor, and respect Richard DeMarco, their father. Emerald still loves Richard. In her eyes, the older he gets, the better he is. Richard is still incredibly dangerously handsome. Emerald waits for Richard. She sits down in his favorite recliner, wearing her favorite lavender bathrobe.

"Hi," She says cheerfully as he enters the room.

"Fancy meeting you here, stranger," Richard says, smiling.

He leans down and gives her a kiss.

"Well, I thought it be nice to hang out here for a while," She told him, smiling. "Is that so?"

"Hmm, mm," She responds.

Emerald stands up, so Richard can sit in his seat. Then Emerald sits down on his lap. He wraps his arms around her.

"It's quiet. Where are the kids?"

"Joseph has a class, and Jackie is at girlfriends'." Emerald answers. "So tell me how that audition went."

"It went," Richard says with a sigh.

"Just went, huh?" Emerald asks.

Richard nods his head.

"Did you get the part?"

"No, but they offered me this role-playing the lead's, wise, but much older mentor."

"Did you take it?"

"I did, but I feel-,"

"Incompetent," Emerald said, finishing the sentence.

"Yeah," Richard said. "I spend years trying to get an acting career, and then Hollywood gets bored with me. I do them a favor and leave. Then years later, I'm back, better than ever, and now it's like Deja Vu. Emmy, write me a movie."

"What?" Emerald asks with a chuckle.

"It's was your work that put me on the spot."

"Richard, it wasn't my movie, it was your performance, and besides, you lived up to your performances with every other movie. And Richard, your reign as Hollywood's action hero is done."

"Thanks, Emerald," Richard said sarcastically.

"No, I mean, every so often, you have a hero. They will only last for a season, and when their season is done, they will pass the torch. Like sports, Magic Johnson passed the torch to Michael Jordan, yet Magic was influential in the game. He is running and owning teams; he was an announcer and with high status. People are willing to listen and let him teach them. Rich, it is your time to pass the torch and advice some young actor who is now coming up. Maybe do a little directing, producing, and the movies you act in now; you just may be the Sean Connery type, you know the suave, debonair type man."

"Where did you learn about basketball?"

"I saw it on T.V. while I was waiting for you," Emerald confessed bashfully.

Richard laughs.

"Every king has to pass the torch someday," Emerald says gently.

"Yeah," Richard said, sighing again.

Richard looks at Emerald. This once painfully shy girl is now a strong, confident woman.

"Em, I want some time-,"

"To be alone?" Emerald said. "Okay, I'll be in my office if you need me."

Richard grins. They lean forward to kiss each other again. Emerald leaves the room. Although her words made some sense, he is still feeling a bit discouraged. Within' the past year, he has been distant, and he's been a bit withdrawn. He would want to be alone. Richard never turned down the company of his wife, but Emerald is not offended; she knows that Richard will come out of this slump sooner or later.

THE LOUD CRASH IN the kitchen causes Emerald to jump. She was in the middle of reading a good mystery. She was caught up in the lives of the characters. The crash startles her and forces her to come back to reality. She chuckles to herself. She knows who is meddling around in the kitchen, one of her children invading the refrigerator looking for leftovers. Emerald walks to the kitchen to see which child is hungry. As she heads to the kitchen, she hears loud laughter. It is her, Joseph.

Her beloved son, Joseph, is nineteen years old and extremely handsome. Like his mother, Joseph wears wire-rimmed glasses. He is quiet and reserved. However, in the past year, Joseph is slowly becoming his father's son. He has a goatee-style mustache, which makes him look like a young version of his father. He has those dark brown eyes that are dangerous like his dad's, and he has his father's charming smile. Joseph and Richard would spend every other day in the gym working out. Richard would be maintaining his sculpted look, and Joseph would be trying to gain one. If Joseph did not have classes, Richard and he would spend all day lounging and loafing in the Sports Room, arguing at the television over a foul play from a football game.

Joseph has two of his friend with him. Michael is a carefree and funny young man that is exceptionally intelligent. He is also a student of Emerald's. The other friend is Raymond, a deep philosophical young man who believes that his personal destiny in life is to bring unity to the world with racial harmony. He constantly makes references to Richard and Emerald's interracial relationship and how their children are a beautiful product of their love. Raymond always says:

"Beautiful,"

"Joseph," Emerald says softly as she enters the kitchen.

"Hey, Mom," Joseph said, smiling at his mother as he kisses her softly on the cheek. "Sorry about the glass."

"It's all right."

As Joseph cleans up the broken glass, Emerald begins to help fix the boys something to eat.

"How you doin' Mrs. DeMarco," Both Raymond and Michael said.

"Good evening, fellas." She said, smiling. "What are you three up to tonight?"

"No much," Joseph said. "We came to grab a bite to eat. We just saw the game."

"What game?"

"The Sylier Vikings versus the Randall Lions," Raymond told her. "It's playoff season, Mrs. DeMarco."

"Oh right," Emerald said, pretending as she cared.

"Joe, how does your mom work at the school and not know what's going on?" Michael asks.

"Because Michael," Emerald said, smiling. "My concern is elsewhere, your paper that is due on Monday."

Joseph and Raymond begin to jeer Michael.

"It's coming, Mrs. D."

"Hmmm," Emerald teases.

Emerald fixes plates of food for Joseph and his friends, and soon they begin eating.

"Where you working on something, Mom?"

"I was just reading, nothing important." Emerald answers.

"I'm reading one of your books, Mrs. DeMarco," Raymond announces. "I really enjoyed the symbolism and how the metaphors-," Raymond notices Michael and Joseph looking at him.

"What?" Raymond asks defensively.

"Stop brown-nosing my mom," Joseph complained.

"Yeah, dude," Michael says, "She's not even your teacher!"

"I'm not," Raymond defends himself. "I'm just saying, Mrs. D, your book is really deep, and it goes beyond literature."

Emerald grins bashfully.

"Which one,"

"*The Topaz Chronicle*," Raymond told her. Emerald grinned. "Mrs. D, that book is crazy." "Crazy?" Emerald asked.

"That is slang for good, Mom," Joseph informs.

"I know what crazy is," Emerald said with a smile, "It's just that I never heard my book described that way before." "Well, look," Raymond said to his friends. "That book made me jump and act all crazy like…," he trails off, lost for words.

Raymond looks at Joseph.

"Oh my god, Joey, that dude, your father, played, he was-,"

"Crazy?" Emerald said with a grin.

"Yes," Raymond exclaims. "Mrs. DeMarco, I was him; Mr. DeMarco. I feel like I can be him. I want to write like you. I want to be deep like you. I want my soul to spy out the universe and rescue the ocean and find my place in the midst of the sand."

"What?" Emerald asks, laughing.

"Mom, let him go; he is getting philosophical," Joseph said, shaking his head.

"I see," Emerald says.

"Mrs. DeMarco, have you ever taught your book in your classes?"

"No," Emerald answered,

"Why not,"

"Because I teach what the school tells me,"

"Sylier University doesn't want *The Topaz Chronicles* taught?" Raymond asked as if he was offended. "Come on, that book is a literature by itself. The movie is off the hook; why wouldn't they want the book studied."

"It is studied, just not at Sylier," Emerald said.

"I've noticed that none of your work is studied at Sylier," Michael said

"Nope," Emerald told them modestly.

"You know what I am going to do? I am going to study your book and write an analysis on it." Raymond said.

"You do that." Emerald encourages and winks at Raymond.

"I mean it, Mrs. DeMarco," Raymond said sternly.

"Okay, Raymond. Ah-Joseph," Emerald politely changes the subject. "your father's birthday is in a few months; any idea on what he wants to do?"

"No, not really; what about your birthday?"

"My birthday," Emerald asks.

"Yes, your birthday is four days after Dad's. Have a party together,"

"A party sounds good. Invite some girls." Michael said.

"There isn't enough time for a party," Emerald suggested.

"Girls?" Joseph asked, appalled. "My dad is going to be sixty-five years old; what girls?"

"Don't underestimate Mr. D.," Michael said. "Your dad can pull some ladies,"

"I'm not hearing this," Joseph said, putting his hands over his ears.

"Joey," Michael said, pulls Joseph's hands away from his ears. "Come on, man; your dad is smooth. He still got your mom smiling."

Emerald starts laughing.

"Man, I don't want to hear about my folks smiling," Joseph complains.

"Anyway," Michael said. "Mrs. D, a party is perfect. Sixty-five years. Have a few close and personal friends, something like a celebrate roast, maybe celebrate Mr. D's career."

"Sounds nice, Michael, but I don't think there is enough time. And schedules can conflict."

Jacqueline enters the kitchen. Both Raymond and Michael smile at her.

"Hello, Miss. Jackie." Michael said, smiling.

"Hello everyone," Jacqueline said, smiling. "What is going on?"

"A party," Raymond answers. "You're dad's birthday, and your mom and Joey are thinking of what to do."

"What about your birthday, Mom?" Jacqueline asks.

"You just passed that Civic exam, and that will be the best present," Emerald says to her daughter sternly.

Jacqueline sighs. Emerald grins.

"Richard's birth date is in three months. That is not enough time to plan a party. Considering that it is his sixty-fifth, I want this to be special." Emerald says.

"How long you two been married, Mrs. D?" Michael asked.

"Twenty-seven wonderful years," Emerald answered, smiling.

"See, Joe, Mom, is still smiling," Michael said, winking at Joseph.

Everyone laughs as Joseph covered his face with embarrassment.

"Jackie, do you want something to eat?" Emerald asks.

"No, thank you."

"Mrs. D, three months is a good time to plan a birthday party," Michael said. "It can be a surprise party." "A surprise party?" Emerald asks.

"Yeah, remember just the close and personal friends. Who wouldn't set some time aside for Mr. D's sixty-fifth? You can invite friends, family, and girls!" Michael says. Everyone laughs.

"Okay, seriously, let us help." Michael offers. "Get a list of names. Jackie, you can make phone calls, me and Ray-," "Raymond and I," Emerald correct.

"Raymond and I can find a spot, and Joey can get his favorite foods. Hire a caterer and decorator, and within three months, Mr. D. can celebrate in style."

"Sounds like a plan; Mr. DeMarco is in the prime of his life? You see his last flick?" Raymond asked. "He is jumping off roofs and riding his Harley. I want to be like Mr. DeMarco."

"Just five minutes ago. You were tryin' to be deep and like Mrs. D.," Michael said.

"I can be fly like Mr. DeMarco and deep like Mrs. DeMarco, just ask Joe." "Ask me?" Joseph asks.

"Yeah, baby," Michael said, smiling. "Mrs. D, let me tell you about junior here. Joey gets all the girls in school. He is cool and smart, and the girls be all over him. They be looking at him all dreamy-eyed. I'm trying to be with Joe, and I don't even swing that way-,"

Everyone laughs. Joseph shakes his head and smiles.

"So the girls, be all Michael?" Emerald asks, teasing Michael's grammar.

"All right, it is time to go; Mrs. D is correcting my grammar. Come on, Ray."

Everyone laughs at Michael, who is tries to run from his teacher.

"Good night, everyone," Both Raymond and Michael said, leaving.

"Good night."

Emerald just laughs.

"Joseph, your friends are something else,"

"I know; tell me about it," Joseph said. "But, Mom, a party sounds real nice."

PREPARATIONS FOR RICHARDS'S SURPRISE party goes under serious consideration. With the help of Joseph and his friends, they are able to deal with the last-minute details while Jacqueline and Emerald keep things hushed from Richard. This wasn't hard because Richard is filming a movie, which he isn't too happy about considering that he did not get the part that he wanted. Night after night, Emerald talks with him. She encourages him and continually tells him that he is still amazing; he is still the man that she will always love.

Richard would be comforted by her words. He kisses Emerald and spends the remainder of the night in her arms. Although Emerald knows that all the love she gives him, Richard needs to feel the confidence in him, his heart, his mind, and his soul.

RICHARD SITS IN HIS chair, reading over his lines when Benjamin Shawl, the young man who is playing the lead role in this movie, the same role that Richard tried out for, approaches. Benjamin is handsome, he has blond hair, and his eyes are so blue that they looked like clear water.

"Mr. DeMarco," Benjamin says.

Richard peeks up from his script and peers over his reading glasses, and gives Benjamin a coy yet friendly grin.

"Yes." He said.

"My name is Benjamin Shawl. I just want to tell you that it is an honor to be working with you."

Hearing those words before, Richard just grins and nods his head.

"Thank you," Richard says.

"I became an actor because of you," Benjamin tells him.

Richard grins, Benjamin continues.

"I was eight years old when I saw *The Topaz Chronicles*. My mom took me to see it, and I saw you, and I told her I want to be him, and ever since then, I've watched every movie you were in. I watch them countless times. I feel like paying homage to you."

"That won't be necessary," Richard tells Benjamin with a chuckle.

Richard is now smiling. Intrigued with this young actor, he sits up in his seat.

"Thank you for those kind words," Richard says.

"I'm only speaking the truth," Benjamin told him. "I followed your career. I got photo clippings of every movie; I almost feel embarrassed to say all this. I feel like a stocker or something,"

Richard is now pleased. It is refreshing hearing encouraging words outside his family.

"You play my mentor in this film maybe you can take me under your wing and show me the dos and don'ts of Hollywood. You know, be my mentor in real life."

"You want me to mentor you?" Richard asks.

"Yeah, show me things, teach me things, whatever."

Richard and Benjamin are interrupted. Standing behind them are Joseph and Michael.

"What's up, Dad," Joseph says.

"How you doin' Mr. D," Michael says, looking at the movie set. "Awe, this is blazin'!" "Blazin?" Richard asks.

"That means nice," Benjamin said.

"Now, you're teaching me," Richard said to Benjamin and then smiles at him.

"I'm Benjamin Shawl." Benjamin introduces himself, shaking Joseph and Michael's hands.

"Yeah, we know you; you do good work," Michael says.
"I'm Michael."

"Joey DeMarco," Joseph said, introducing himself.

"What do I owe this honor of my son and his homey?"

"Homey?" Michael said with a laugh, "Nice one, Mr. D."

"We were in the neighborhood, and we just wanted to stop by," Joseph said smiling.

Richard nods his head with a grin.

"How much do you want?"

Richard knows his son too well. Although Joseph admires, his father acting is not his thing. He is usually found in the library or in a local coffee shop, or a book store. Therefore Richard knows that his beloved son wants something.

"A couple of dollars," Joseph said with a grin.

"Excuse me, Ben," Richard says, getting up from his chair.

Together Richard leads Joseph and Michael to his dressing room.

"Tell me the truth Mr. D, you the type of man who gets a limo to take you to your trailer and then to the studio, you know, across the street?" Richard laughs.

"No, Mike, I walk over."

Inside the trailer, Michael is astonished at what he sees inside the trailer. However, it looks like a camper from the outside, the inside looks like a small living room. There is a mini refrigerator that is stocked with bottled waters and Richard's favorite soda root beer. A creamed-colored sofa is in the center, and in front of the sofa is a small coffee table with a large jar of Peanut M&M's. Also, three are large bags of fan mail that Richard has yet to open.

"Do they let you keep the wardrobe?" Michael asks.

"It depends," Richard said as he gets into his wallet. He pulls out his credit card and hands it to Joseph. "Don't go crazy."

"Come on, Dad; I'm not Jackie."

"Right, you're the good twin."

"Okay, thanks, Dad, we're out," Joseph said, tapping his father on the shoulder.

Within' moments, Joseph and Michael are gone, and Richard returns to Benjamin, his number one fan.

A DOZEN OF GOLD AND and gray balloons are placed at each corner of the ballroom. Two hundred guests wait, sitting at the tables that are covered with white table cloth and white roses are the centerpieces. Caterers are waiting in the back to serve the guest. The local jazz band that Jacqueline hired plays in the background. There is a separate table for the presents that are wrapped in shiny paper. Emerald and Jacqueline wait for Joseph to bring Richard.

The guest is a mixture of young adults and older adults. The party's theme is to symbolize that Richard is a legend.

Jacqueline's cell phone buzzes; it is Joseph texting her that he and Richard are in the parking lot. Joseph had told Richard that they are going to a seminar that Emerald is giving.

"I never heard of this seminar," Richard said.

"You know how Mom is always keeping this hush, hush," Joseph said. "Besides, you were so busy with your new son, Benny, that you probably forgot." Joseph jokes.

Joseph and Richard enter the banquet hall, and suddenly everyone yells:

"SURPRISE!"

Richard is overwhelmed by the sudden noise, and the confetti is thrown in his face. Jacqueline approaches and gives her father a hug. Many friends and familiar faces hug and shake Richard's hand and wish him a Happy Birthday.

"Got you, Dad," Joseph said, smiling at his father.

Richard never expected this. Usually, he would spend a quiet evening at home with his wife and children for his birthday.

Although Richard is pleased to see all the friendly and smiling faces, he scans the room for Emerald. Slowly she is making her way to her husband. Finally, they approach each other. Richard takes Emerald in his arms and holds her.

"Whose idea was this?" he asks her, smiling.

"The kids," Emerald tells him with a grin.

MUSIC PLAYS IN THE background. The guests are dancing and having a good time mingling with each other. Coming along beside Richard and Emerald dancing is Michael. He starts to do the Bump with Emerald and Richard, making them laugh.

"What is going on, Mr. and Mrs. D," Michael asks. "Nice little turnout,"

"Michael, what's going on?" Richard asks, smiling.

"Just enjoying the party, happy twenty-fifth, Mr. D."

"Twenty-five, no-," Emerald began to say.

"Relax, Emmy, let the man speak," Richard said, shaking Michael's hand.

"You're such a little brown noser," Emerald said, smiling at Michael.

"I do what I can," Michael says and then leaves, dancing his way back into the crowd.

Richard and Emerald shake their head laugh.

JACQUELINE STANDS ON THE stage in front of the ballroom and speaks into the microphone.

"Ladies and gentlemen," she begins.

The guest takes their seats in preparations for the evening.

"This is part of the evening where we like to honor our guests. Daddy, you have made a mark in Hollywood, so the drama class at Sylier University has got together for a little performance for you."

The Sylier Drama Class does a rendition of Richard's career from his first movie to his most recent by acting out the most known scenes. This performance truly touches Richard because he is now feeling that although he is getting older, he is not forgotten. The performance moves Richard to tears. Emerald takes his hand and squeezes kiss him.

AFTER THE PERFORMANCES, JOSEPH introduces the next course of events; a celebrity roasts which included friends and fellow actors and actresses who are friends of Richards or may have starred alongside in movies.

IT IS TIME FOR remarks from the guest of honor. Everyone stands clapping their hands as he takes the microphone. As he looks at the crowd that is full of friends and family smiling at him, he feels as if he won the best award, better than an Oscar or Golden Globes. This award is the Honor Award, the Love Award, and the Respect Award. Looking at the sea of faces, he feels so much honor, love, and respect.

The crowds clap and cheers loudly. Richard put his head down to hide the tears that are welling up in his eyes. He takes a deep breath steps to the microphone;

"I am so thankful and grateful for all of you tonight." Richard said,

"We love you, DeMarco!" various people shout from the audience.

"I love you too,"

The crowd cheers.

"You truly made my birthday special for me." Richard begins
He looks over at Joseph and Jacqueline.

"My two children Joseph and Jacqueline, thank you so
much. My lovely wife, thank you, Emmy, and my friends and
family, thank you."

RICHARD AND EMERALD arrive home at three in the
morning.

"So, did you have a nice time?" Emerald asks as
Richard helped her unlatch her necklace.

"I had a wonderful time," Richard said, kissing her
neck.

"I was so nervous," Emerald tells him.

"Why?" Richard asked, putting his arm around her
waist.

"Well, you've been so down lately about not getting the
parts you want and turning sixty-five,"

"I feel good," Richard said. "I feel appreciated, not only
from my family but from the world. All those young kids,"
"Joseph and Jacqueline's friends are your true fans,
Richard." Emerald said. "I also am a true fan,"

She turned around to face him. She wraps her arms
around his shoulders.

"I am a fan of Richard DeMarco, the movie star. I am in
love with Richard DeMarco, my husband. I have much respect
for Richard DeMarco, the father, and the friend."

"You are amazing," Richard said. "Simply amazing."

Richard leans forward to kiss her. Slowly he began to
undo her clothes. Emerald pulls back and gave him a
flirtatious grin.

"I don't think this is a good idea, Mr. DeMarco."

"Why not,"

"Well, is a man at your age up to such rigorous
activity?" Emerald asked.

Richard grins.

"I am up to anything and everything," He answered with a grin.

As he walks towards his wife he says.

"See, baby, I only just begun."

Epilogue

Full Circle

RICHARD AND JOSEPH GOT tired of waiting for Jacqueline and Emerald, so they decided to go to the film festival without them and meet the girls later. Tonight is a special night. Tonight marks the thirty-year anniversary of the release of *The Topaz Chronicle*. For the past year, fans have been celebrating the re-releasing of the movie. And with the re-issuing, there is new footage added. Also, within the past year, the director of *The Topaz Chronicle* is being honored with a lifetime achievement award. Thirty years ago, the world was hit with not only a movie but a book that took action-adventure to a whole new level. *The Topaz Chronicle* has made Richard DeMarco and his co-stars household names forever. In honor of the spectacular event, *The Topaz Chronicle* movie has been selected to be featured at the Film Festival.

From old fans to new, everyone has united in coming out to celebrate this event. On a personal note, this anniversary also marks the beginning of Richard and Emerald's relationship.

As Richard and Joseph arrive at the party, many people from the media rushed to take pictures of Richard and Joseph. The two men look handsome. Richard wears a navy blue suit with a royal blue shirt. He no longer has a beard, but he has his goat-tee, his trademark that many young men try to imitate. Joseph's look is more relaxed. Tonight he wears dark blue jeans and a white button-up shirt. The entire world wonders what is to become of Joseph DeMarco. Will he become an actor like his father, or does he enjoy writing like his mother? Knowing that everyone wonders about him, Joseph enjoys playing coy and hard to get with the world.

Richard looks at his watch; it reads eight-fifteen. Emerald and Jacqueline are late. He told Emerald to be at the party at eight. This is an important event, and it is not good for the creator of this whole empire to be late. She is going to miss the walk on the red carpet. Richard knows why she is late. She is trying to find the right outfit, then match it up with the right shoes, and of course, the proper hairstyle, and to set things off the right kind of jewelry, and he knows that Jacqueline is doing just the same,

Women, he said to himself, *Women, women, women.*

Richard begins to remember that Emerald was late at the first movie premier; Richard had waited impatiently for her and wondered why he cared that she was late. To him, that night was not a date. Little did he know then that it was only the beginning of their relationship. He remembers wondering if Emerald had the guts to show up. She was painfully shy, but that night, she showed. Her spell-bounding beauty took him by surprise, and her charm rapture up his soul forever.

Tonight, there are more people at this premier than at the last one thirty years ago. Everyone is here tonight to be a part of this empire. Thirty years ago, the people that came out were just going along with the flow of things to see the summer new box office hit. Now the people that were at the movie premiere party thirty years ago and are here now can honestly say that they were a part of history.

EMERALD STANDS IN FRONT of a mirror wearing a tan colored dress. Jacqueline looks at the dresses that lay across the bed then she looks at the stylist.

"Where did these dresses come from?" Jacqueline asks in disgust.

"They looked good on the runway." The stylist replies. "They make my mother look like some old politician!"

"Jacqueline," Emerald admonishes.

Jacqueline looks at her mother. Emerald shakes her head, indicating that she is rude. Jacqueline takes in a deep breath. She walks into the walk-in closet for a perfect dress for her mother. In Jacqueline's eyes, her mother is too beautiful to dress like a politician or librarian. To Jacqueline, her mother is the most beautiful woman in the world.

Far in the back of the closet is a dress. It has a dry cleaners bag over it. Interested in seeing the dress, Jacqueline pulls it from off the curtain rod. It is a long, silk, red dress with spaghetti straps.

This is nice, Jacqueline, she said to herself.

Jacqueline walks out of the closet and holds the dress up to her mother.

"What do you think?" Jacqueline asks.

Emerald is surprised to see the dress.

"Jackie, was that in the back?"

"Yes,"

Emerald examines the dress.

"I haven't worn this dress in a long time. In fact, I only wore it once,"

"Then wear it again." Jacqueline orders.

"Jackie, I can't fit this dress." Emerald shakes her head.

"Yes, you can; it's a size five,"

"I'm too old for a dress like that." Emerald insisted.

"No, you're not." Jacqueline almost begs, "Come on, Mom, at least try it on."

"Is that Versace?" the stylist asks.

"No, DeMarco," Jacqueline said quickly.

Emerald chuckles. Jacqueline dangles the dress in front of Emerald. Just to amuse her daughter, Emerald tries the dress on, and to her surprise, it is a perfect fit.

"Oh my-," the stylist replies.

"Mom," Jacqueline says. "You look beautiful,"

Emerald smiles bashfully.

"It's not too much?"

"No, it's just right," Jacqueline says, smiling.

Jacqueline and the stylist share a smile.

"Pin your hair up," Jacqueline said.

As Emerald sits down at her vanity, Jacqueline looks at the stylist.

"You can go," Jacqueline says to the stylist.

"Jacqueline," Emerald admonishes again.

"No, no, Emerald." The stylist says with a grin.

The stylist takes a deep breath. She should be offended, but she's not. She gathers the dresses that are on the bed.

"Call me on Monday," the stylist said to Jacqueline. "Emerald, have a good time. I'll see myself out." Emerald and Jacqueline watch as the stylist leaves. "Looks like you'll have a job for the summer," Emerald said, smiling.

Jacqueline grins as she begins to brush her mother's long thick hair.

"You said that you only wore the dress once," Jacqueline asks.

"Yes, I wore it to the movie premiere of *The Topaz Chronicles*," Emerald answers.

Immediately Emerald looks up in the mirror and watches how Jacqueline does her hair. She is putting her hair in a bun; for a moment, Emerald goes back in time. She looks at an image in the mirror. It is not her reflection or Jacqueline's image, but it is an image of herself when she was younger. Emerald looks at Jacqueline's reflection. Jacqueline sees the confused look in her mother's eyes. "What?" Jacqueline asks.

"This dress, my hair, everything is repeating itself; I wore this dress thirty years ago tonight. Funny, isn't it? I was meeting your dad at the premiere party. I wasn't going to go, but your dad talked me into it, and that night ended up being our first date."

"So not only is this a celebration of your movie, but your relationship," Jacqueline said smiling.

"Yes, I suppose,"

"And you wearing that dress only confirms that your two are meant to be."

"If a thirty-year relationship doesn't confirm things Jackie, then-,"

"No, Mom, I mean it's just destiny, letting you know that it is still here," Jacqueline said.

"So your first date with Daddy, tell me what was it like?"

Emerald sighs and begins to remember how it all took place.

"Well, as I said, it was at the movie premiere. I was supposed to meet your dad because he told me that I needed to be there as the creator. So that night was not a date. So when I got there, your dad and I talked, and we got on the dance floor, and I was so nervous because I never really danced with a man before, and to top things off, it was a slow song came on. Plus, I was dancing with Richard DeMarco, the movie star. So I was extremely nervous. Yet, we danced, and your dad kept looking at me. I avoided eye contact, but our eyes locked, and before I knew it, we were kissing on the dance floor." "Mom!" Jacqueline said, smiling.

Emerald blushes and looks away.

"Did you know that Daddy was going to kiss you?"

"No, I never knew your dad like me, other than as a friend. I guess we got caught up in the song."

"What song was it?"

"*Lady in Red*," Emerald told her. "An older but goodie,"

"Was it nice, the kiss?"

"Yes, it was nice," Emerald says, smiling.

"Then what," Jacqueline asks.

"Then the song was over, we mingled with the fans and co-stars, and before long, we went back to your dad's, well here, and he showed me around his home. We talked about the kiss, and we've been together ever since."

"Nothing juicier?" Jacqueline asks in a prying manner.

"No, Jackie, that was it."

"Something else had to happen," Jacqueline asks suspiciously.

Jacqueline looks at her mother, trying to read more into her story. Together the two girls laugh.

AT THE CLUB, RICHARD grows more impatient, yet, he doesn't let it show. He talks with reporters, fans, and fellow costars. This is a magical night, and when Emerald gets arrives, then it will be spectacular.

RICHARD HEARS LOUD CHEERS at the front entrance of the club. Richard turns around and walks to see what is going on. It is Emerald and Jacqueline. The media, the press, and fans are yelling with excitement. Emerald smiles as she makes her way through the crowd of people.

Richard cannot believe his eyes. Emerald is dressed in the same dress that captured him thirty years ago. The same dress that made him take notice. Richard went back thirty years, but the only difference is this Emerald is more cool and comfortable battling the crowd, and this time she has someone behind her, Jacqueline. Jacqueline stands back in awe as she watches her mother handle the over-excited crowd. Tonight, Jacqueline wears a black sleeveless blouse with a pair of black Capri pants and black sandals, and like her mother, she too wears her hair in a bun.

"Mom, everyone loves you," Jacqueline says, smiling.

Emerald smiles at her daughter, and together they walk further into the club.

They see Richard approaching them. He extends his hand to Emerald. She smiles and takes his hand.

"I'm sorry, we're late," Emerald said.

"What happened?" Richard asked.

"I couldn't decide what to wear, and then our transportation didn't show. So I was going to drive, but the car wouldn't start. So we took a cab."

Again, like thirty years ago, Emerald takes a cab.

Richard shakes his head.

Richard leads Emerald to a vacant table. Together they sat down. Again, like thirty years ago, Richard is nervous sitting across from Emerald. He can't get over how she looks in that dress now and how she looked then. He is truly living in

274

Deja Vu. He takes her hands and holds them. Emerald can tell by his hands that he is nervous.

"Rich, do you want a ginger ale?" she asks, smiling.

"No, I'm okay." He said, smiling at her. "Would you like to dance?"

Emerald grins as Richard leads her onto the dance floor. Emerald begins to feel her stomach tie into knots. Why is she so nervous? She danced with Richard before. Emerald minds go to the first time she danced with Richard; it was thirty years ago tonight. Tonight she is dancing with Richard DeMarco. As they begin to dance, Richard looks into Emerald's eyes and sees that she has something on her mind.

"What's the matter?" Richard asks.

"This night. This night is where this all began, where we began. Did you have any idea that it would come to all this, that we would come to this?"

"Honestly, Emmy, I didn't know what to think." Richard begins, "I was nervous for so many reasons. I was coming out of a ten-year hiatus; there was so much pressure and then seeing you. I expected you to come with your hair in your eyes, hiding, but you came in that dress; this dress,"

"Jackie found it in the closet. Can you believe it still fits?"

"You look beautiful," Richard tells her. "Tonight, baby is confirmation that all of this has come into full circle. Without you, *The Topaz Chronicles* would have never been. Without you, Emerald, I would not be here. I am blessed that you have allowed me to be a part of your journey. I love you, Emerald."

"I love you, Richard DeMarco," Emerald said as tears form in her eyes.

They look into each other eyes, and like the first time, they are able to read each other as if they are reading a book. His eyes said that he still feels that new first-time love, and Emerald's eyes said that she is still in love. Like before, he wants to kiss her. Emerald lips are still enticing with that lip gloss.

Should I kiss her here? He asks himself. *Should I kiss her now?*

Then slowly, he begins to kiss Emerald softly on the lips. She is still a good kisser, and still, in Emerald's eyes, kissing Richard DeMarco is a dream come true.

JOSEPH AND JACQUELINE WATCH their parents from a table not too far away.

"Look at them." Joseph said, "Does it get any grosser?"

"No," Jacqueline says, smiling.

Jacqueline begins to tell her brother about their parents' first date that was thirty years ago day, at this club, at this hour. As she narrates the fairy tale, Joseph sees this beautiful young girl slowly entering the nightclub wearing this sexy yet classy red dress. Then Joseph sees a handsome man quickly approaches this girl, and as he approaches, he is immediately struck by her beauty. This girl bashfully smiles at the gentleman, and he escorts her through the crowd to a vacant table. Then this man and this girl walk to the dance floor, and instinctively they dance to a song that was before his and his sister's time.

"Can you see them now?" Jacqueline asks, smiling.

"I can see them then." Joseph answers.

MANY PEOPLE IN THE watch as Emerald and Richard dance. They ignore the world around them. They can see the people but cannot hear them, as if a mute button had been pushed. However, to the crowd, it is like watching a beloved king dance with his enchanted lady. Everyone watches and observes the charming couple. Thirty years ago, those in the crowd barely noticed them then, but now realize that thirty years ago was the making of a fairy tale, an unfailing love story. Thirty years ago, no one cared what was to become of Richard and Emerald when they first got together; thirty years now, it is a celebration of their love that began once upon a time.

JOSEPH AND JACQUELINE look at their surroundings in detail. There are large posters with images of the characters from the movie. Once upon a time, this movie must have been something big. Why else would there be such a turnout of people? The club is packed. Thirty years ago, it was just a movie premiere. Tonight is more than just an anniversary party; it was their season coming into full circle. Tonight it's a celebration of history, their chronicles, right before everyone's eyes.

www.ingramcontent.com/pod-product-compliance
Lightning Source LLC
Chambersburg PA
CBHW071317090426
42738CB00012B/2717